THE PENGUIN POETS

D 37

ITALIAN VERSE

THE PENGUIN BOOK OF
ITALIAN VERSE

INTRODUCED AND EDITED BY

GEORGE R. KAY

*

WITH PLAIN PROSE TRANSLATIONS
OF EACH POEM

PENGUIN BOOKS

Penguin Books Ltd, Harmondsworth, Middlesex

u.s.a.: Penguin Books Inc., 3300 Clipper Mill Road, Baltimore 11, Md

australia: Penguin Books Pty Ltd, 762 Whitehorse Road,
Mitcham, Victoria

—

First published 1958

Made and printed in Great Britain
by Richard Clay & Company, Ltd,
Bungay, Suffolk

GENERAL EDITOR'S FOREWORD

THE purpose of these Penguin books of verse in the chief European languages is to make a fair selection of the world's finest poetry available to readers who could not, but for the translations at the foot of each page, approach it without dictionaries and a slow plodding from line to line. They offer even to those with fair linguistic knowledge the readiest introduction to each country's lyrical inheritance, and a sound base from which to make further explorations. The anthologist too gains a considerable advantage from this method, since he can choose much more freely among medieval, dialect, and difficult modern poems when he knows that all the reader's problems can be solved by a glance at the bottom of the page.

But these anthologies are not intended only for those with a command of languages. They should appeal also to the adventurous who, for sheer love of poetry, will attack a poem in a tongue almost unknown to them, guided only by their previous reading and some Latin or French. In this way, if they are willing to start with a careful word for word comparison, they will soon dispense with the English, and read a poem by Petrarch, Campanella, or Montale, by Garcilaso, Góngora, or Lorca, straight through. Even German poetry can be approached in this unorthodox way. Something will, of course, always be lost, but not so much as will be gained.

The selections in each book have been made by the anthologist alone. But all alike reflect contemporary trends in taste, and include only poetry that can be read for pleasure. No specimens have been included for their historical interest, or to represent some particular school or phase of literary history.

J. M. COHEN

THE PENGUIN
FOREIGN VERSE ANTHOLOGIES

The following foreign verse anthologies have already been published in this series:

The Penguin Book of Spanish Verse, edited by J. M. Cohen

The Penguin Book of French Verse: (3) The Nineteenth Century, edited by Anthony Hartley

The Penguin Book of German Verse, edited by L. W. Forster

TO

DIANA BONACOSSA

TO MARK OUR COMING OF AGE

TABLE OF CONTENTS

*

TABLE OF CONTENTS

TABLE OF CONTENTS

xi

FOLGÒRE DA SAN GIMIGNANO (alive between the years 1309 and 1317). This poet, Giacomo da Michele by name, is remembered as Folgòre for the splendour of his life in San Gimignano, which is still much as he knew it – a little, walled medieval city with its crown of towers. As he lived, so he wrote. Few have evoked the pleasures of life in such colours.

DANTE ALIGHIERI (1265–1321). Dante has been much praised in our country; but his shorter poems have still to be known as well as they deserve.

FRANCESCO PETRARCA (1304–74). The great occasion for Petrarch's three hundred sonnets, *canzoni*, and other poems, was his devotion to Laura. The works are incredibly rich. Petrarch is the poet who is 'most poet'.

FAZIO DEGLI UBERTI (1310–70). The single work given in
this poet's name has a fine turn of phrase – *Soave va in guisa di
pavone*. . .

GIOVANNI BOCCACCIO (1313–75). Boccaccio wrote
poems, as well as wonderful prose, and in the best of them his
originality shows a new face. Particularly touching is the sonnet written after he had learned, at a distance of months, of
Petrarch's death: *caro signor mio* – his great friend, his colla-
borator in hastening the Renaissance.

FRANCO SACCHETTI (1335?–1400). Sacchetti's shorter
poems stir like the Greek lyric, and close as mildly. In his
poetry, even more than in Petrarch's, the medieval city with

its darkened streets, on which the Madonna of Dante and his friends appeared 'like a sudden star, is left behind, and the country, which seems so fresh and clean and new, welcomes the poet.

MATTEO MARIO BOIARDO (1434–94). Boiardo's most famous work is the *Orlando innamorato*, a fantastic saga with Childe Roland as hero. It has passages of brilliant freshness, a quality found in the best of his short poems as well.

LORENZO DE MEDICI (1449–92). The greatest member of the family in which the vital sap 'mounted to the higher branches' so remarkably. Gifted statesman, befriender rather than patron of artists like Leonardo and Michelangelo, the intelligent companion of such Renaissance wits as Politian, Ficino, Pico della Mirandola, Lorenzo was also the poet whose 'songs for dances' have all the charm of the dance.

ANGELO POLIZIANO (1454–94). The distinguished Latin scholar, close friend of Lorenzo, and, like him, a most natural poet in the Italian tongue. He too wrote 'songs for dances', wonderfully easy compositions that rival Lorenzo's own; and in the space of a day threw off the *Orfeo*, a lively ballad-play for the Carnival, today considered the first libretto in the real sense of the word.

LUDOVICO ARIOSTO (1474–1533). Ariosto is a great name in Italian poetry, but his shorter poems, with few exceptions, lack the satisfying oneness. The *Capitolo* given is a thing of warm breath, but, to know Ariosto's range, the reader must open the *Orlando furioso*, and be caught up with Angelica as she gallops away into that vivid, fantastic world.

MICHELANGELO BUONARROTI (1475–1564). Michelangelo's wrestle with his own desires has given his sonnets their form; always nervous, sometimes too muscular from the struggle. The unhappiness incidental to his devotions (the majority of his love poems are to the good-looking young Roman, Tommaso Cavalieri: the others to the unassailably virtuous Vittoria Colonna) does much to determine their tone, a questioning, light-begging tone. But if the poet can call both Christ and Cavalieri 'my dear Lord', and ask the selfsame help from God and Vittoria Colonna, it is always Love he serves. The lines *In me la morte, in te la vita mia* are fittingly untitled.

VITTORIA COLONNA (1490–1547). This excellent lady recorded her love for her husband in numerous sonnets, several of which speak to everyone.

GASPARA STAMPA (1523–54). Little more than a girl, she fell in love with Collatino, conte di Collalto, and her poems have caught the reflection of the violence with which she burned. The whole story of her passion is told in a long series of sonnets – from first maddening to professed disillusion. The beating heart is never far beneath.

TORQUATO TASSO (1544–95). After he fell in love with Laura Peperara, Tasso wrote madrigals and songs which for cadence, cunning simplicity, tenderness, and pause are incomparable. The unhappy, uncertain life of his after years is too involved to be summarized; but it was right that he should die outside Rome, before they could crown him with a partisan or patronizing laurel.

GIORDANO BRUNO (1548–1600). Bruno illustrated parts of his challenging philosophy in sonnets, and these give a sense of the cosmic journey, the soul launched towards the infinite, as no other poetry does. The Romantics have not his swift directness. As a poet he is virtually unknown in this country. As a philosopher, the interest which began when he discussed with Philip Sidney, Fulke Greville, and their friends at London, and continued in Coleridge's awareness of him as a 'dynamic' thinker, has hardly come to full recognition.

TOMMASO CAMPANELLA (1568–1639). The great friar of the Counter Reformation who suffered much for the reasonableness of his faith and his impassioned conviction that religion was still catholic. The dangers, the assurances, the despairs, and ecstasies his soul knew breathe in the madrigals of his *Cantica*, grouped into 'Psalms' that can be compared to the divine Psalms of David.

GIOVAN BATTISTA MARINO (1569–1625). Marino has suffered much for hearsay judgements of his gift and use of it. His ease of melody, his twining of images to give works of curious, sensuous delight, are not the devices of a pallid Arcadian. Marino could describe, frankly and with humour, a love-encounter with some shepherdess who was no empty classic name. And Marino could see himself as he was. Witness the singing lines to *L'amore incostante*.

PIETRO METASTASIO (1698–1782). The flower of the Arcadian sports. That *Libertà* should be freedom from a woman, and that this should be rhymed in fifty different ways is a comment upon the spirit of the age – neatly caught by Metastasio in the sonnet on the *Olimpiade*. That the long poem holds us, or, rather, makes us move with it, although itself it hardly moves, is a tribute to his mastery. Even Thomas Gray thought him a great lyric poet.

UGO FOSCOLO (1778–1827). Foscolo's life speaks of generosity and impulsiveness: a forthright, combative spirit that won him no few loves and enemies. His campaigning with Napoleon's armies, his quick disillusionment with the man as 'Emperor', his daring addresses for the Italian cause during the weeks of his professorship at Pavia, his flight to exile in Switzerland and then England, these experiences meant a life at the centre of his time – what many of his foreign contemporaries longed for in the depths of their Romantic souls. Few of the Englishmen he met appreciated his genius. We gladly remember Hobhouse's tribute, that Foscolo never uttered a commonplace, and Lord Holland's gift of a favourite wine as the poet lay dying. His memory grows in brightness.

GIOVANNI BERCHET (1783–1851). In Berchet we have a typical and attractive figure of the early *Risorgimento*: an ardent patriot who suffered for his love of country, a dabbler in letters, possessed of some wit and fire. *Il trovatore* is a pleasant ballad of the 'Germanic' kind. In its own day it was taken for an allegory, such was the dismal identification of poetic with political affinities.

ALESSANDRO MANZONI (1785–1873). Manzoni is a novelist. It is in his prose that he touches on the poetic. But the choruses of his plays enjoy a well-earned popularity, and the best of them is given here.

GIACOMO LEOPARDI (1798–1837). A great modern poet. The Italians consider him an immortal.

GIUSEPPE GIUSTI (1809–50). The best of the strictly *Risorgimento* poets, who measured against injustices on the part of the Austrian government, the humour, quick and cruel, of the poor-born Italian, tempered by the restraint of the well-bred one. When he turned to the Italians themselves, Giusti could be biting. *La chiocciola* strips once for all the 'whatever-the-catastrophe-we-survive' attitude in some ungenerous spirits of his Italy. But his best poem, *Sant'Ambrogio*, does not stop at being correction by laughter. In it Giusti sounds a deep and painful quarrel of man with his own world.

TABLE OF CONTENTS

GIOSUÈ CARDUCCI (1835–1907). Carducci's preoccupation
with political small-life and a pedestrian strain of thinking that
was twin to it, often came in his way when he wished to write
poetry. He would cut at the tame followers of Manzoni in the
very act of mounting Pegasus: he would indulge week-end reflections about the simple life just after he had summoned up
the love of his youth, the vivid *Maria bionda*. In his shorter
poems and a few long sustained pieces like *Alla stazione in una
mattina d'autunno* (remarkable both for its broken sincerity
and its shadowiness – early Impressionist), he shows the fullness of his gift.

GIOVANNI PASCOLI (1855–1912). Pascoli is among the first
of minor poets. His gift is so evident (listen to the *cader fragile*
of the leaves in *Novembre*): and yet the reader is impelled to
demand something more as soon as the shadowy music passes.
His ear for words that lull is almost as exquisite as Tasso's, but
his melancholy does not stem from some uncertainty in his
time. The bereavements he suffered left him to gentle sadness
and, inevitably, to the desire for a quiet life. They also did
much to shape his modest, wondering poetry.

GABRIELE D'ANNUNZIO (1863–1938). D'Annunzio's
poetry is to be rescued from that grotesque, encrusted mauso-
leum, his complete works. The small body that emerges shows
irresistible youth, a maturer, questioning sensuality, and always a vigour, not unshadowed by the Romantic's dissatis-
faction with the world and its promises.

DINO CAMPANA (1885–1932). Campana was outspanned by
D'Annunzio in years, not in achievement. He left only two
collections of poems: *Canti orfici* and *Quaderno*. These give a
fair impression of the man: devil-ridden, though his phantoms
are no more than mildly evil; self-driven from theme to theme
as he, in his waking life, was from one place to another; bearing an unforgettable identity. At times his poems share the de-
fects of D'Annunzio's poorer work, the baroque excesses of
sweetness and violence. But the best of them set the reader
trembling with a new, half-recognized experience.

GIUSEPPE UNGARETTI (1888–   ). Ungaretti's poetry
was born before the 1914–18 war, but it came of age in the
middle of it, when he was a soldier. The tremendous pressures

that the new style of warfare put upon individualities – and Ungaretti's is a rare one – forced poetry from him: the long, spare forms, the short, clean-broken utterances we associate with his name. Some of these poems, *I fiumi* for instance, have a dazzling completeness about them, and defy comparison with all but the very best of his later works. But *La pietà* and a few from *Il dolore* can take their place by the diamonds of his first conceiving.

EUGENIO MONTALE (1896–   ). Montale's poetry is in itself a life. It can be said to 'come like leaves to the tree'. He found himself early as a poet. Before the First World War, when he was still a youth, he had already come alive on the Ligurian coast where he spent his summers, the Liguria of Esterina. So it was that, after the war, in which his voice was muffled, he could return to the Mediterranean, and meet himself again. *Ossi di seppia* (1925) was followed by *La casa dei doganieri* (1932) which was then incorporated in *Le occasioni* (1939), just as *Finisterre* (1943) now becomes the first part of *La bufera e altro* (1956). These volumes enclose some forty years of poetry, and no small share of Europe's best today.

SALVATORE QUASIMODO (1901–   ). Quasimodo brings us the luxurious harmonies of the South which, in Italian poetry of the past, has meant the sickly as well as the exquisite. He looks to Tasso as his ideal. Tasso himself erred this way. But Quasimodo's own lyric form – *quasi un madrigale* – has given something new to Italian poetry. Occasionally he romanticises his childhood Sicily, looking back at it from misty Milan; but in poems like *Lettera alla madre* or *Vento a Tìndari* he is finely moving.

INTRODUCTION

THIS is a good moment for putting together an anthology of Italian poetry. Today we are beginning to see the importance of Italy's living poets, because the best of these are older men who have already given us a substantial body of works. We can look at the achievement-to-date of Eugenio Montale, of Giuseppe Ungaretti, of Salvatore Quasimodo, against the background of all Italian poetry, and their contribution in turn throws a new light on what has gone before. The river has taken another bend. From this point the whole course looks different. As I write, Montale's new volume *La bufera e altro* is being put out in the bookshops, and I remember with gratitude that, thanks to the poet's kindness in lending me a typescript, I have managed to include something from these *recentissime* in the present collection.

So this book really grows from its last part of all. It is modern taste and modern questionings which have determined my selection. Similarly it has been in translating the works of the last forty years (reputedly so difficult, though the essays, or rather articles, written to illustrate this are much more obscure) that I have learned how far a literal translator of poetry can help the reader with small knowledge of the language. He reports faithfully, he may at times be obliged to choose one interpretation rather than another, but he should stop short of explanation. Again, however cleanly he may deliver the poet's meaning into his own tongue, he does not pretend to transmit to the understanding the poetic shock with which his original is charged. These translations, then, should serve to make Italy's lyric wealth accessible to all who value poetry; and to those who are already acquainted with the various *Rime*, something new will, I hope, be shown.

To find Saint Francis listed as the first Italian poet will probably surprise those who have only glanced at Italian literature before. This placing is no innovation of mine. Numerous collections published in Italy begin with his inspired hymn. It is not given this honour here for its art or supposed lack of art – its 'primitive charm', as some would say, a weak recommendation, little more suggestive than the popular adjective 'nice'. Saint Francis comes first because, already in his distant time, he displays the virtues of the best Italian poets. He is simple, passionate, meaningful. His words are marked by an unspectacular urgency. Yet he commands our wonder, and not only when he says that God is to be praised for 'our sister, bodily death'. From Saint Francis, too, we learn something of the character of the masters of Italian poetry. They are great individuals who have dominated the word, each in his own special way. They are never professionals of verse.

Italian poetry is the work of individuals who in their own lives were original and who, to translate an expression, 'breathed more deeply' than other men. But these poets have not always grown in isolation. Lone Leopardi, the born stranger, stands today as the figure of the Italian poet. His is only half the story. To illustrate this from the earliest age – immediately after Saint Francis another solitary religious emerged, Iacopone da Todi, himself a Franciscan. He stands alone, in torment, in joy, in quiet gladness – *Fiorito è Cristo nella carne pura*. But contemporary with Iacopone the first 'school' of poets was gathering in the South, in Sicily. And however much 'school' may suggest one style or a common programme, the important ones in Italian poetry have never been more than groups of individuals.

The names of the leading Sicilians, Rinaldo d'Aquino, Giacomino Pugliese, Giacomo da Lentini, are constellated about that of the great emperor, Frederick II, himself a poet. A distinctive poetic accent gives them a family likeness. So, too, does the way they sing of love. In fact, no poets have ever revealed a greater intimacy with love as it is known to lovers. Rinaldo d'Aquino can write, with perfect sympathy, poems for the woman's voice: take that wonderful complaint, *Già mai non mi conforto*. But perhaps the Sicilian gift of knowing both voices, both hearts of love is best displayed in the popular *contrasto* (or 'contest in words') by Cielo d'Alcamo – a window dialogue, the most natural thing

in the world. No one could say that these two works, or any of
the best Sicilian poems, were 'essays in a style'. The accent may
be the same in all, the voices are quite different.

With the Tuscan poets the reader's impression could be that
they form a school in the accepted sense of the word. Their
colours are easily recognized. They accept much of their imagery
in common. Each gazes at his lady with adoring fixity. But where
they have liberated themselves from their own conventions, the
Tuscans are far more original than the Sicilians. In some of them
the creative moment illuminates a few poems only. Lapo Gianni
would be simply an excellent craftsman if he had not written a
piece like his wonderful day-dream *Amor, eo chero mia donna in
domino*. But two poets stand out, high above the others, like
towers overshadowing a compact medieval city: a major poet
and a great one: Guido Cavalcanti and Dante. The poet who
wrote sonnets such as *Chi è questa che ven* and the incomparable
Perch'i' no' spero di tornar giammai is still the companion, after
these seven hundred years, of the one who wrote the *Vita nuova*
and the Divine Comedy.

Dante's originality is as astonishing as his achievement. As a
young man he put himself to school with Guido Guinizelli, re-
garding himself as a follower of Bologna's 'sage of love'. But no
word of the story of his youthful heart, the *Vita nuova*, is
prompted. In middle age Dante was overtaken by a new passion,
when he lost his heart to a mere girl and was rejected. The experience was violent. It caught and shook him by the neck.
No part of the poetic language he had mastered could ade-
quately suggest it. Dante found new words, a new way of speak-
ing: *Così nel mio parlar voglio esser aspro | com'è ne li atti questa
bella petra*. This, certainly, is what it is to be a poet.

I have included several of the poems to the 'young girl of
stone' in the present selection. They are not generally known in
this country, even to readers for whom Dante is the one Italian
poet. With Petrarch, by contrast, no neglected works have still
to be honoured. Complete editions of his poems have been
made and read from his own life-time to the present day, and

much has been translated, meantime, into English. The reader has simply to try what readers through six centuries have known and admired. The wonder is that, in reading Petrarch, the sense of discovery never fails us. The simplicity, the new devices with which he expressed devotion to Laura lay hold of us as they did of his contemporaries and successors. We see why he was universally recognized while he lived. When they crowned him with laurel on the Capitol hill, it was no idle ceremony. We see why generations of would-be poets longed to write sonnets, *canzoni*, poems, as he had done – 'Frances Petrarke the Laureat hight'.

Petrarch left poems that are almost perfect (what finer setting of a thought is to be found than *Di pensier in pensier, di monte in monte?*); and his example dazzled. This is particularly true of the sonnet and *canzone*. Before his time these forms were still growing. The Tuscans did not take them as the Sicilians had shaped them. But once Petrarch's sonnets and *canzoni* came to be known, the forms themselves were thought of as Petrarchan. So we should not be surprised if, in all the works of his imitators, we find little innocence of vision. They only wanted a likeness of their great original. They had nothing to add. Nor is it strange that the new impulses in Italian poetry should come in forms that Petrarch had not 'appropriated': the *ballata* and the madrigal.

The moment for the *ballata* came in Florence during the early Renaissance. *Ballata* is best translated 'song for a dance', a sort of composition that, always popular, was especially so during Carnival, when the procession, cars and people, wound through the streets. The *canti carnescialeschi* of that time move with a new, a pagan abandon, but they move with grace. They are not rough-spun folk-song, because the masters of the form were not crude rhymers, but Lorenzo de' Medici, lord of the city, and Angelo Poliziano, a leading scholar of the time. These public men composed their words in the intervals of pressing duties; and, by a happy chance, gave them just the lightness, simplicity, fire that have kept them glowing to this day. How Lorenzo and

Politian enjoyed these entertainments of theirs is shown by a wood-cut of the time that depicts them looking on, while some girls dance, fair as the Graces, singing one of their songs. Lorenzo seems to be saying to his friend:

> *Queste ninfe ed altra gente*
> *son allegre tuttavia.*
> *Chi vuol esser lieta, sia:*
> *di doman non c'è certezza.*

In the hundred years after Lorenzo's time lyrical poetry is poorly served. Ariosto, master of a new, mixed, narrative style, uses it to create idyllic moments in his long verse-tale about Childe Roland. Boiardo, another story-teller, does produce some 'song', but this is not free of the Petrarchan canon. It is not until Tasso's madrigals, that the short poem comes into its own again.

These last named works offer a pleasure far different from that of the Florentine Carnival songs. They have risen in the isolated lover. They could never be taken up by the crowd, though they ask to be sung, so pure is the line of verbal melody in them. Tasso is the most musical of Italian poets. But we would wrong him if we saw him merely as the best of courtly song-writers. The very unrestraint, the recurrent sadness of his short poems betray some quarrel deep within him. In fact, it is his life and work that show how the 'heavy change' that followed the Reformation and the Catholic reaction to it affected one who was, first and last, a poet; how, after he had written his youthful poems, among them the *Aminta*, a charming pastoral entertainment with a hint of the elegiac about it, he felt he must undertake an epic defence of Christendom, and gave us the irresolute and troubled *Gerusalemme liberata*. The best poems of his contemporaries lets us see how great individuals, Michelangelo Buonarroti, Gaspara Stampa, to name two, used poetry more as a kind of diary to record how they suffered, and gladly burned (the phoenix is their image), in the new era of uncertainty. Greatest of all, in a sense, is Campanella, the friar who could accept prison, torture, oblivion, from his church and still write:

La dubbia guerra fa le virtù conte.
Breve è verso l'eterno ogn'altro tempo,
e nulla è più leggier ch'un grato peso.
Porto dell'amor mio l'imago in fronte,
sicuro d'arrivar lieto per tempo,
ove io senza parlar sia sempre inteso.

Tasso's younger contemporary, Marino, went further with curious images or 'conceits', wrote with a musicality hardly less enchanting, could suggest a most caressing pleasure (look at *L'Amore incostante*) but, as a poet, stops there. If we pass over his followers, the *Marinisti*, who are occasionally rewarding to the lover of pure style, little that can be called poetry is met with in the next two hundred years or so. Take Metastasio, the delight of the eighteenth century. His quatrains move quite perfectly, turning upon themselves with the precise and fluid movement of the brass weights revolving in a six-day clock. But what does he sing? Liberty. And what does he mean? Freedom from a woman he has doted upon. His own work can be of a seductive monotony, but, as an influence, he proved more disastrous than Marino. Not before Foscolo – great Ugo – is the small, dulcet, chiming tone lost to Italian poetry, as if it had never been. Parini and Alfieri seem, in their shorter poems, too conscious of what they are writing against.

Already in Foscolo's gallant odes *A Luigia Pallavicini* and *All'amica risanata*, the eighteenth century is behind us. Their form is still, in a sense, neo-classic, but although Foscolo handles it correctly, and even enhances the flattering style, we have the feeling that he is playing: brilliantly, not without some heat of passion, but, first and last, to show that, as a poet, he can make a far more taking bow than any of his betters. Turn to the sonnets. The impression is different. Here an unquiet strength rises and strains at the fourteen lines. It strains at them as long as they follow the honoured pattern set by Petrarch. Once Foscolo leaves this for a sonnet of his own making, something swift and incandescent is created. How the lines *A Zante* speed to their fateful end – *illacrimata sepoltura*! But sonnets could not, in the end, contain his more powerful impulses to poetry. Only in the surges of *De' Sepolcri* that gather and lunge forward until they touch their glittering horizon – *finchè il Sole | risplenderà su le sciagure umane* –, does he give his utmost as a poet.

Foscolo's Italian, with its inversions and lengthy constructions, occasionally presents difficulties to the foreign reader and to the native one as well – much as Milton's English does. The extreme instance is the image in that verse of *A Luigia Pallavicini* beginning *Tal nel lavacro immersa*. That takes unravelling. At points like this the reader will probably turn to the translation for more support than ever, but he must turn back to the original and catch the true Foscolian phrase: *O bella Musa, ove sei tu? Non sento|spirar l'ambrosia…: …te beata gridai…: e pianto, ed inni, e delle Parche il canto: …l'isolette | stupefatte l'udiro ed i continenti*: the whole of that perfect lyric, *Io dal mio poggio*, to give just a few examples.

If Foscolo's style of expression calls for close appreciation, so in a more special way does Leopardi's. Here the question is no longer of difficulty of language. The English reader is asked instead to see the rightness of Leopardi's phrase, the simple finality of his forms, the purity of his line: in *L'infinito*, the wonderfully youthful *Sera del dì di festa*, in *Silvia*, the passage about the stars in *Il canto notturno*, or the unearthly description of Pompei in *La ginestra*, and that poem's tender close. It is in the last-named work that Leopardi shows the modern temper – which does not break through even once in Foscolo's *De' sepolcri*, though the poem's import is perfectly 'modern'. He is willing to discuss, refute, observe life; but he still thirsts for some sublimer touch – all in one and the same poem. Clearly it was because Leopardi was too modern that he did not become a master for his contemporaries or those in the century following.

This is the background to modern Italian poetry. Leopardi was not recognized in his day for the supreme poet that he is: the century after him was spanned by three who were much less inspired, Carducci, Pascoli, D'Annunzio: and, then, with the vivid disintegration of Campana, the new age opens. As I write,

Montale's newest volume, *La bufera e altro*, is propped on the bookshop counters. The printing is not of the finest and the book may not look impressive, but I, for one, feel that this is, for now and the future, a memorable production. The poet who had already given us *Falsetto*, *Delta*, the series of *Mediterraneo* and *Motteti*, *La casa dei doganieri*, has added to these richly, and in one poem at least, *L'Anguilla*, seems to have mounted higher than ever – like the *anguilla* itself, thrashing its way upstream in defiant joy. This is a good moment for Italian poetry.

G.R.K.

Rome, October 1956

My first decision with this anthology was to choose no quotations from longer works – the *Commedia*, *Trionfi*, *Orlando*, *Gerusalemme*, and so on. The poets who have suffered most for this are Ariosto, who did not master shorter forms, and Vicenzo Monti, whose tracts of blank-verse include such excellent passages. For texts I have trusted, in the absence of one complete series of definitive editions, to the best of the series: Laterza, the handsome new Ricciardo Ricciardi, the older, red-bound Rizzolis, at times to the *Classici Italiani*, not to mention numerous other best editions for single poets. My practice with the earlier schools, Sicilians and Tuscans, has been to adopt the clean spelling of the Bianchi Govoni volumes (*La magna curia* and *Il dolce stil nuovo*), neither modernized nor fussily authentic. Coming to the moderns, I might have included younger men than Quasimodo, but Italian poetry, after the three, is an anarchic province; though I think highly of works by Maria Luisa Spazziani, Vittorio Gasparini and those new Sicilians, Bartolo Cataffi, Enrico de' Miceli, and Michele Spina. Of Italian anthologies, my favourites have long been Bontempelli's *Lirica italiana* (1182–1837) and Spagnoletti's *Antologia della poesia italiana 1909–1949*, and these have doubtless influenced some of my minor decisions.

My first acknowledgements must be to Dr Antonia Sansica Stott, the kind tutor who saw and trained my interest in Italian poetry, giving me both the books I mention, each at the right moment: to my other Italian masters at Edinburgh University, John Purves, whose *First Book of Italian Verse* is still the best student introduction to the poetic subtleties of the language, and Doctor Mario Manlio Rossi, philosopher and liveliest of teachers. Latterly I have been greatly helped, particularly with my Montale translations, by Dr Filippo Donini of the Italian Institute in London. My debt to him in the present instance is immeasurable. If it had not been for Dr Donini, I would never have had the chance of undertaking the present work. I must thank others of the Institute, its director, Count Morra, Miss Lucia Pallavicini, Mr Mallia, who were so kind in affording me books, information, every kind of facility, even during the holiday month of August: Mrs A. Walker and Magda King for valuable assistance with typing: Rafaele Fernando Squirru and the Reverend Doctor Alexander King for timely aid: J. M. Cohen for suggestions in the later stages. Lastly I would record my friends in Italy: Carlo Candi, the sculptor, who years ago in Florence let me hear *Ed è subito sera* and *Mattina* for the first time: those who, the other day, lent me books – the painters Angelo Verga and Giorgio de Gaspari, the distinguished critic, Marco Valsecchi: the others interested in my work, be they of Piazza Roma in Bibbiena or Signora Lina's *Giamaica* in Milan.

The following publishing-houses are to be thanked for permission to print modern Italian works: Nicola Zanichelli of Bologna for Carducci's poems; Vallecchi of Florence for Campana's; and Arnoldo Mondadori of Milan for those of Pascoli, D'Annunzio, Ungaretti, Quasimodo, and the earlier Montale.

THE PENGUIN BOOK OF
ITALIAN VERSE

SAN FRANCESCO

Cantico delle creature

ALTISSUMU, onnipotente, bon Signore
tue so le laude la gloria e l'honore
et onne benedictione.
Ad te solo, Altissimo, se confano
et nullu homo ene dignu te mentovare.

Laudato sie, mi Signore, cun tutte le tue creature
spetialmente messor lo frate sole
lo qual jorna et allumini noi per loi.
Et ellu è bellu e radiante cun grande splendore
de te, altissimo, porta significatione.

Laudato si', mi Signore, per sora luna e le stelle,
in celu l'ai formate clarite et pretiose et belle.

Laudato si', mi Signore, per frate vento
et per aere et nubilo et sereno et onne tempo,
per lo quale a le tue creature dai sustentamento.

Canticle of All Created Things

LORD, most high, almighty, good, yours are the praises, the glory,
and the honour, and every blessing. To you alone, most high, do
they fittingly belong, and no man is worthy to mention you.

Be praised, my Lord, with all your creatures, especially master
brother sun, who brings day, and you give us light by him. And he
is fair and radiant with a great shining – he draws his meaning, most
high, from you.

Be praised, my Lord, for sister moon and the stars, in heaven you
have made them clear and precious and lovely.

Be praised, my Lord, for brother wind and for the air, cloudy
and fair and in all weathers – by which you give sustenance to your
creatures.

I

Laudato si', mi Signore, per sor'aqua
la quale è multo utile et humile et pretiosa et casta.

Laudato si', mi Signore, per frate focu
per lo quale ennallumini la nocte
et ello è bello et iocundo et robustoso et forte.

Laudato si', mi Signore, per sora nostra matre terra,
la quale ne sustenta et governa
et produce diversi fructi con coloriti fiori et herba.

Laudato si', mi Signore, per quelli che perdonano per lo
    tuo amore
et sostengo infirmitate et tribulatione,
beati quelli che sosterranno in pace
ca da te, altissimo, sirano incoronati.

Laudato si', mi Signore, per sora nostra morte corporale
da la quale nullu homo vivente po scappare,
guai a quelli che morranno ne le peccata mortali,
beati quelli che trovarà ne le tue sanctissime voluntati
ca la morte secunda nol farrà male.

Be praised, my Lord, for sister water, who is very useful and
humble and rare and chaste.

Be praised, my Lord, for brother fire, by whom you illuminate
the night, and he is comely and joyful and vigorous and strong.

Be praised, my Lord, for sister our mother earth, who maintains
and governs us and puts forth different fruits with coloured flowers
and grass.

Be praised, my Lord, for those who forgive because of your love
and bear infirmity and trials; blessed are those who will bear in
peace, for by you, most high, they will be crowned.

Be praised, my Lord, for sister our bodily death, from which no
living man can escape; woe to those who die in mortal sin; blessed
are those whom it will find living by your most holy wishes, for
the second death will do them no harm.

Laudate et benedicete mi Signore et rengratiate
et serviteli cun grande humilitate.

IACOPONE DA TODI

De la diversità de contemplazione de croce

– Fuggo la croce che me devora,
la sua calura non posso portare.

Non posso portare sì grande calore
che getta la croce: fuggendo vo amore;
non trovo loco, ca porto nel core
la remembranza me fa consumare. –

– Frate, co fuggi la sua delettanza?
io vo chirendo la sua amistanza;
parme che facci grande vilanza
de gir fugendo lo suo delettare. –

– Frate io fuggo, chè io son ferito:
venuto m'è 'l colpo, e 'l cor m'ha partito;
non par che senti de quel c'ho sentito,
però non par che ne sacci parlare. –

Praise and bless my Lord and give thanks to him and serve him
with great humility.

Of the Various Ways of Contemplating the Cross

'I FLEE the cross which devours me, I cannot bear its heat.
'I cannot bear a heat as great as that the cross sends out: I keep
flying from love; I find no refuge, for I bear the memory in my
heart and that consumes me.'
'Brother, why do you fly its delightfulness? I keep asking for its
friendship; it seems that you do a very base wrong to keep fleeing
its power to delight.'
'Brother, I flee because I am wounded: the blow has fallen on me
and split my heart; it does not seem that you feel what I feel, because you do not seem to be capable of talking of it.'

– Frate, io sì trovo la croce fiorita,
de soi pensieri me sono vestita;
non ce trovai ancora ferita,
'nante m'è gioia lo suo delettare. –

– Ed io la trovo piena de sagitte
ch'escon del lato; nel cor me son fitte:
el balestrier en ver me l'ha diritte,
on arme ch'aggio me fa perforare. –

– Io ero cieco ed or veggio luce:
questo m'avenne per sguardo de cruce;
ella me guida, chè gaio m'aduce,
e senza lei son en tormentare. –

– E me la luce sì m'ha acecato:
tanto lustrore de lei me fo dato,
che me fa gire co abacinato,
c'ha li bel occhi e non pote mirare. –

– Io posso parlar, chè stato so muto,
e questo ella croce sì m'è apparuto:

'Brother, I find the cross so flourishing, that I have clothed myself with its thoughts: I do not find I am wounded in this, rather is its sweetness my joy.'

'And I find it full of arrows that fly out from its side; they have stuck in my heart: the bowman has aimed them at me, and shot them through every piece of armour I have.'

'I was blind and now I see the light: this has come about from my gazing on the cross; it leads me, that blithely leads me on, and without it I am in torment.'

'And the light has equally blinded me: it shone so strongly upon me, that it makes me go about like those blind people who have fine eyes and cannot gaze.'

'I can talk who have been dumb, and it is because of the way this

tanto de lei sì aggio sentuto,
ch'a molta gente ne pos predicare. –

– E me fatt'ha muto, che fui parlatore:
en sì grande abisso entrat 'è el mio core,
ch'io non trovo quasi auditore
con chi ne possa de ciò ragionare. –

– Io era morto ed or aggio vita,
e questo è la croce sì m'è apparita:
parme esser morto de la partita
ed aggio vita nel suo demorare. –

– Ed io non so morto, ma faccio el tratto,
e Dio lo volesse ch'el fosse ratto!
star sempremai en estremo fatto
e non poterme mai liberare! –

– Frate, la croce m'è delettamento:
nollo dir mai ch'en lei sia tormento;
forsa non èi al suo giognemento
che tu la vogli per sposa abracciare. –

cross appeared to me: I have felt so much from it, that I can declare
this to many people.'
    'And it has made me dumb who was such a talker: my heart has
come into so great an abyss, that I can hardly find a listener with
whom to speak of this.'
    'I was dead and now have life, and it is because of the way this
cross appeared to me: I seem to be dead at its leaving me, and I have
life in its sojourning.'
    'And I am not dead, but suffer the last spasms, and God grant
that they may be over quick! always in extremities and never able
to free myself!'
    'Brother, the cross is my delight: never say it is torment for you;
perhaps you are not in union with the cross that you want to embrace as your bride.'

– Tu stai al caldo, ma io sto nel fuoco:
a te è diletto, ma io tutto cuoco;
con la fornace trovar non pò loco:
se non c'èi entrato non sai quegn' è stare.

– Frate, tu parli che io non t'entendo,
como l'amor gir vòi fugendo:
questo tuo stato verrìa conoscendo
se tu el me potessi en cuore splanare. –

– Frate, el tuo stato è en sapor de gusto:
ma io c'ho bevuto, portar non pò el musto;
non aggio cerchio che sia tanto tusto
che la fortuna non faccia alentare. –

Del iubilo del core che esce in voce

O IUBILO del core, · che fai cantar d'amore!

Quando iubilo se scalda, · sì fa l'uomo cantare;
e la lengua barbaglia · e non sa que parlare:
dentro non pò celare, · tanto è grande el dolzore!

'You are in the heat, but I stand in the fire: it is delight to you,
but I am quite roasted; I can find no refuge with this furnace: if you
have not entered it, you do not know what it is to stay there.'

'Brother, you speak in a way I don't understand, of how you
wish to keep fleeing from love: I should like to know your state,
if you could lay it open to my heart.'

'Brother, your state takes the form of joy: but I who have drunk,
cannot bear the taste of must; I have no hoop that is so stout that
my ferment does not loosen it.'

Of the Heart's Rejoicing which Comes Forth in the Voice

O REJOICING of the heart that makes us sing from love.

When rejoicing warms, it makes man sing; and the tongue
babbles and does not know what to say; this joy cannot be hid
within, so very great is its sweetness.

Quando iubilo è acceso, · sì fa l'omo clamare;
lo cor d'amore è preso · che nol pò comportare:
stridendo el fa gridare, · e non vergogna allore.

Quando iubilo ha preso · lo cor enamorato,
la gente l'ha en deriso, · pensando suo parlato,
parlando smesurato · de que sente calore.

O iubil, dolce gaudio, · ched entri ne la mente,
lo cor deventa savio · celar suo convenente:
non può esser soffrente · che non faccia clamore.

Chi non ha constumanza · te reputa empazito,
vedendo svalianza · com omo ch'è desvanito:
dentro lo cor ferito · non se sente de fuore.

When rejoicing is in flame, it makes man cry out; his heart is seized with love, so that he cannot bear it: it makes him shout out piercingly and he is not then ashamed.

When rejoicing has possessed the heart in love, people hold a man in derision, thinking of his speech, for he speaks beyond all measure of what he feels inflaming him.

O rejoicing, sweet joy, that comes into the mind, the heart grows wise in hiding its state: it cannot bear to the point of not making itself heard.

He who has no acquaintance with this considers you mad, seeing your distractedness, like that of a man out of his senses: the wounded heart does not feel what is outside it.

Pianto de la madonna de la passione del figliolo Iesù Cristo

NUNZIO

DONNA del paradiso,
lo tuo filgiolo è priso · Iesù Cristo beato.

Accurre, donna, e vide · che la gente l'allide!
credo che llo s'occide, · tanto l'on flagellato.

VERGINE

Como esser porria, · che non fece mai follia,
Cristo, la spene mia, · omo l'avesse pigliato?

NUNZIO

Madonna, egli è traduto: · Iuda sì l'ha venduto,
trenta denari n'ha 'vuto, · fatto n'ha gran mercato.

VERGINE

Succurri, Magdalena: · gionta m'è adosso piena!
Cristo figlio se mena, · como m'è annunziato!

Lament of the Virgin at the Suffering of Her Son Jesus Christ

MESSENGER: Lady of Paradise, your son is taken, blessed Jesus
Christ. Run, woman, and see for the people strike him. I believe
he is being killed, they have so whipped him.

THE VIRGIN: How could this be when he never did wrong? Christ,
my hope, how could any one have seized him?

MESSENGER: Lady, he is betrayed: Judas has sold him, he has had
thirty pieces of silver for it, he has struck a great bargain.

THE VIRGIN: Help, Magdalen, pain has come upon me! Christ,
my son, is being led along, as was foretold me.

NUNZIO

Succurri, Madonna, aiuta! · ch'al tuo figlio se sputa
e la gente lo muta: · hanlo dato a Pilato.

VERGINE

O Pilato, non fare · lo figlio mio tormentare:
ch'io te posso mostrare · como a torto è accusato.

TURBA

Crucifige, crucifige! · Omo che se fa rege,
secondo nostra lege, · contradice al senato.

VERGINE

Priego che m'entendàti, · nel mio dolor pensàti:
forsa mò ve mutati · da quel ch'avete pensato.

NUNZIO

Tràgon fuor li ladroni · che sian suoi compagnoni:

TURBA

De spine se coroni! · chè rege s'è chiamato.

MESSENGER: Help, lady, lend aid! for they spit upon your son,
and the people push him along: they have given him to Pilate.

THE VIRGIN: O Pilate, do not cause my son to be tormented: for
I can show you how wrongly he is accused.

THE CROWD: Crucify, crucify! A man who makes himself king, by
our law, defies the senate.

THE VIRGIN: I beg you to hear me, think of my grief: perhaps
even now you begin to have misgivings.

MESSENGER: They are dragging out the thieves to be his companions.

THE CROWD: Let him be crowned with thorns! he who called
himself king.

VERGINE

O figlio, figlio, figlio! · figlio, amoroso giglio,
figlio, chi dà consiglio · al cor mio angustiato?

Figlio, occhi giocondi, · figlio, co non respondi?
figlio, perchè t'ascondi · dal petto ove se' lattato?

NUNZIO

Madonna, ecco la cruce, · che la gente l'aduce,
ove la vera luce · dèi essere levato.

VERGINE

O croce, que farai? · el figlio mio torrai?
e que ci aponerai, · chè non ha en sè peccato?

NUNZIO

Succurri, piena de doglia: · chè 'l tuo figliuol se spoglia,
e la gente par che voglia · che sia en croce chiavato.

VERGINE

Se glie tollete 'l vestire, · lassatemel vedire
come 'l crudel ferire · tutto l'ha 'nsanguinato.

THE VIRGIN: O my son, son, son! my son, lovesome lily, who
will counsel my heart in anguish?
    Son, joyful eyes, son, why do you not answer? Son, why do
you hide from the breast that has suckled you?
MESSENGER: Lady, here is the cross, being brought by the people,
upon which the true light is to be raised.
THE VIRGIN: O cross, what will you do? Will you take my son?
And what will you charge him with? That he has no sin in him?
MESSENGER: O help, thou full of grief: for thy son is being
stripped, and the people seem to wish that he be nailed to the
cross.
THE VIRGIN: If they have taken off his clothes, let me see – how the
cruel wounding has stained him all with blood.

NUNZIO

Donna, la man gli è presa · e nella croce gli è stesa:
con un bollon gli è fesa, · tanto ci l'on ficcato!

L'altra mano se prende, · nella croce se stende,
e lo dolor s'accende, · che più è multiplicato.

Donna, li piè se prenno · e chiavellanse al lenno:
onne iontura aprenno · tutto l'han desnodato.

VERGINE

Ed io comencio el corrotto: · Figliolo, mio deporto,
figlio, chi me t'ha morto, · figlio mio delicato?

Meglio averìen fatto · che'l cor m'avesser tratto,
che, nella croce tratto, · starce desciliato.

CRISTO

Mamma, o' sei venuta? · mortal me dài feruta,
chè 'l tuo pianger me stuta, · che 'l veggio sì afferrato.

MESSENGER: Lady, his hand has been taken and stretched upon
the cross; it is pierced through by a nail, in such a way have they
fixed him! The other hand is taken, and is being stretched upon
the cross, and the pain burns that is ever more multiplied. Lady,
his feet are taken and nailed to the wood; every joint is opened,
they have so wrenched him.
THE VIRGIN: And I shall begin the lament: son, my comfort, son,
who has made you dead to me, my delicate son?
They would have done better to have taken out my heart,
than for it to be torn there, set upon the cross.
CHRIST: Mother, why have you come? You give me a mortal
wound, since your weeping casts me down when I see it gripping
you so.

VERGINE

Figlio, che m'agio anvito, · figlio, patre e marito,
figlio, chi t'ha ferito? · figlio, chi t'ha spogliato?

CRISTO

Mamma, perchè te lagni? · voglio che tu remagni,
che serve i miei compagni · ch'al mondo agio acquistato.

VERGINE

Figlio, questo non dire: · voglio teco morire,
non me voglio partire, · fin che mo m'esce 'l fiato.

Ch'una agiam sepultura, · figlio de mamma scura!
trovarse en affrantura · matre e figlio affogato.

CRISTO

Mamma, col core affletto, · entro a le man te metto
de Ioanne, mio eletto; · sia il tuo figlio appellato.

Ioanne, esta mia mate · tollela en caritate:
aggine pietate, · ca lo core ha forato.

THE VIRGIN: My son, I have good cause, son, father, and husband,
son, who has wounded you? my son, who has stripped you?
CHRIST: Mother, why do you lament? I want you to stay behind
and care for the companions whom I have gained in the world.
THE VIRGIN: My son, do not say that: I want to die with you, I do
not want to leave you, until, in a little while, my breath leaves
me.
   Let us have one burial, son of a darkened mother! Mother and
son were found overcome by anguish.
CHRIST: Mother, with a stricken heart I put you into the hands of
John, my chosen: let him be called your son.
   John, keep this my mother in all love: have pity on her, for
her heart has been pierced.

VERGINE

Figlio, l'alma t'è uscita, · figlio de la smarrita,
figlio de la sparita, · figlio attossicato!

Figlio bianco e vermiglio, · figlio senza simiglio,
figlio, a chi m'apiglio? · figlio, pur m'hai lassato.

Figlio bianco e biondo, · figlio, volto iocondo,
figlio, perchè t'ha el mondo, · figlio, cusì sprezato?

Figlio, dolce e piacente, · figlio de la dolente,
figlio, hatte la gente · malamente tratto!

O Ioanne, figlio novello, · morto è lo tuo fratello:
sentito aggio 'l coltello · che fo profetizato,

che morto ha figlio e mate · de dura morte afferrate:
trovarse abracciate · mate e figlio abracciato.

De la incarnazione del verbo divino

FIORITO è Cristo nella carne pura:
or se ralegri l'umana natura.

THE VIRGIN: My son, your soul has gone, son of the lost woman,
son of the lifeless one, who have been poisoned.

My son, white and red, son without compare, son, whom
shall I hold to? son, you have left me then?

My son, white and fair, son of joyful face, son, why has the
world so despised you?

My son, sweet and pleasant, son of the grieving one, son, the
people have used you wickedly.

O John, my new son, your brother is dead: I have felt the
blade that was prophesied,

Which has killed son and mother, both seized by hard death:
they were found embraced, mother and son embraced.

Of the Incarnation of the Divine Word

CHRIST has flowered in the pure flesh: now let human nature
rejoice.

Natura umana, quanto eri scurata,
ch'al secco fieno tu eri arsimigliata!
Ma lo tuo sposo t'ha renovellata!
or non sie ingrata · de tale amadore.

Tal amador è fior de puritade,
nato nel campo de verginitade:
egli è lo giglio de l'umanitade,
de suavitate · e de perfetto odore.

Odor divino da ciel n'ha recato,
da quel giardino là ove era piantato:
esso Dio dal Padre beato
ce fo mandato · conserto de fiore.

Fior de Nazzareth si fece chiamare,
de la Giesse virgo vuols pullulare:
nel tempo del fior se volse mostrare,
per confermare · lo suo grande amore.

Amore immenso e carità infinita
m'ha demostrato Cristo, la mia vita;
prese umanitate in deità unita:
gioia compita · n'aggio e grande onore.

Human nature, you were so darkened that you had become like
burnt hay! But your bridegroom has renewed you: do not be ungrateful for such a lover.

Such a lover is the flower of purity, born in the field of virginity:
he is the lily of humankind, of sweetness, and of perfect fragrance.

Divine fragrance he has brought us from heaven, from the garden where he was planted: this God was sent to us from the blessed
Father, a twining of flowers.

He took the name Flower of Nazareth, in the Virgin of Jesse he
chose to stir: in the season of flowers he chose to grow, to testify
his great love.

Christ, my life, has shown me immense love and infinite charity;
he has taken humanity upon himself, joined to his godhead: this
gives me full joy and great honour.

Onor con umiltà volse recepere:
con solennità la turba fe' venire,
la via e la cittade refiorire
tutta, e reverire · lui como Signore.

Signor venerato con gran reverenza,
poi condannato de grave sentenza:
popolo mutato senza providenza,
per molta amenza · cadesti in errore.

Error prendesti contra veritade
quando lo facesti viola de viltade:
la rosa rossa de penalitate
per caritate · remutò el colore.

Color natural ch'avea de bellezza
molta in viltade prese lividezza:
sua suavitade portò amarezza,
tornò in bassezza · lo suo gran valore.

Valor potente fo umiliato,
quel fiore aulente tra piè conculcato,
de spine pungente tutto circundato,
e fu velato · lo grande splendore.

He chose to receive honour with humility: solemnly he made the
crowd come to him, the ways and the populace reflower together,
and revere him as Lord.

Lord venerated with a great reverence, and then condemned to a
grievous penalty: o people, inconstant and without vision, you fell
into error through great stupidity.

You took error's part against truth when, reviling him, you left
his flesh purple with bruises: the red rose changed its colour in
suffering for love.

The natural colour of beauty he had took on dire lividness when
he was reviled: he bore bitterness sweetly, and let his great worth
be humiliated.

Mighty worth was brought low, that breathing flower was
trampled underfoot, surrounded by piercing thorns, and its great
splendour covered.

Splendor che illustra onne tenebroso
fo oscurato per dolor penoso,
e lo suo lume tutto fo renchioso
en un sepolcro · nell'orto del fiore.

Lo fior reposto giacque e sì dormìo;
renacque tosto e resurressìo,
beato corpo e puro refiorìo,
ed apparìo · con grande fulgore.

Fulgore ameno apparìo nell'orto
a Magdalena che 'l piangea morto,
e del gran pianto donògli conforto,
sì che fo absorto · l'amoroso core.

Lo core confortò agli suoi fratelli,
e resuscitò molti fior novelli,
e demorò nello giardin con elli,
con quelli agnelli · cantando d'amore.

Con amor reformasti Tomaso non credente,
quando li mostrasti li tuoi fiori aulente,
quali reservasti, o rosa rubente:
sì che incontinente · gridò con fervore.

Splendour that lightens any shade was darkened by painful grief,
and his light was quite obscured in a sepulchre in the flower-garden.
  The flower placed there lay and slept; it soon came to life again
and arose, blessed body and pure reflowering, and appeared with
great brightness.
  A kindly brightness appeared to Magdalen in the garden who
lamented him as dead, and comforted her in her great weeping so
that her loving heart was wrapt.
  Her heart comforted the brethren, and raised up many new
flowers, and stayed in the garden with them, with those lambs
singing for love.
  With love you remade doubting Thomas, when you showed
him the fragrant flowers which you kept, o embodied rose: so that
at once he cried with fervour.

Fervore amoroso ebbe inebriato,
lo cor gioioso fo esilarato:
quando glorioso t'ebbe contemplato,
allora t'ebbe vocato · Dio e signore.

Signor de gloria sopra al ciel salisti,
con voce sonora degli angeli ascendisti:
con segni di vittoria al Padre redisti,
e resedisti · in sedia ad onore.

Onor ne donasti a servi veraci,
la via demostrasti a li tuoi sequaci:
lo spirito mandasti acciò che infiammati
fussero i sequaci · con perfetto ardore.

Como è somma sapienzia essere reputato pazo per l'amor
de Cristo

Senno me pare e cortesia · empazir per lo bel Messia.

Ello me sa sì gran sapere · a chi per Dio vol empazire,
en Parige non se vidde · ancor sì gran filosofia.

Loving fervour had made him drunk, his joyous heart was ex-
hilarated: when he looked upon you in your glory, he cried – my
Lord and my God.

Lord of Glory, you ascended to heaven, went up to the ringing
voice of angels: you returned to the Father with symbols of victory, and sat again in the place of honour.

You gave honour to your true servants, showed the way to your
followers: sent the Spirit so that your followers were inflamed with
a perfect ardour.

That it Is the Highest Wisdom to Be Thought Mad for
Love of Christ

Sense and nobleness it seems to me, to go mad for the fair Messiah.

It seems to me great wisdom in a man if he wish to go mad for
God, no philosophy so great as this has yet been seen in Paris.

Chi per Cristo va empazato, · par afflitto e tribulato:
ma è maestro conventato · en natura e teologia.

Chi per Cristo ne va pazo, · a la gente sì par matto;
chi non ha provato el fatto, · pare che sia fuor de la via.

Chi vol entrare en questa scola, · troverà dottrina nova:
la pazia, chi non la prova, · già non sa que ben se sia.

Chi vol entrar en questa danza, · trova amor d'esme-
   suranza:
cento dì de perdonanza · a chi li dice villania.

Ma chi va cercando onore, · non è degno del suo amore,
chè Iesù fra doi latrone · en mezo la croce staìa.

Ma chi cerca per vergogna, · ben me par che cetto iogna:
ià, non vada più a Bologna · a 'mparar altra mastria.

He who goes mad for Christ seems afflicted and in tribulation:
but he is an exalted master of nature and theology.

He who goes mad for Christ, certainly seems insane to people;
it seems that he is off the road to whoever has not experienced the
state.

He who wishes to enter this school, will discover new learning:
he who has not experienced madness does not yet know what it is
exactly.

He who wishes to come into this dance will find unbounded
love: a hundred days' indulgence to whoever reviles him.

But he who goes seeking honour is not worthy of His love, for
Jesus stayed upon the cross between two thieves.

But he who seeks in humbleness, will arrive quickly, I am sure:
let him not go to Bologna any more to learn another doctrine.

FEDERIGO II

Oi lasso! non pensai
sì forte mi parisse
lo dipartire da Madonna mia;
ca poi che m'alontai,
ben paria ch'eo morisse,
membrando di sua dolze compagnia;
e giammai tanta pena non durai
se non quando a la nave adimorai.
Ed or mi crio morire certamente,
se la lei non ritorno prestamente.

Tutto quanto eo vio
sì forte mi dispiace,
che non mi lassa in posa in nessun loco;
sì mi stringe el disio,
che non posso aver pace,
e fami reo parere riso e gioco:
membrandomi suo' dolzi 'nsegnamenti,
tutti diporti m'escono di menti;
e non mi vanto ch'eo disdotto sia,
se non là ov'è la dolze donna mia.

ALAS! I did not think that leaving my Lady would cast me down like this; for since I took myself away, it has truly seemed that I've died, remembering her sweet society; and I have never endured such pain unless it was when I was aboard ship. And now I believe I shall die indeed, if I do not speedily go back to where she is.

Everything I see repels me so strongly that it leaves me no rest in any place; desire so oppresses me that I can enjoy no peace, and it makes laughter and sport wrong for me: remembering her sweet graces, every pleasure goes from my mind: and I do not claim to know delight, except where my sweet lady is.

O Deo, como fui matto,
quando mi dipartivi
là ov'era stato in tanta dignitate!
Ed io caro l'accatto,
e scioglio como nivi,
pensando c'altri l'aia 'm potestate!
Ed e' mi pare mille anni la dia
ched eo ritorni a voi, Madonna mia;
lo reo pensero sì forte m'atassa,
che rider nè giucare non mi lassa.

Canzonetta gioiosa,
va a la fior di Soria,
a quella c'à in prigione lo mio core:
di' a la più amorosa
ca per sua cortesia
si rimembri de lo suo servidore,
quello che per suo amore va penando
mentre non faccia tutto 'l suo comando;
e priegalami per la sua bontate
ch'ella mi degia tener lealtate.

O God, how mad I was when I left the place where I had lived in such eminence! And I am paying dearly for it, and melt like snow, when I think that some one else may have her in his power! And the day when I may return to you, my Lady, seems a thousand years away; that evil thought so poisons me, that it does not let me laugh or sport.

Joyous song, go to the flower of Syria, to her who keeps my heart in prison: tell her, the most loving of all, to remember her servant in her courtesy, him who keeps suffering for love of her as long as he cannot be entirely at her command; and beg her in her goodness to keep faith with me.

GIACOMO DA LENTINI

MERAVILLOSAMENTE
un amor mi distringe · e soven ad ogn'ora,
com omo che ten mente
in altra parte e pinge · la simile pintura.
Così, bella, facc'eo:
dentr'a lo core meo · porto la tua figura.

In cor par ch'eo vi porte
pinta como parete, · e non pare di fore.
O Deo, co mi par forte!
Non so se lo savete · com'io v'amo a bon core;
ca son sì vergognoso
ch'eo pur vi guardo ascoso · e non vi mostro amore.

Avendo gran disio
dipinsi una pintura, · bella, voi simigliante;
e quando voi non vio,
guardo in quella figura · e par ch'eo v'agia avante,
sì com om che si crede
salvarsi per sua fede, · ancor non vegia inante.

A LOVE has seized on me wonderfully and makes me remember at all times, like a man who has his mind elsewhere and keeps painting the one picture. So is it with me, my fair: within my heart I bear your image.

It seems I bear you in my heart, painted as you look, and that this does not appear outwardly. O God, how hard this seems! I cannot tell if you know with what a good heart I love you: for I am so hesitant that I even look at you in a covert way, and do not show you love.

Feeling great desire, I painted a picture, my fair, your likeness; and when I do not see you, I look upon that image, and it seems that I have you before me, like a man who thinks to save himself by his faith, although he does not see before him.

Al cor m'arde una doglia
com om che tene 'l foco · a lo suo seno ascoso,
e quando più lo 'nvoglia
alora arde più loco · e non po' stare incluso;
similmente eo ardo
quando passo e non guardo · a voi, viso amoroso.

Se siete, quando passo,
in ver voi non mi giro, · bella, per risguardare.
Andando, ad ogne passo
gittone uno sospiro · che mi facie angosciare.
E certo bene angoscio,
c'a pena mi conosco, · tanto forte mi pare.

Assai v'aggio laudata,
Madonna, in molte parte, · di belleze c'avete.
Non so se v'è contato
ch'eo lo faccia per arte, · chè voi ve ne dolete.
Sacciatelo per singna,
zo ch'e' vòi dire a lingua · quando voi mi vedete.

In my heart a sorrow burns, I am like a man who keeps fire hidden in his bosom, which the more he wraps it round, burns the more fiercely, and cannot be contained; similarly do I burn when I pass and do not look at you, o face of love.

If you are there, I do not turn towards you to gaze, as I pass, my fair. At each step I take, I heave a sigh that puts me in agony. And truly I suffer agony, for I hardly know myself, the feeling seems so strong.

Much have I praised you, in many places, my Lady, for the beauty that is yours. I cannot tell if it is clear to you that I do it with a purpose, since you are distressed by it. Learn from the signs that appear in me when you look, what I wish to say with my lips.

Canzonetta novella,
va e canta nova cosa; · levati da maitino
davanti a la più bella
fiore d'ogn'amorosa, · bionda più c'auro fino.
Lo vostro amor ch'è caro
donatelo al Notaro · ch'è nato da Lentino.

Io m'agio posto in core a Dio servire
com'io potesse gire in paradiso,
all'auto loco c'agio audito dire
si mantiene sollazo, gioco e riso:
sanza Madonna non vi voria gire,
quella c'à blonda testa e claro viso,
chè sanza lei non poteria gaudire,
estando da la mia donna diviso.

Ma no lo dico a tale intendimento
perch'io peccato ci volesse fare,
se non veder lo suo bel portamento,
lo bel viso e lo morbido sguardare:
chè lo mi teria 'n gran consolamento,
vegiendo la mia donna in ghiora stare.

My newborn song, go and sing something new; rise up in the morning and go before the loveliest, the flower of all loving women, more finely fair than gold: 'give your love that is dear to the Notary who was born at Lentino'.

I HAVE set my heart to serving God so that I may go to Paradise, to the holy place where, as I have heard, there is always entertainment, play, and laughter: without my lady I would not want to go there, she who has the fair hair and clear brow, as without her I could not rejoice, being separated from my lady.

But I do not say this with the intention of committing a sin, if I do not see her graceful mien, her lovely face, and soft gaze: for it would keep me in great contentment to see my lady standing there in glory.

RINALDO D'AQUINO

Già mai non mi conforto
nè mi vo' ralegrare,
le navi sono al porto
e vogliono colare:
vassene lo più giente
in terra d'oltra mare,
oi me lassa, dolente,
como deg'io fare?

Vassen 'n altra contrata
e nol mi manda a dire,
io rimangno ingannata;
tanti son li sospire
che mi fanno gran guerra
la notte co' la dia!
Nè in cielo ned in terra
non mi pare ch'io sia.

O Santus, santus Deo
che 'n la Vergin venisti,
tu guarda l'amor meo
poi da me 'l dipartisti.

I'LL never more take comfort, nor do I wish to be gay. The ships
are at the roadstead, and they want to set sail. The gentlest man is
going away, to a land beyond the sea. Alas, wearied and sorrowing,
what am I to do?

He's going to another country, and he did not let me know. I
have been deceived and left; how thick come the sighs that wage
war on me both night and day. And I seem to be neither in heaven
nor on earth.

Holy, holy God who came in the Virgin, watch over my love

Oit alta potestate,
temuta e dottata,
la dolze mi' amore
ti sia raccomandata!

La crocie salva giente
e me facie disviare,
la crocie m' fa dolente:
non mi val Dio pregare.
Oi, crocie pellegrina,
perchè m'ài sì distrutta?
oimè, lassa tapina,
ch'io ardo e 'nciendo tutta.

Lo 'mperador com pacie
tutto 'l mondo mantene
ed a me guerra facie:
m'à tolta la mia spene.
Oit alta potestate
temuta e dottata,
la mia dolze amore
vi sia raccomandata.

now that you have sent him away from me. O high, dread, awful power, may my sweet love enjoy thy care.

The cross saves people and makes me lose my way, the cross makes me sorrowful: praying to God is of no avail. O, excellent cross, why have you destroyed me so? O wearied and wretched woman, for I altogether burn and flame.

The Emperor keeps the whole world at peace and makes war upon me: he has taken my dear hope away. O high, dread, awful power, may my sweet love enjoy your care.

Quando crocie pigliao
cierto nol mi pensai,
quel che tanto m'amao,
ed i' lui tanto amai,
ch'io ne fui batuta
e messa in presgionia
e in cielata tenuta
per tutta vita mia!

Le navi so' a le celle,
'm bon or possan andare,
e la mia amor con elle
la giente che v'à andare.
Oi Padre Criatore,
a porto le conducie,
chè vanno a servidore
de la tua santa crucie.

Però priego, Dolcietto,
che sai la pena mia,
che men facie un sonetto
e mandilo in Soria,
ch'io non posso abentare
la notte nè la dia:
in terra d'oltra mare
istà la vita mia

His becoming a Crusader was so unexpected, he who loved me so much, and I loved him so much that I was beaten for it and put into prison and kept in confinement – for life!

The ships are at the roadsteads, and they can soon depart, and my love with them, the people who are to go. Father Creator, lead them to safe port who go in service to thy holy cross.

So I beg you, Sweetling, who know my grief, to write a sonnet and send it to Syria, as I can have no peace neither by night nor by day: my true love is now in a land beyond the seas.

ORMAI quando flore · e mostrano verdura
le prata e la rivera,
li ausei fanno isbaldore · dentro da la frondura
cantando in lor manera,
infra la primavera · che vene presente
frescamente · sì frondita
ciasuno invita · d'aver gioja intera.

Confortami d'amore · l'aulimento dei fiori
e 'l canto de li auselli.
Quando lo giorno appare · sento li dolci amori
e li versi novelli
che fan sì dolci e belli · e divisati
lor trovati · a provasione;
a gran tençone · stan per li arbuscelli.

Quando l'aloda intendo · e 'l rusignuol vernare,
d'amor lo cor m'afina,
e magiormente intendo · ch'è llegno d'altr'affare,
che d'arder non rifina.
Vedendo quell'ombrina · del fresco bosco,
ben cognosco · c'acortamente
serà gaudente · l'amor che m'inchina.

Now when meadow and bank show flower and greenery, the birds make merry among the leaves, singing in their different ways, while spring that comes here freshly, so leafy, invites each one to have joy entire.

The scent breathed by the flowers and the song of birds encourage me to love. When day appears I hear their sweet loves and the new songs which they make so sweet and fine and their rhyming diversified in rivalry; they vie with one another greatly among the bushes.

When I hear the lark and the nightingale first warbling, my heart is purified with love, and I know better than ever then that it is wood of another sort that is not refined in burning. Seeing that little shade of fresh woodland, I am sure that the love that bends me will be joyful in a subtle way.

China, ch'eo sono amata · e giamai non amai;
ma 'l tempo m'inamora
e fami star pensata · d'aver merzè ormai
d'un fante che m'adora,
e sacio che tortura · per me sostene
e gran pene; · l'un cor mi dice
che si disdice · e l'altro m'incora.

Però prego l'amore · che m'intenda e mi svollia
come la follia vento,
che no mi facie fore · quel che presio mi tollia,
e stia di me contento.
Quelli c'à intendimento · d'avere intera
gioja e cera · del mio amore
senza romore, · nonde à compimento.

GUIDERDONE aspetto avire
da voi, donna, cui servire
non m'è noia;
ancor che mi siate altera,
sempre spero d'avere intera
d'amor gioia.

Bent, since I am loved and have never loved: but the season fills
me with sweetness, so that I think of taking pity now on a youth
who adores me, and I know that he bears torture and great pains for
me; one part of my heart tells me to deny and the other sets me on.
So I pray love for him to understand me and bend my will as
wind does the leaf, and not to do anything publicly that will
cheapen me, and to be content with me. A man who thinks of having the bloom and joy of my love by stealth will not have his way.

I EXPECT a reward from you, my lady, whom to serve is no burden
for me; although you are haughty, still I hope to have complete joy

Non vivo in disperanza,
ancor che mi diffidi
la vostra disdegnanza;
ca spesse volte vidi, · ed è provato,
omo di poco affare
pervenire in gran loco,
s'ello sape avanzare,
moltiplicar lo poco · conquistato.

In disperanza non mi gietto,
ch'io medesmo m'imprometto
d'aver bene:
di bon core è la leanza
ch'i' vi porto, e la speranza
mi mantene.
Però non mi scoragio
d'Amor che m'à distretto:
sì com'omo salvagio,
faragio, ch'el' è detto · ch'ello facie:
per lo reo tempo ride,
sperando che poi pèra
la laida ara che vide:
di donna troppo fera · spero pacie.

of love. I do not live in despair, although your disdain daunts me;
for often have I seen (it is common experience) a man of small
means attain a great place, if he knows how to take advantage and
multiply the little gained.

I'm not thrown into despair, for I promise myself much. I preserve my loyalty to you cheerfully, and hope sustains me.   So I do
not despond because of Love which has caught me fast; I shall act
like a savage – as it is said he acts: he laughs at the evil weather,
hoping the sullen clouds he has seen will pass away: I hope for
peace from a too cruel fair.

S'io pur spero in allegranza,
fina donna, pietanza
in voi si mova;
fina donna, non siate
fera, poi tanta bieltate
in voi si trova.
Ca donna c'à belleze
ed è sanza pietade,
com'omo è, c'à richeze
e usa scarsitade · di ciò c'ave:
se non è bene apreso
nè dritto nè insegnato,
da ogn'omo n'è ripreso,
onuto e dispregiato · e posto a grave.

Donna mia, ch'io non perisca!
s'io vi prego, non v'incrisca
mia preghera:
le belleze ch'en voi pare
mi distringie e lo sguardare
de la ciera.
La figura piagiente
lo core mi diranca:
quando vi tegno mente,
lo spirito mi manca · e torna in ghiaccio.

If I still trust in joy, fine lady, let pity stir in you; fine lady, do not be fierce with me, since you have so much beauty in you. For a woman who is beautiful and without pity is like a man who has riches but practises meanness with what he has: if he is not well advised, or right or enlightened, he is reproved for it by every man, and shamed and despised and put in a sorry position.

My lady, do not let me perish! If I pray to you, may my prayer not displease you: the beauty that shows in you and the very way you look have caught me fast. Your pleasant face lays waste my heart: when I think of you, my spirit fails and turns to ice. Nor am

Nè mica mi spaventa
l'amoroso volere
di ciò che m'ardenta,
ch'io no lo posso avere · ond'io mi sfaccio.

GIACOMINO PUGLIESE

La dolze ciera piagente
e li amorosi semblanti
lo cor m'allegra e la mente
quando mi pare davanti,
sì volentieri la vio
quella cui eo amai;
la bocca ch'eo basciai
ancor l'astetto e disio!

L'aulente bocca e le menne
de lo petto ciercai,
fra le mie braza la tenne;
basciando mi dimandai:
«Messer, se venite a gire,
non facciate adimoranza,
chè non esti bona usanza
lassar l'amore e partire.»

I in the least scared in my passionate desire for what burns me – I
am undone because it is not mine.

Her sweet and pleasant face and her loving expression delight
my heart and mind when she comes before me; so readily I look on
her whom I have loved; I still desire and long for the mouth I
kissed.
    I sought her fragrant mouth and both her breasts, I held her in
my arms; kissing, she asked me: 'Sir, if you call in passing, do not
stay, for it is not mannerly to leave love and depart.'

Allotta ch'eo mi partivi
e dissi: «A Deo v'accomando»
la bella guardò 'nver mivi,
sospirava lagrimiando;
tant'erano li sospiri
ch'a pena mi rispondia:
e la dolze donna mia
non mi lassava partiri.

Eo non fùivi sì lontano
che lo meo amor v'ubriasse,
nè non credo che Tristano
Isaotta tanto amasse.
Quando vio venir l'aulente,
infra le donne apariri,
lo cor mi trae di martiri
e ralegrami la mente.

ISPLENDIENTE
stella d'albore
e piagiente
donna d'amore!

Then when I separated from her and said, 'I commend you to God', that fair one looked towards me, sighing and weeping; so frequent were her sighs that she hardly answered me: that sweet fair of mine did not let me leave.

I was not so far away that my love had left me, and I do not think that Tristan loved Iseult as much. When I see that fragrant one appear among the women, my heart leads me from sufferings and my mind rejoices.

SHINING star of dawn and pleasant mistress!

Bella, 'l mio core, · c'ài in tua ballìa
non si diparte · da voi, in fidanza;
or ti rimembri, · bella, la dia
che noi fermammo · la dolze amanza.

Bella, or ti sia
a rimembranza
la dolze dia
e l'alegranza,

che in diportanza · istava con vui:
Basciando dicia: · «Anima mia,
lo dolze amore · ch'è 'ntra noi dui,
non falsiasse · cosa che sia.»

Lo tuo splendore
mi à priso,
di gioia d'amore
mi à conquiso,

sì che non auso · da voi partire
e non faria · se Dio volesse:
ben mi poria · doblar martire
se fallimento · 'nver voi facesse.

My heart, that you have in your keeping, my fair, does not leave
you, in faith: remember now, my fair, the day when we affirmed
our sweet love.
My fair, let that sweet day now come back to you and the joy
when I stayed dallying with you: kissing, you said to me: 'My
soul, the sweet love that is between us two would not prove false
for anything that is.'
Your brightness has so taken me, has overcome me with joy of
love
so that I dare not leave you, and I would not if God were to will
it: well might He double my torments if I really failed you.

Donna valente,
la mia vita
per voi, più gente,
è ismarita:

la dolze aita · è conforto
membrando ch'èite · a lo mio brazo,
quando scendesti · a me in diporto
per la finestra · de lo palazo.

Alor t'ei, bella,
in mia ballìa,
rosa novella,
per me temìa.

Di voi, amorosa, · presi vengianza:
o in fide rosa, · fosti patuta!
Se 'n ballìa avesse · e Spagna e Franza
non averìa · sì rica tenuta.

Quand'io partìa
da voi, intando
dicivi a mia
in sospirando:

Rare woman, my life has gone astray for pleasant you:
My sweet help is my comfort in remembering that I had you in
my arms, my fair, when you slipped down to me in delight from
the window of your high house.
Then, my fair, I had you in my power, new rose, you feared because of me.
I took revenge upon you, loving creature: o rose indeed, you
suffered! If I had in my power Spain and France, I would not have
so rich an estate.
When I took myself from you, you said the while with sighs:

34

«Se vai, meo sire · fai dimoranza
ve' ch'io m'arendo · e faccio altra vita,
giamai non entro · in gioco e danza,
ma sto rinchiusa · più che romita.»

Or vi sia a mente,
Madonna mia,
che 'ntra la gente
v'èi in ballìa.

Lo vostro core · non falsiasse:
di me vi sia · ben rimembranza.
Tu sai, amore, · pene ch'io trasse:
chi ne diparte · more in tristanza!

Chi ne diparte,
fiore di rosa,
non abbia parte
di buona cosa,

chè Deo fecie amore · dolcie e fino.
Di due amanti · che amar di core,
canta asai · versi Giacomino
e' che si parte · di reo amore.

'If you go, my lord, and stay away, see if I do not give myself up
and lead a different life, never enter into game or dance, but live
more cloistered than a nun.'

Now remember, mistress mine, that I am the one who has you in
his power.

Do not let your heart be false: let the memory of me stay with
you. You know, love, the pains I have undergone: let him who
parts us die in sadness!

Let whoever parts us, flower of the rose, have no part in anything good,

since God made sweet and tempered love. Giacomino, he who
shuns wicked love, rhymes out many lines for two lovers who have
loved with all their hearts.

MORTE, perchè m'ài fatta sì gran guerra
che m'ài tolta Madonna, ond'io mi doglio?
La fior de le bellezze mort'ài 'n terra,
per che lo mondo non amo nè voglio.
Villana morte, che non ài pietanza,
disparti amore e togli l'allegranza
e dài cordoglio.
La mia alegranza post'ài in gran tristanza,
chè m'ài tolto la gioia e l'alegranza
ch'aver soglio.

Sollea aver sollazo e gioco e riso
più che null'altro cavalier che sia;
or n'è gita Madonna in Paradiso:
portòne la dolze speranza mia,
lasciòmi in pene e con sospiri e pianti,
levòmi da sollazo, gioco e canti
e compagnia;
or no la vegio, nè le sto davanti
e non mi mostra li dolzi sembianti
che far solìa.

DEATH, why have you waged so great a war against me, taking my
lady from me, at which I grieve? You have killed the flower of the
beauties of earth, so that I no longer love nor desire the world. Base
death, who have no pity, you divide love, take away delight and
give sorrowing. You have turned my delight to great sadness, for
you have taken away the joy and delight I used to have.

I used to enjoy ease and sport and laughter, more than any other
knight living; now my lady has gone to Paradise, she has borne
away my sweet hopes, left me in pain, sighing and weeping, plucked
me from ease, sport and songs and company: now I do not see her,
nor stand before her, and she does not show me the sweet looks
she was wont to.

Oi Deo, perchè m'ài posto in tale iranza?
ch'io son smaruto, non so ove mi sia,
che m'ài levata la dolze speranza.
Partit'ài la più dolze compagnia,
che sia in nulla parte, ciò m'è aviso.
Oimè, Madonna, chi tene tuo viso
in sua ballìa?
lo vostro insegnamento dond'è miso?
e lo tuo franco cor chi lo mi à priso,
o donna mia?

Ov'è Madonna e lo suo insegnamento,
la sua bellezza e la gran canoscianza,
lo dolze riso e lo bel parlamento,
gli ochi e la boca e la bella sembianza,
lo adornamento e la sua cortesia?
Madonna, per cui stava tutavia
in alegranza,
or no la vegio nè notte, nè dia,
e non m'abella, sì com' far solia,
in sua sembianza.

O God, why have you set me in such wrath? I am bewildered, not knowing where I am, for you have taken away my sweet hope. You have taken the sweetest company that can ever be, I am sure. O my Lady, who has your face in his keeping? your influence, where is it turned? And who has robbed me of your generous heart, O my love?

Where is my Lady and her influence, her beauty and great wit, her sweet laugh and lovely speech, her eyes and mouth and her comely appearance, her grace and courtesy? My Lady, for whose sake I spent my days in gladness, I no longer see by night or day, and I am not ennobled, as I was wont to be, in her gaze.

Se fosse mio lo regno d'Ungaria,
con Greza e la Magna infino in Franza,
lo gran tesoro di Santa Sofia,
nom poria ristorar sì gran perdanza
come fu in quella dia che si n'andao.
Madonna de sta vita trapassao,
con gran tristanza
sospiri e pene e pianti mi lasciao,
e giamai nulla gioia mi mandao
per confortanza.

Se fosse al meo voler, donna, di voi,
diciesse a Dio sovran, che tuto face,
che giorno e notte istessimo amboduoi.
Or sia voler di Dio, da c'a lui piace.
Membro e ricordo quand'era con mico,
sovente m'apellava «dolze amico»,
ed or nol face,
poi Dio la prese e menolla con sico.
La sua verute sia, bella, con tico
e la sua pace.

If the kingdom of Hungary were mine, with Greece and Germany all the way to France, the great treasure of Santa Sophia, they would not make good the great loss it was the day she went away. My Lady passed on from this life, with great sadness, sighs, and pain and tears she left me, and never sent me any joy to comfort me.

If your being were in my hands, lady, I would say to God the king, who orders all things, that we should stay together day and night. Now let it be as God wills, since she delights him. I remember and dwell on the time she was with me, she often called me 'sweet friend', and now she does not, since God took her and led her away with him. His goodness be with you, my fair, and his peace.

PIER DELLA VIGNA

AMORE, in cui disio ed ò speranza,
di voi, bella, m'à dato guiderdone;
guardomi infin che vegna la speranza,
pur aspetando bon tempo e stagione:
com'om ch'è in mare ed à spene di gire,
quando vede lo tempo ed ello spanna,
e giamai la speranza no lo 'nganna:
così faccio, Madonna, in voi venire.

Or potess'eo venire a voi, amorosa,
come larone ascoso e non paresse!
be 'l mi teria in gioia aventurosa,
se l'amor tanto bene mi faciesse.
Sì bel parlante, donna, con voi fora,
e direi come v'amai lungiamente
più ca Piramo Tisbia dolzemente,
ed ameragio infin ch'eo vivo ancora.

Vostro amor è che mi tene in disio,
e donami speranza con gran gioia,
ch'eo non curo s'io dollio od ò martiro
membrando l'ora ched io vegno a voi;

LOVE, in whom I wish and hope, has given me, my fair, the reward
of you. I save myself, awaiting good weather and season, until hope
becomes real: as a man who is on the seas trusts to make way when
he sees the weather for it, and spreads his sails, and that hope never
deceives him; I do the same, my Lady, to come to you.

If I could come to you now, loving creature, like an undercover
thief and never be seen! It would be such luck and joy for me, if
love were to do me so great a favour. I would be so eloquent, love,
and tell you I have loved you long, more sweetly than Pyramus,
Thisbe, and I will love you as long as I live.

It is love of you that makes me desire, and gives me hope accompanied with great joy, for I do not care if I sorrow and suffer while
I can think of the moment when I shall come to you; for if I delay

ca s'io troppo dimoro, aulente lena,
pare ch'io pera, e voi me perderete.
Adunque, bella, se ben mi volete,
guardate ch'eo no mora in vostra spera.

In vostra spera vivo, donna mia,
e lo mio core adesso a voi dimando,
e l'ora tardi mi pare che sia
che fino amore a vostro cor mi manda;
e guardo tempo che mi sia a piaciere
e spanda le mie vele inver voi, rosa,
e prendo porto là 've si riposa
lo meo core al vostro insegnamento.

Mia canzonetta, porta esti compianti
a quella c'à 'n balìa lo meo core,
e le mie pene contale davanti
e dille com eo moro per su' amore,
e mandimi per suo messaggio a dire
com io conforti l'amor ch'i' lei porto;
e s'io ver lei feci alcuno torto,
donimi penitenza al suo valore.

too long, o fragrant breath, it seems I die, and that you will lose
me. So, my fair, if you love me, watch lest I die hoping for you.

I live hoping for you, my lady, and now I ask my heart back
from you, and it seems late for fine love to bring me to your heart;
and I watch for the time that will favour my hope, when I may
spread my sails towards you, rose, and harbour where my heart
rests under your sway.

My little song, bear these complaints to her who has my heart in
her power, and lay my sufferings before her and tell her how I am
dying for love of her, and let her send a message to tell how I am to
console the love I bear her, and if I have done her any wrong, let
her impose penance upon me according to her worth.

CIELO D'ALCAMO

Contrasto

«Rosa fresca aulentissima · c'apar' inver la state,
le donne ti disiano · pulzelle e maritate,
trami d'esti focora · se t'este a bolontate.
    Per te non aio abento notte e dia,
    penzando pur di voi, Madonna mia.»

«Se di meve trabagliti, · follia lo ti fa fare.
Lo mar potresti arompere · a' venti asemenare,
l'abere d'esto secolo · tutto quanto asembrare:
    avèreme non pòteri a esto monno.
    Avanti li cavelli m'aritonno.»

«Se li cavelli artoniti · avanti foss'io morto,
ca i' sì mi perdera · lo solaccio e diporto.
Quando ci passo e vejoti · rosa fresca de l'orto,
    bono conforto donimi tut'ore:
    poniamo che s'ajunga nostro amore.»

Contest in Words (between a man and a woman, the man
speaking first)

'Rose, fresh and most fragrant, that appears about the summertime, the women envy you, the young and the married, bring me out
of this fire, if it please you. For you I have no rest, night or day, as
I think of you always, my lady.'

    'If you worry yourself for my sake, folly makes you do so. You
might delve the sea and sow the wind, bring together all the wealth
of temporality: you could not have me in this world. I would shave
off my hair first.'

    'If you are to shave off your hair, may I be dead first, for then I
should lose all solace and delight. When I pass by and see you,
fresh rose of the garden, you give me great comfort at all times:
what do you say to joining ourselves in love?'

«Che nostro amore ajungasi · non boglio m'atalenti.
Se ti ci trova pàremo · cogli altri miei parenti,
guarda non t'arigolgano · questi forti correnti.
    Como ti sappe bona la venuta,
    consiglio che ti guardi a la partuta.»

«Se i tuoi parenti trovammi · e che mi pozzon fari?
Una difensa mettoci · di dumilia agostari,
Non mi tocàra padreto · per quanto avere à 'm Bari,
    Vive lo 'mperadore, graz' a Deo!
    Intendi, bella, quel che ti dico eo?»

«Tu me no lasci vivere · nè sera nè maitino.
Donna mi son di perperi · d'auro massamotino.
Se tanto aver donassemi · quanto à lo Saladino
    e per ajunta quant'à lo Soldano,
    tocàreme nom pòteri la mano.»

«Molte sono le femine · c'ànno dura la testa,
e l'omo com parabole · l'adimina e amonesta:
tanto intorno percàzala · fin che l'à in sua podesta.

'I won't have you persuading me to join ourselves in love. If my father and relatives find you here, watch that they do not lay hold of you: they are good runners. As the road here was well known to you, I advise you to look to the road away.'

'If your relatives find me here, what can they do to me? They'll risk a fine of two thousand Augustans, so your father will not touch me for all the wealth there is in Bari: long live the Emperor, thanks be to God! Do you understand what I mean, my fair?'

'You will not let me be, morning or evening. I am a woman of Greek coin and Arabian gold. If you were to bring me as much substance as Saladin has with what the Sultan has to boot, you should not touch my hand.'

'Many are the women who have hard heads, and man masters them and controls them with his words: pursues them until he has

Femina d'omo non si può tenere:
guardati, bella, pur di ripentere.»

«Ch'eo me ne pentesse · davanti foss'io aucisa,
ca nulla bona femina · per me fosse riprisa!
Aersera passastici, · còremo, a la distisa,
   Acquestiti riposo, canzoneri:
   le tue paràole a me non piaccion gueri.»

«Doi! quante son le schiantora · che m'ài mise a lo core,
e solo pur penzànnone: · la dia quanno vo fore!
Femina d'esto secolo · non amai tanto ancore,
   quant'amo teve, rosa invidiata:
   ben credo che mi fosti distinata.»

«Se distinata fosseti · caderia de l'alteze,
che male messe forano · en teve mie belleze.
Se tanto addivenissemi · tagliàrami le treze,
   e comsore m'arenno a una magione,
   avanti che m'artocchi 'n la persone.»

them in his power. Woman cannot keep herself from man: watch,
my fair, you may be repentant yet.'

'I repent! first let me be killed, so that no good woman may be
reproved for my sake. Last night, you kept passing this way, take a
rest, minstrel: your words do not please me one bit.'

'Ah, how many wounds have you inflicted on my heart, as I
know when I am alone and think! – but when I go out by day! I
never yet loved a woman in this world as I love you, coveted rose:
I do believe you were destined for me.'

'If I were destined for you, I should fall from on high, for ill
would my beauties be entrusted to you. If that were to happen to
me, I should cut all my hair and enter a religious house as a sister,
before you touched my person.'

«Se tu comsore arenneti, · donna col viso cleri,
a lo mostero vènoci · e rènnomi confreri.
Per tanta prova vèncere · faràlo volonteri.
    Con teco stao la sera e lo maitino:
    besogn'è ch'io ti tenga al meo dimino.»

«Boimè, tapina misera, · com'ao reo distinato!
Gieso Cristo l'altissimo · del tutto m'è airato:
conciepistimi a abàttere · in omo blestiemato!
    Cerca la terra ch'este granne assai,
    chiù bella donna di me troverai.»

«Ciercat'aio Calabria · Toscana e Lombardia,
Puglia, Costantinopoli · Gienoa, Pisa, Soria,
Lamagna e Babilonia, · e tuta Barberia:
    donna non ci trovai tanto cortese,
    perchè sovrana di meve te prese.»

«Poi tanto trabagliastiti · facioti meo pregheri
che tu vadi adomànimi · a mia mare e a mon peri.
Se dare mi ti degnano, · menami a lo mosteri,

'If you make yourself a sister, lady of the clear brow, I will go to
the monastery and offer myself as a friar. To win you by so great a
trial, I will submit willingly. I will stay with you evening and
morning: I must have you in my power.'

'Alas! miserable creature, what an evil fate is mine! Jesus Christ
on high is altogether angered against me: you have brought me
forth to encounter a man self-damned! Search the earth which is
large enough, you will find a woman more beautiful than I.'

'I have searched Calabria, Tuscany and Lombardy, Puglia, Con-
stantinople, Genoa, Pisa, Syria, Germany, and Babylon, and all
Barbary: I have not found a woman so gracious. I have taken you
to be my queen.'

'As you have endured so much for my sake, I shall request this
of you: that you go and ask for me from my mother and father: if

e sposami davanti de la jenti,
e poi farò li tuo comannamenti.»

«Di ciò che dici, vitama, · neiente non ti bale,
ca de le tuo' parabole · fatto n'ò ponti e scale.
Penne penzasti metere, · sonti cadute l'ale;
   e dato t'aio la bolta sotana.
   Dunque, se pòi, teniti villana.»

«En paura non metermi · di nullo manganiello:
istomi 'n esta groria · d'esto forte castiello.
Prezo le tue parabole · meno che d'un zitiello.
   Se tu no' levi e vaitine di quaci,
   se tu ci fosse morto ben mi chiaci.»

«Dunque voresti, vitama, · ca per te fosse strutto?
Se morto essere deboci · od intagliato tutto,
di quaci non mi mosera · se non ài de lo frutto
   lo quale stao ne lo tuo jardino:
   disiolo la sera e lo maitino.»

they deign to give me to you, lead me to the monastery and marry
me before the world, and then I shall do your bidding.'

'Nothing of what you say, my life, will do you any good, for I
have made a ladder and bridge of your words. You thought to put
out feathers, your wings have fallen; and I have battered down your
defences. Then save yourself, country girl, if you can.'

'You do not frighten me with any engine of war: I stay in the
fastness of this strong castle. I value your words less than a boy's.
If you do not stir and go away from here, I should like to see you
dead.'

'So, my life, you would have me destroyed for you? If I must
meet my death, be cut to pieces, I shall not move from here until
I have the fruit that is in your garden; I long for it morning and
evening.'

«Di quel frutto non àbero · conti nè cabalieri
molto lo disiano · marchesi e justizieri,
avere nonde pòtero, · gironde molto feri.
    Intendi bene ciò che bole dire?
    Men'este di mill'onze lo tuo avire!»

«Molti son li garofani · ma non che salma 'ndai.
Bella, non dispregiaremi · s'avanti non m'assai!
Se vento è im proda e girasi · e giungeti a le prai,
    a rimembrare t'ao este parole:
    ca d'esta animella assai mi dole.»

«Macàra se doleseti · ca cadesse angosciato,
la giente ci corresoro · da traverso e da lato,
tutt'a meve diciessono: · Acorri esto malnato!
    Non ti degnàra porgiere la mano
    per quanto avere à 'l Papa e lo Soldano.»

«Deo lo volesse, vitama, · te fosse morto in casa!
L'arma n'anderia cònsola · ca dì e notte pantasa.
La jente ti chaimàrano: · Oi perjura malvasa,

‘Lords and knights have had none of that fruit; marquises and justices have much desired it, they could not have it, and went away angered. Do you understand just what I mean? Your substance is less than a thousand gold ounces.’

‘Many are the carnations, but you haven't a bushel of them. My fair, do not despise me before you try me! If the wind is against your prow and turns and you come to shore, you will have these words to remember. I am sorely stricken for this little soul of yours.’

‘My dear, well may you be stricken, for if you were to fall in anguish, and people ran from this side and that, and everyone said to me: Help this wretch! I would not condescend to stretch my hand to you, for all the wealth the Pope and Sultan have.’

‘Pray God my life should leave me in your house! My soul would be comforted that wanders day and night: people would cry

c'ài morto l'omo in càsata, traita!
Sanz'onni colpo levimi la vita.»

«Se tu no' levi e vàtine   co la maledizione,
li frati miei ti trovano · dentro chissa magione.
Bello, ben lo mi sofero · perdici la persone;
   c'a meve se' venuto a sormonare:
   parente ned amico non t'ave a aitare.»

«A meve non aitano · amici nè parenti:
istrano mi son, càrama · enfra esta bona jenti.
Or fa un anno, vitama, · ch'entrata mi se' 'n menti.
   Di canno ti vististi lo majuto,
   bella, da quello jorno son feruto.»

«Ai, tanno namorastiti, · ahi Juda lo traito!
como se fosse porpore, · iscarlato o sciamito?
S'a le Vangelie jurimi · che mi si' a marito,
   avereme non poteri a esto monno.
   Avanti in mare jittomi al perfonno.»

at you: O evil and foresworn, who have killed that man in your
house, traitress. You take my life without a blow.'
   'If you don't stir and go away with my curse upon your head,
my brothers may find you in this house. My handsome friend, if
you are to lose your life, I could well bear it; you have come to
harangue me: you have neither relative nor friend to help you.'
   'Neither friends nor relatives aid me: I am a stranger, my life,
among these good people. It is a year now since you came into my
mind. From the time I saw you in your brocade dress, my fair, since
then have I been wounded.'
   'What, you fell in love for that, O Judas the traitor, as if it were
the purple, scarlet, or samite? If you swear on the gospels you will
be my husband, you shall not have me in this world. I had sooner
throw myself into the depths of the sea.'

«Se tu nel mare jititi, · donna cortese e fina,
dereto mi ti misera · per tuta la marina,
e poi c'anegasseti · trobàrati a la rina;
    solo per questa cosa adimpretare:
    con teco m'aio a jiungere a pecare.»

«Segnomi in Patre e 'n Filio · ed in santo Matteo!
So ca non se' tu retico · o figlio di giudeo,
e cotale parabole · non udì dire anch'eo!
    Mortasi la femina a lo 'ntutto
    perdeci lo sabore e lo disdutto.»

«Ben lo saccio, càrama; · altro non pozzo fare!
Se quisso non arcomplimi, · lassone lo cantare.
Fallo, mia donna, plazati, · chè bene lo puoi fare!
    Ancora tu nomm'ami, molto t'amo,
    sì preso m'ài como lo pesce a l'amo.»

«Sazzo che m'ami, e amoti · di core paladino.
Levati suso e vatene, · tornaci a lo matino,
Se ciò che dico faciemi, · di bon cor t'amo e fino.

'If you throw yourself into the sea, my gracious, fine lady, I shall keep myself behind you through all its breadth, and when you have drowned, I shall find you on the sand only to win this: that I join myself with you in sin.'

'I sign myself in the name of the Father, the Son, and Saint Matthew! I know you are not a heretic or the son of a Jew, but I have never heard such words. Once a woman is dead, she loses flavour and delightfulness altogether.'

'I know that perfectly well, dearest; I can do nothing else! If you do not grant me my will, I leave off singing. Do it, lady, be pleased to, as you can perfectly well. Even if you don't love me, I love you greatly. You have taken me like a fish with the hook.'

'I know that you love me, and I love you with perfect heart. Rise up and go, come back in the morning. If you do what I say, I

Quisso t'imprometto eo sanza faglia:
te' la mia fede che m'ài in tua baglia.»

«Per zo che dici, càrama, · neiente non mi muvo.
Inanti prenni e scannami: · tolli esto cortel nuvo.
Esto fatto far potesi · inanti scalfi un uovo:
   Arcompli mi' talento, amica bella,
   chè l'arma co lo core mi s'infella.»

«Ben sazzo, l'arma doleti, · com'omo c'ave arsura.
Esto fatto non potesi · per null'altra misura.
Se non a le Vangelie, · che mo ti dico, jura,
   avere me non puoi in tua podesta:
   innanti prenni e tagliami la testa.»

«L'Evangiele, càrama? · ca io le porto in sino!
A lo mostero presile: · non ci era lo patrino.
Sovr'esto libro juroti · mai non ti vegno mino.
   Arcompli mi' talento in caritate
   che l'arma me ne sta in suttilitate.»

shall love you with a good and gentle heart. This I promise without deception: keep faith with me for you have me in your power.'

'I am not moving in the least for all you say. First take and finish me: draw this new knife. It can be done quicker than you peel an egg. Fulfill my desire, fair mistress, for soul and heart are filling me with bitterness.'

'I know perfectly well, your soul torments you, like a man who suffers from a burn. This thing cannot be done in any other way — if you do not swear on the Gospel, as I tell you now, you cannot possess me. First take me and cut off my head.'

'The Gospel, dearest? I have it here in my bosom! I took it from the monastery: the priest wasn't there. Upon this book I swear never to fail you. Do what I want for mercy's sake, as my soul grows faint at all this.'

«Meo sire, poi jurastimi · eo tuta quanna incenno.
Sono a la tua presenza · da voi non mi difenno.
S'eo minespreso àioti, · merzè, a voi m'arrenno.
    A lo letto ne gimo a la bon'ura,
    chè chissà cosa n'è data in ventura.»

ANONIMO

PÀRTITE, amore, adeo,
chè troppo ce se' stato;
lo maitino è sonato,
giorno mi par che sia.

Pàrtite, amore, adeo,
che non fossi trovato
in sì fina cellata
come nui semo stati.
Or me bacia, occhio meo;
tosto sia l'andata
tenendo la tornata
come d'innamorati,
sì che per spesso usato
nostra gioia renovi,
nostro stato non trovi
la mala gelosia.

'My lord, since you have sworn to me, I am all on fire. I am with you, and do not defend myself from you. If I have slighted you, pardon, I surrender to you. Let us to bed speedily, for who knows what the future holds for us.'

LEAVE, my love, farewell, for you have tarried too long; morning has rung, I think it is full day.
    Leave, my love, farewell, lest you be found in so fine a retreat as we have been in. Now kiss me, apple of my eye; let your going be quick, looking to the return, as lovers do, so that our joy, often proved, may be renewed, let our sweet state encounter no evil jealousy.

Pàrtite, amore, adeo,
e vanne tostamente,
ch'ogni tua cosa t'aggio
parecchiata in presente.

FOR de la bella caiba · fugge lo lusignolo.
Piange lo fantino · però che non trova
lo so usilino · ne la gaiba nova,
e dice con duolo: · chi gli avrì l'usolo?
e dice con duolo: · chi gli avrì l'usolo?
E in un boschetto · se mise ad andare
sentì l'osoletto · sì dolce cantare.
– Oi bel lusignolo · torne nel mio brolo
oi bel lusignolo · torna nel mio brolo.

Leave, my love, farewell, and go speedily away, for I have made everything of yours ready for you.

OUT from the fine cage flies the nightingale. The little child is crying because he does not find his little bird in the new cage, and he says with grief: who opened the door for him? and he says with grief: who opened the door for him? And he started walking in a little wood, he heard the fledgling that so sweetly sang. O lovely nightingale, come back into my garden: O lovely nightingale, come back into my garden.

TAPINA oi me, ch'amava uno sparviero,
amaval tanto ch'io me ne moria;
a lo richiamo ben m'era manero
ed umque troppo pascer nol dovia.
Or è montato e salito sì altero
assai più alto che far non solia,
ed è assiso dentro a un verziero,
un'altra donna lo tene in balia.

Isparver mio, ch'io t'aveo nodrito,
sonaglio d'oro ti facea portare
perchè dell'ucellar fosse più ardito;
or se' salito siccome lo mare,
ed a' rotti li geti e se' fuggito,
quando eri fermo nel tuo ucellare.

COMPIUTA DONZELLA

A LA stagion che il mondo foglia e fiora
accresce gioia a tutt'i fini amanti;
vanno insieme a li giardini allora
che gli augelletti fanno dolci canti:

MISERABLE that I am, I loved a sparrow-hawk, loved him so
much that I was dying for love of him: he was very obedient to my
call, and I never had to give him too much. Now he has flown up
and mounted so proudly, higher far than he used to do, and he has
perched in a garden, another woman keeps him in.

Sparrow-hawk mine, I have fed you, I gave you a bell of gold to
wear, so that you might be bolder in your hawking. Now you have
risen up like the sea, and have broken your chains, and have flown
when you were secure in your preserve.

IN the season when the world puts out leaf and flower, the joy of
gentle lovers grows; they go to the gardens together when the
little birds make sweet song: all feeling people fall in love, and each

la franca gente tutta s'innamora,
ed in servir ciascun traggesi inanti,
ed ogni damigella in gioi' dimora;
a me n'abbondan marrimenti e pianti.

Ca lo mio padre m'ha messa in errore
e tenemi sovente in forte doglia:
donar mi vuole, a mia forza, segnore.
Ed io di ciò non ho disio nè voglia,
e 'n gran tormento vivo a tutte l'ore:
però non mi rallegra fior nè foglia.

GUIDO GUINIZELLI

Vedut' ho la lucente stella diana,
ch'appare anzi che 'l giorno rend'albore,
c'ha preso forma di figura umana,
sovr'ogni'altra mi par che dea splendore;
viso di neve colorato in grana
occhi lucenti gai e pien d'amore;
non credo che nel mondo sia cristiana
sì piena di beltate e di valore.

man passes his days in doing service, and every maiden lives in joy;
but my bitterness and tears are multiplied.

For my father has wronged me, and often keeps me in deep anguish: he wishes to give me a husband against my will. And I have no wish or desire for that, and spend every hour in great torment: so that no joy comes to me from either flower or leaf.

I HAVE seen the shining star of morning which shows before day yields its first light, and which has taken the shape of a human being, I think she gives more brightness than any other. Face like snow tinged with red, shining eyes that are gay and full of love; I do not believe that in the world there is a Christian girl so full of beauty and worth.

Ed io da lo su' amor son assalito
con sì fera battaglia di sospiri
ch'avanti a lei di dir non seri' ardito:
così conoscess'ella i miei disiri,
chè, senza dir, di lei seria servito
per la pietà ch'avrebbe de' martiri.

I' vo' del ver la mia donna laudare
ed assembrargli la rosa e lo giglio:
più che la stella diana splende e pare,
e ciò ch'è lassù bello a lei somiglio.
Verde rivera a lei rassembro e l'aire,
tutti color di fior, giallo e vermiglio,
oro e azzurro e ricche gioi' per dare,
medesmo amor per lei raffina miglio.

Passa per via adorna e sì gentile;
ch'abbassa orgoglio a cui dona salute
e fa 'l di nostra fè se non la crede;
e non si pò appressar omo ch'è vile;
ancor vi dico c'ha maggior vertute:
null'om pò mal pensar fin che la vede.

And I am beset by love of her with so fierce a battle of sighs that
I would not dare say anything in her presence. Then, would that
she knew my desires, so that, without speaking, I should be re-
quited by the pity she would take upon my torments.

I wish to praise my lady most truly and compare her to the rose
and the lily: she shines and appears like the morning star, and I
liken to her what is lovely on high. I compare green banks and the
air to her, all colours of flowers, yellow and crimson, gold and blue
and rich jewels to be offered, love itself is made purer through her.
  She goes by, comely and so kind, that she humbles the pride of
whom she greets and makes him of our faith if he does not already
believe it; and no man who is base can approach; and more, I tell
you she has greater power: no man can think evil from the time
he has seen her.

GUIDO CAVALCANTI

Avete 'n voi li fiori e la verdura
e ciò che luce od è bello a vedere;
risplende più che sol vostra figura,
chi voi non vede mai non può valere.
In questo mondo non ha creatura
sì piena di bieltà nè di piacere:
e chi d'amor si teme, l'assicura
vostro bel viso a tanto in sè volere.

Le donne che vi fanno compagnia,
assai mi piaccion per lo vostro amore:
ed i' le prego, per lor cortesia,
che qual più puote, più vi faccia onore,
ed aggia cara vostra segnoria,
perchè di tutte siete la migliore.

Chi è questa che ven, ch'ogn'om la mira,
e fa tremar di chiaritate l'a're,
e mena seco Amor, sì che parlare
null'omo pote, ma ciascun sospira?

You have in you the flowers and all green things and what shines or is fair to see; your face is more resplendent than the sun, he who does not see you can never know your worth. In this world there is no creature so full of beauty or of pleasantness: and he who fears love, is reassured by your lovely face so as to desire as much in himself.

The women who accompany you, are dear to me because of your loving regard: and I beg them, in their courtesy, that the one who best can, should do you most honour, and hold your sovereignty dear, because of them all you are the best.

Who is this who comes, that every man looks on her, who makes the air tremble with brightness, and brings Love with her, so that no man can speak, but each one sighs? O, just how she looks when

Deh, che rassembla quando li occhi gira,
dical Amor, ch'i' no 'l savria contare:
cotanto d'umiltà donna mi pare,
che ciascun'altra inver' di lei chiam'ira.

Non si porìa contar la sua piagenza,
ch'a lei s'inchina ogni gentil vertute,
e la beltate per sua dea la mostra.
Non fu sì alta già la mente nostra,
e non si pose in noi tanta salute,
che propriamente n'aviam canoscenza.

FRESCA rosa novella,
piacente Primavera,
per prata e per rivera
gaiamente cantando,
vostro fin pregio mando · a la verdura.

Lo vostro pregio fino
in gio' si rinovelli
da grandi e da zitelli
per ciascuno cammino;

she glances round, let love say, for I could never describe it: she seems so much a woman of modesty, that every other one beside her is to be called a thing of wrath.

Her pleasantness could not be described, since every gentle virtue bends to her, and beauty shows her for its goddess. Our minds have never been so exalted, nor have we in ourselves so much grace, that we can ever rightly have knowledge of this.

FRESH new rose, delighting Spring, gaily singing by meadow and bank, I declare your rare gifts to the greenery.

Let your rare gifts be celebrated anew by grown men and youths

e càntine gli augelli
ciascuno in suo latino
da sera e da matino
su li verdi arbuscelli.
Tutto lo mondo canti
(poi che lo tempo vène)
sì come si convene,
vostr'altezza pregiata;
chè siete angelicata · criatura.

Angelica sembianza
in voi, donna, riposa;
Dio, quanto aventurosa
fue la mia disianza!
Vostra cera gioiosa,
poi che passa e avanza
natura e costumanza,
ben è mirabil cosa.
Fra lor le donne dea
via chiaman come siete:
tanto adorna parete
ch'eo non saccio contare;
e chi poria pensare · oltr'a natura?

and let birds sing of them, each in his own tongue, evening and morning, in the green bushes. Let the whole world sing (now that the time is come), as is right, of your varied excellence; for you are an angelic creature.

The likeness of an angel is in you, my lady; God, how lucky my desire was! Your glad look is certainly a wonderful thing when it surpasses both nature and wont. Among themselves the women call you goddess, as indeed you are: you appear so favoured that I cannot describe it; and who could think beyond nature?

Oltr'a natura umana
vostra fina piagenza
fece Dio, per essenza
che voi foste sovrana:
per che vostra parvenza
ver' me non sia lontana;
or non mi sia villana
la dolce provedenza.
E se vi pare oltraggio
ch'ad amarvi sia dato,
non sia da voi blasmato:
chè solo Amor mi sforza,
contra cui non val forza · nè misura.

O DONNA mia, non vedestù colui
che 'n su lo core mi tenea la mano,
quando ti rispondea fiochetto e piano
per la temenza delli colpi sui?
Elli fu Amore che, trovando nui,
meco restette che venia lontano,
a guisa d'un arcier presto soriano,
acconcio sol per uccider altrui.

God made your fine comeliness above human nature so that you should be queen: so do not let your look be distant to me; do not let your sweet benevolence be rude to me. And if you think it an outrage that I should be given to loving you, do not let me be blamed by you: for Love alone forces me on, against whom neither strength nor moderation has any power.

O MY lady, did you not see him who held his hand upon my heart when I answered you, feeble and low for fear of his blows? He was Love who, on discovering us, stayed with me since he came from afar, in the form of a swift Syrian archer, girded only to kill people.

E trasse poi de gli occhi tuoi sospiri,
i quai mi saettò nel cor sì forte,
ch'i' mi partii sbigottito fuggendo.
Allor m'apparve di sicur la Morte
accompagnata di quelli martiri
che soglion consumare altrui piangendo.

ERA in penser d'amor quand'i' trovai
due foresette nove;
l'un cantava: «E' piove
gioco d'amore in nui.»

Era la vista lor tanto soave
e tanto queta, cortese ed umìle
ch'i' dissi lor: «Vo' portate la chiave
di ciascuna vertù alta e gentile.
Deh, foresette, no m'abbiate a vile
per lo colpo ch'io porto:
questo cor mi fu morto,
poi che 'n Tolosa fui.»

And he drew sighs from your eyes then, which he shot so violently into my heart that I fled terrified. Then suddenly Death appeared to me accompanied by those agonies that are wont to consume us in weeping.

I WAS deep in thoughts of love when I came upon two young
country girls; one was singing: 'Joy of love rains upon us.'
   Their look was so sweet and so calm, courteous and modest that
I said to them: 'You have the key of every high and gentle virtue.
O, country girls, do not despise me for the wound I bear: this heart
has been dead to me, since I was in Toulouse.'

Elle con gli occhi lor si volser tanto,
che vider come 'l cor era ferito
e come un spiritel nato di pianto
era per mezzo de lo colpo uscito.
Poi che mi vider così sbigottito,
disse l'una che rise:
«Guarda come conquise
forza d'amor costui!»

L'altra pietosa, piena di mercede,
fatta di gioco, in figura d'Amore,
disse: «Il tuo colpo, che nel cor si vede,
fu tratto d'occhi di troppo valore,
che dentro vi lasciaro uno splendore
ch'i' nol posso mirare;
dimmi se ricordare
di quegli occhi ti pui.»

Alla dura questione e paurosa
la qual mi fece questa foresetta,
i' dissi: «E' mi ricorda che 'n Tolosa
donna m'apparve accordellata istretta,

They turned their eyes so, that they saw how my heart was
wounded and how a little spirit born of tears had come out from the
wound itself. When they saw I was so frightened, one of them
said, laughing: 'See how the power of love has overcome this
man!'

The other pitying, full of mercy, made for joy, in the form of
Love, said: 'The wound, which is seen in your heart, came from
eyes of too great power, which left a splendour within that I cannot
gaze at; tell me if you can remember those eyes.'

To the hard and fearful question which this country girl put to
me, I said: 'I remember in Toulouse a woman appeared before me,

la quale Amor chiamava la Mandetta:
giunse sì presta e forte
che 'n fin dentro, a la morte,
mi colpir gli occhi sui.»

Molto cortesemente mi rispose
quella che di me prima aveva riso;
disse: «La donna che nel cor ti pose
co' la forza d'Amor tutto 'l su' viso,
dentro per li occhi ti mirò sì fiso,
ch'Amor fece apparire.
Se t'è greve 'l soffrire
raccomàndati a lui.»

Vanne a Tolosa, ballatetta mia,
ed entra quetamente a la Dorata:
ed ivi chiama che, per cortesia
d'alcuna bella donna, sia menata
dinanzi a quella di cui t'ho pregata;
e s'ella ti riceve,
dille con voce leve:
«Per merzè vegno a vui.»

tightly laced, whom Love called la Mandetta: she came so quick
and strong that her eyes struck me inwardly and deep, to the point
of death.'

She who had first laughed at me replied most courteously; she
said: 'The woman who, with the power of Love, impressed all her
features upon your heart gazed so fixedly through your eyes that
she made Love come there. If your suffering is heavy, turn to him.'

Go to Toulouse, my little song, and quietly enter the 'Gilded'
church: and there ask aloud for some lovely woman, in her kindness, to take you before her about whom I have charged you; if she
will see you, tell her in a low voice: 'I come to you for mercy.'

PERCHI'I' no spero di tornar giammai,
ballatetta, in Toscana,
va tu, leggera e piana,
dritt'a la donna mia,
che per sua cortesia
ti farà molto onore.

Tu porterai novelle di sospiri,
piene di doglia e di molta paura;
ma guarda che persona non ti miri
che sia nemica di gentil natura;
chè certo per la mia disaventura
tu saresti contesa,
tanto da lei ripresa,
che mi sarebbe agnoscia;
dopo la morte poscia,
pianto e novel dolore.

Tu senti, ballatetta, che la morte
mi stringe sì che vita m'abbandona,
e senti come 'l cor si sbatte forte
per quel che ciascun spirito ragiona.
Tanto è distrutta già la mia persona

SINCE I do not hope ever to return, little song, go, lightly and
quiet, to Tuscany, straight to my lady, who, in her courtesy, will
do you much honour.

You will carry tidings of sighs, tidings full of pain and great
fear: but watch that no one sees you who is hostile to a gentle
nature; as certainly, to my misfortune you would be opposed, and
so reproved by her, that it would be agony for me; then, after
death, weeping and fresh grief.

You feel, little song, that death grapples me so that life deserts
me, and feel how my heart beats strong because of what every
spirit in me says. So much of my being is destroyed already that I

ch'i' non posso soffrire:
se tu mi vuo' servire,
mena l'anima teco,
molto di ciò ti preco,
quando uscirà del core.

Deh, ballatetta, alla tua amistate
quest'anima che trema raccomando:
menala teco nella sua pietate
a quella bella donna a cui ti mando.
Deh, ballatetta, dille sospirando,
quando le se' presente:
«Questa vostra servente
vien per istar con vui,
partita da colui
che fu servo d'amore.»

Tu, voce sbigottita e deboletta,
ch'esci piangendo de lo cor dolente,
coll'anima e con questa ballatetta
va ragionando della strutta mente.
Voi troverete una donna piacente

can suffer no more: if you wish to help me, take my soul with you,
I beg you fervently, when it has left my heart.

O, little song, I commend to your friendship this soul that
trembles: take it with you in its misery to the lovely woman to
whom I send you. O, little song, tell her with sighs, when you are
before her: 'This your servant has come to live with you, having
left him who was the servant of love.'

You, frightened, small-weakened voice, that come weeping from
the heart that grieves, go with my soul and with this little song and
tell of my mind destroyed. You will find a pleasant woman of so

di sì dolce intelletto,
che vi sarà diletto
davanti starle ognora.
Anima, e tu l'adora
sempre nel su' valore.

LAPO GIANNI

Dolc'è 'l pensier che mi notrica il core
d'una giovane donna che disia,
per cui si fè gentil l'anima mia,
poichè sposata la congiunse Amore.

I' non posso leggeramente trare
il novo esemplo ched ella simiglia
quest'angela che par di ciel venuta;
d'Amor sorella mi sembr'al parlare
ed ogni su' atterello è maraviglia:
beata l'alma che questa saluta!
In colei si può dir che sia piovuta
allegrezza, speranza e gioi' compita
ed ogni rama di virtù fiorita,
la qual procede dal su' gran valore.

sweet an understanding, that it will be a delight for you all to stay by her always. My soul, adore her for ever in her worthiness.

Sweet is the thought which my heart nourishes, of a young woman whom I desire, for whom my soul has been ennobled, since Love took her in marriage.

I cannot easily evoke the so new image that this angel who seems to have come from heaven resembles; she seems Love's sister by her speech and every least gesture of hers is a marvel: blessed is the soul this woman greets! To her, it can be said, has gladness flowed, hope and joy entire, and every flowering branch of virtue, which comes from her great worth.

Il nobile intelletto ched i' porto
per questa gioven donna ch'è apparita,
mi fa spregiar viltate e villania;
e 'l dolce ragionar mi dà conforto
ch' i' fe' con lei de l'amorosa vita,
essendo già in sua nova signoria.
Ella mi fè tanta di cortesia
che no sdegnò mio soave parlare;
ond'i' voglio Amor dolce ringraziare
che mi fè degno di cotanto onore.

Com'i' son scritto nel libro d'amore
conterai, ballatetta, in cortesia,
quando tu vederai la donna mia;
poi che di lei fui fatto servidore.

AMOR, eo chero mia donna in domìno,
l'Arno balsamo fino,
le mura di Firenze inargentate,
le rughe di cristallo lastricate,
fortezze alte, merlate,

The gentle mind I have because of this young woman who has
appeared makes me scorn vileness and base dealings; and the sweet
converse I had with her about the life of love, when I was fresh to
her service, comforts me. She showed me such courtesy that she
did not scorn my soft talking; so that I want to thank sweet Love
who made me worthy of so great an honour.

As I am inscribed in the book of Love, my song, you will tell
your tale with courtesy, when you see my lady; since I have been
made her servant.

LOVE, I ask to have my mistress in my power, for the Arno to be
fine balsam, the walls of Florence silvered, the streets paved with
crystal, high, battlemented fortresses, every Italian to be my bonds-

mio fedel fosse ciaschedun latino;
il mondo 'n pace, securo 'l cammino;
non mi noccia vicino;
e l'aira temperata verno e state;
e mille donne e donzelle adornate,
sempre d'amor pregiate,
meco cantasser la sera e 'l mattino;
e giardin fruttuosi di gran giro,
con grande uccellagione,
pien di condotti d'acqua e cacciagione;
bel mi trovasse come fu Assalone;
Sansone pareggiasse e Salomone;
servaggi de barone;
sonar viole, chitarre e canzone;
poscia dover entrar nel ciel empiro.
Giovane sana allegra e secura
fosse mia vita fin che 'l mondo dura.

CINO DA PISTOIA

Io guardo per li prati ogni fior bianco,
per rimembranza di quel che mi face
sì vago di sospir ch'io ne chieggo anco.

man; the world at peace, the roads free; no neighbour harming me; the air mild both summer and winter; a thousand comely women made more beautiful by love, to sing with me night and morning; and flourishing gardens of great compass, with great preserve of fowl, full of little channels and hunting places; I ask to be as handsome as Absalom; equal Samson and Solomon; with barons for servants; with playing of viols, guitars, and songs; then to be sure of entering highest heaven: ask for a young woman, fresh, happy, and faithful, to be my life as longs as the world lasts.

I LOOK at every white flower through the fields, remembering what makes me so eager to sigh that I ask for more.

E' mi rimembra de la bianca parte
che fa col verdebrun la bella taglia,
la qual vestio Amore
nel tempo che, guardando Vener Marte,
con quell sua saetta che più taglia
mi diè per mezzo il core:
e quando l'aura move il bianco fiore,
rimembro de' begli occhi il dolce bianco
per cui lo mio desir mai non fie stanco.

Io fui 'n su l'alto e 'n sul beato monte,
ch'i' adorai, baciando il santo sasso;
e caddi 'n su di quella pietra, lasso,
ove l' Onestà pose la sua fronte,
e che là chiuse d'ogni vertù 'l fonte
quel giorno che di morte acerbo passo
fece la donna de lo meo cor, lasso!
già piena tutta d'adornezze conte.

I remember the white part of her dress which, with the dark-green, makes up its fair shape, which Love donned at the season when, Mars and Venus gazing, he struck me through the heart with the arrow that cuts deepest: and when the breeze moves the white flower, I remember the sweet whites of her lovely eyes for which my desire will never falter.

I WAS upon the high and blessed mountain, which I worshipped, kissing the holy stone; and fell upon that headstone, weary, where Honesty laid her forehead, and which shut off the fountainhead of every virtue that day when the woman of my heart went through death's bitter pass, alas! she who was once full of every brighter charm.

Quivi chiamai a questa guisa Amore:
– Dolce mio iddio, fa che qui mi traggia
la morte a sè, chè qui giace 'l mio core. –
Ma poi che non m'intese 'l mio Signore,
mi dipartii, pur chiamando Selvaggia:
l'alpe passai con voce di dolore.

CECCO ANGIOLIERI

– Accorri accorri accorri, uom, a la strada!
– Che ha', fi' de la putta? – I' son rubato.
– Chi t'ha rubato? – Una, che par che rada
come rasoi', sì m'ha netto lasciato.
– Or come non le davi de la spada?
– I' dare' anzi a me. – Or se' 'mpazzato?
– Non so; che 'l dà? – Così mi par che vada:
or t'avess'ella cieco, sciagurato! –

– E vedi che ne pare a que' che 'l sanno?
– Di' quel, che tu mi rubi. – Or va' con Dio!
– Ma ando pian, ch' i' vo' pianger lo danno.

There I called on Love in this manner: 'My sweet god, let death
take me here, since my heart lies here.' But when my Lord did not
hear me, I left, still calling on Selvaggia: I passed over the mountain with the voice of grief.

'Run, run, run, man, along that street!' 'What's wrong, whore-
son?' 'I've been robbed.' 'Who robbed you?' 'A woman, who
shears like a razor, she's left me so bare.' 'Well, why didn't you
have at her with your sword?' 'I'd sooner turn it on myself.' 'Are
you mad?' 'I don't know; what makes you think so?' 'The way
you are going on: it's as good as if she had blinded you, you
wretch!'

'See how it appears to people who understand?' 'Let them know
that you rob me.' 'O go away!' 'I'm going, but slowly, for I must

– Che ti diparti? – Con animo rio.
– Tu abbi 'l danno con tutto 'l malanno!
– Or chi m'ha morto? – E che diavol sacc'io? –

MALEDETTO e distrutto sia da Dio
lo primo punto, ch'io innamorai
di quella, che dilettasi di guai
darmi, ed ogn'altro sollazzo ha in oblio;
e si fa tanto tormento esser mio,
che 'n corpo d'uòm non ne fu tanto mai:
e non le pare aver fatto anco assai,
tant'è 'l su' cor giude', pessimo e rio.

E non pensa se non com'ella possa
far a me cosa, che mi scoppi'l cuore:
di questa oppinion ma' non fu mossa.
E di lei non mi posso gittar fuore,
tant'ho la ment' abbarbagliat'e grossa,
c'ho men sentor, che non ha l'uom, che mòre.

weep my loss.' 'How do you leave me?' 'In bad heart.' 'Well, you can suffer your "loss" and every illness with it, for all I care!' 'Who is killing me now?' 'How the devil should I know?'

MAY God curse and destroy the first moment that I fell in love with her who takes pleasure in bringing me woes, and is oblivious of every other delight; and causes me so much torment, that never before was there so much in the body of man: and she doesn't seem to think she has done much yet, so pitiless, evil, and utterly bad is her heart.

And she thinks of nothing but how she may do things that will break my heart: she has never been budged from this fixed idea. And I cannot get beyond her reach, my mind is so bedazzled and stupefied, that I have less feeling in me than a dying man.

S' i' fosse foco, arderei 'l mondo;
s' i' fosse vento, lo tempesterei;
s' i' fosse acqua, i' l'annegherei;
s' i' fosse Dio, mandereil' en profondo;
s' i' fosse papa, sare' allor giocondo,
che tutt' i cristiani imbrigherei;
s' i' fosse 'mperator, sa' che farei?
A tutti mozzarei lo capo a tondo.

S' i' fosse morte, andarei da mio padre;
s' i' fosse vita, fuggirei da lui:
similmente farìa da mi' madre.
S' i' fosse Cecco, com' i' sono e fui,
torrei le donne giovani e leggiadre:
e vecchie e laide lasserei altrui.

TRE cose solamente mi so' in grado,
le quali posso non ben ben fornire:
ciò è la donna, la taverna e 'l dado;
queste mi fanno 'l cuor lieto sentire.

IF I were fire, I'd burn up the world; if I were wind, I'd storm it;
if I were water, I'd drown it; if I were God, I'd send it into the
abyss; if I were Pope, then I'd be happy, for I'd cheat all the
Christians; if I were emperor, 'know what I'd do? I'd chop off
everyone's head.

   If I were death, I would go to my father; if I were life, I'd fly
from him: likewise would I do with my mother. If I were Cecco, as
I am and was, I would take the women who are young and gay, and
leave the old and ugly to other men.

THREE things only please me, which I cannot easily provide: that
is, women, the tavern, and dicing; these gladden my heart. But I

Ma sì me le convèn usar di rado,
chè la mie borsa mi mett'al mentire;
e, quando mi sovvien, tutto mi sbrado,
ch' i' perdo per moneta 'l mie disire.

E dico: – Dato li sia d'una lancia! –
Ciò a mi' padre, che mi tien si magro,
che tornare' senza logro di Francia.
Trarl' un denai' di man serìa più agro,
la man di pasqua, che si dà la mancia,
che far pigliar la gru ad un bozzagro!

FOLGORE DA SAN GIMIGNANO

De gennaio

I' DOTO voi nel mese de gennaio
corte con fochi di salette accese,
camere e letta d'ogni bello arnese,
lenzuol de seta e copertoi di vaio;
tregèa, confetti e mescere arazzaio,
vestiti di doagio e di rascese,
e 'n questo modo stare a le difese,
mova sirocco garbino e rovaio.

am obliged to indulge them so rarely, for my purse makes me put them away from me; and, when I think of this, I rage at losing my pleasures for money.

And I say: – let him get it with a lance! – that is, my father, who keeps me so meagrely, that I would come back from far France with never an enticement. Getting one coin from his hand, on Easter morning, too, when largess is general, would be harder than taking a crane with a mousing-hawk.

For January

I MAKE you a present in the month of January of a courtyard with fires kindled with straw, rooms, and beds with every fine furnishing, silk sheets, and coverlets of vair; sugared nuts, sweets, and sparkling wine, clothes of Douai and Rascia, and in this way you would be fortified, should the Sirocco, the South-West, or the North wind blow.

Uscir di for'alcuna volta il giorno
gittando de la neve bella e bianca
a le donzelle che staran da torno;
e quando fosse la compagna stanca
a questa corte facciase ritorno
e si riposi la brigata franca.

D'aprile

D'APRIL vi dono la gentil campagna
tutta fiorita di bell'erba fresca,
fontane d'acqua che non vi rincresca,
donne e donzelle per vostra compagna;
ambianti palafren, destrier di Spagna
e gente costumata a la francesca,
cantar danzar a la provenzalesca
con istormenti novi d'Alemagna.

E da torno vi sia molti giardini
e giachita vi sia ogni persona,
ciascun con reverenza adori e 'nchini
a quel gentil ch'ò dato la corona
de pietre preziose le piu fini
ch'à 'l presto Gianni o 'l re di Babilona.

Going out several times in the day, to throw the lovely white
snow at the girls who are standing about; and when the company
was tired, they would return to this court, and the generous band
find rest.

For April

FOR April I give you the gentle countryside all flowering with
fresh grass, fountains of water that will not displease you, women
and girls for company; nimble horses, chargers from Spain, and
people dressed in the French style, singing and dancing in the
manner of Provence, with new instruments from Germany.

And round about there will be many gardens, and everyone will
be stretched out at ease there, each will worship and bow with
reverence to that gentle one to whom I have given the crown of
precious stones, the finest that Prester John or the King of Babylon
has.

Di maggio

Di maggio sì vi do molti cavagli
e tutti quanti siano affrenatori,
portanti tutti, dritti corritori,
pettorali e testiere con sonagli;
bandiere e coverte a molti 'ntagli
di zendadi e di tutti li colori,
le targhe a modo degli armeggiatori,
viole rose e fior c'ogni uom abbagli;

Rompere e fiaccar bigordi e lance
e piover da finestre e da balconi
en giù ghirlande e 'n su melerance;
e pulcellette giovene e garzoni
baciarsi ne la bocca e ne le guance,
d'amor e di goder vi si ragioni.

Di giugno

Di giugno dòvi una montagnetta
coverta di bellissimi arboscelli,
con trenta ville e dodici castelli
che siano entorno ad una cittadetta;

For May

For May I give you this – many horses and all of them will be
manageable, each trained, with upright riders, breast- and head-
pieces, with bells; flags, and other trappings in silk and all colours,
shields in the style of the jousters, violets, roses, and other flowers
to dazzle everyone;

    and there will be breaking and shattering of jousting-spears and
lances, and from windows and balconies will rain garlands, and
oranges fly up in the air; and young maids and youths kissing one
another on the mouth and on the cheeks, and everyone intent on
loving and enjoying.

For June

For June I give you a small mountain covered with fairest trees,
with thirty country-houses and twelve castles standing about a little

ch'abbia nel mezzo una so' fontanetta
e faccia mille rami e fiumicelli,
ferendo per giardini e praticelli
e rinfrescando la minuta erbetta.

Aranci cedri dattili e lumìe
e tutte l'altre frutte savorose
empergolate siano per le vie;
e le gente vi sian tutte amorose,
e faccianvisi tante cortesie
ch'a tutto 'l mondo siano graziose.

DANTE ALIGHIERI

A CIASCUN'ALMA presa e gentil core
nel cui cospetto ven lo dir presente,
in ciò che mi rescrivan suo parvente,
salute in lor segnor, cioè Amore.
Già eran quasi che atterzate l'ore
del tempo che onne stella n'è lucente,
quando m'apparve Amor subitamente,
cui essenza membrar mi dà orrore.

city; that has in its midst a sweet fountain and turns this into a
thousand branches and little streams striking through gardens and
meads, and freshening the tiny grass.

Oranges, lemons, dates, and limes, and all other succulent fruits,
would overarch the walks at the roadside; and everyone be ready
for love, and pay one another many fine compliments there which
should delight everyone.

To every soul possessed and gentle heart into whose gaze the present words come, greetings in the name of their lord, that is Love,
that they may write me in return their opinion of this. The hours of
the time when every star is shining were almost passed by a third,
when Love suddenly appeared to me in a form which is horrifying
to recall.

Allegro mi sembrava Amor tenendo
meo core in mano, e ne le braccia avea
madonna involta in un drappo dormendo.
Poi la svegliava, e d'esto core ardendo
lei paventosa umilmente pascea:
appresso gir lo ne vedea piangendo.

O voi che per la via d'Amor passate,
attendete e guardate
s'elli è dolore alcun, quanto 'l mio, grave;
e prego sol ch'audir mi sofferiate,
e poi imaginate
s'io son d'ogni tormento ostale e chiave.
Amor, non già per mia poca bontate,
ma per sua nobiltate,
mi pose in vita sì dolce e soave,
ch'io mi sentia dir dietro spesse fiate:
«Deo, per qual dignitate
così leggiadro questi lo core have?»

Happy Love seemed holding my heart in his hand, and in his
arms he had my lady wrapped in a mantle, asleep. Then he woke
her, and submissively, in fear, she ate this heart that burned; there-
after I saw him go away weeping.

O you who pass along the way of Love, pause and see if there is
any grief as heavy as mine, and I ask you only to give me a hearing,
and then consider if I am not the abode and key of every anguish.
Love (not in the least for my slight worth, but in his nobleness) set
me in a life so delightful and sweet that I heard people say behind
me many times: 'God, by what grace is that man's heart so lightsome?'

Or ho perduta tutta mia baldanza,
che si movea d'amoroso tesoro;
ond'io pover dimoro,
in guisa che di dir mi ven dottanza.
Sì che volendo far come coloro
che per vergogna celan lor mancanza,
di fuor mostro allegranza,
e dentro da lo core struggo e ploro.

DONNE ch'avete intelletto d'amore,
i' vo' con voi de la mia donna dire,
non perch'io creda sua laude finire,
ma ragionar per isfogar la mente.
Io dico che pensando il suo valore,
Amor sì dolce mi si fa sentire,
che s'io allora non perdessi ardire,
farei parlando innamorar la gente.
E io non vo' parlar sì altamente,
ch'io divenisse per temenza vile;
ma tratterò del suo stato gentile
a respetto di lei leggeramente,
donne e donzelle amorose, con vui,
chè non è cosa da parlarne altrui.

Now I have lost all the easy pride that came from my loving treasure, and I am left so poor that a fear to speak has come upon me. So that wishing to do as those who hide what they lack from shame, I show gladness outwardly, and in my heart am torn and weep.

LADIES who have an understanding of love, I wish to speak with you of my lady, not because I think to exhaust her praise, but only to talk so as to unburden my mind. I tell you that when I think of her worth, Love makes himself known to me so sweetly, that if I did not then lose heart, I should make everyone fall in love simply by talking. And I do not wish to speak so exaltedly that I become faint-hearted from fear, but I shall treat of her gentle condition lightly out of respect for her, loving women and maids, with you, since it is not a thing to talk of with others.

Angelo clama in divino intelleto
e dice: «Sire, nel mondo si vede
maraviglia ne l'atto che procede
d'un'anima che 'nfin qua su risplende.»
Lo cielo, che non have altro difetto
che d'aver lei, al suo segnor la chiede,
e ciascun santo ne grida merzede.
Sola Pietà nostra parte difende,
che parla Dio, che di madonna intende:
«Diletti miei, or sofferite in pace
che vostra spene sia quanto me piace
là 'v'è alcun che perder lei s'attende,
e che dirà ne lo inferno: – O mal nati,
io vidi la speranza de' beati.»

Madonna è disiata in sommo cielo:
or voi di sua virtù farvi savere.
Dico, qual vuol gentil donna parere
vada con lei, che quando va per via,
gitta nei cor villani Amore un gelo:
per che onne lor pensero agghiaccia e pere;
e qual soffrisse di starla a veder
diverria nobil cosa, o si morria.

An angel exclaims in the Divine Intelligence and says: 'Lord, a marvel is seen on earth in the grace that comes from a soul that shines up to this height.' Heaven, which has no other blemish but to want her, asks her from its lord, and each saint cries out for this boon. Only Pity takes our part, speaking in God, who comprehends my lady: 'Dearly beloved, suffer in peace, for, however much your hope is pleasing to me, there is one down there who is soon to lose her, and who will say in hell: "O you evil-born, I have seen the hope of the blessed."'

My lady is desired in highest heaven; make yourselves acquainted with her virtue then. I say whoever of you wants to appear as a gentle woman, let her go with her, as when she goes along the street, Love throws a frost upon every base heart, so that every thought of theirs freezes and perishes; and whoever could bear to stand and gaze at her would become a noble thing, or die. And

E quando trova alcun che degno sia
di veder lei, quei prova sua vertute,
chè li avvien, ciò che li dona, in salute,
e sì umilia, ch'ogni offesa oblia.
Ancor l'ha Dio per maggior grazia dato
che non pò mal finir chi l'ha parlato.

Dice di lei Amor: «Cosa mortale
come esser pò sì adorna e sì pura,»
Poi la reguarda, e fra se stesso giura
che Dio ne 'ntenda di far cosa nova.
Color di perle ha quasi, in forma quale
convene a donna aver, non for misura:
ella è quanto de ben pò far natura;
per esemplo di lei bieltà si prove.
De li occhi suoi, come ch'ella li mova,
escono spirti d'amore infiammati,
che feron li occhi a qual che allor la guati,
e passan sì che 'l cor ciascun retrova:
voi le vedete Amor pinto nel viso,
là 've non pote alcun mirarla fiso.

when Love finds one who is worthy to look upon her, that man
feels her power so that it comes to him (as she grants it) as a gift of
grace, and so humbles him that he forgets everything hurtful. God
has also granted as a greater blessing that whoever speaks to her
cannot end badly.

Love says of her: 'How can any mortal thing be so comely and
so pure?' Then he looks at her, and swears in himself that God intended in her to create something new. She has the colour almost
of the pearl, in the degree that is right for a woman to have, not
beyond measure: she is that sum of goodness that Nature can make;
beauty is proved by her being. From her eyes, when she moves
them, come flaming spirits of love which wound the eyes of whoever looks at them then, and they penetrate so that each one finds
out the heart. You see Love painted on her face there where no one
can look at her steadily.

Canzone, io so che tu girai parlando
a donne assai, quand'io t'avrò avanzata.
Or t'ammonisco, perch'io t'ho allevata
per figliuola d'Amor giovane e piana,
che là 've giugni tu dichi pregando:
«Insegnatemi gir, ch'io son mandata
a quella di cui laude so' adornata.»
E se non vuoli andar sì come vana,
non restare ove sia gente villana:
ingegnati, se puoi, d'esser palese
solo con donne o con omo cortese,
che ti merranno là per via tostana.
Tu troverai Amor con esso lei;
raccomandami a lui come tu dei.

Tanto gentile e tanto onesta pare
la donna mia quand'ella altrui saluta,
ch'ogne lingua deven tremando muta,
e li occhi no l'ardiscon di guardare.

My song, I know you will go about speaking to many women
when I have once sped you. Now I enjoin you, because I have
brought you up as the simple, young daughter of Love, to make
this request in whatever place you come to: 'Show me where to
go, as I am being sent to that fair whose praise adorns me.' And if
you do not want to go about like a vain thing, do not stay where
they are low people: contrive, if you can, to be open only with
women and courteous men, who will lead you by the quick way.
You will find Love and with him her; remind him of me as you
ought.

My lady is so gentle and modest when she greets others that
every tongue trembles and is still, and eyes do not dare to look upon

Ella si va, sentendosi laudare,
benignamente d'umiltà vestuta;
e par che sia una cosa venuta
da cielo in terra a miracol mostrare.

Mostrasi sì piacente a chi la mira,
che dà per li occhi una dolcezza al core,
che 'ntender no la può chi no la prova:
e par che de la sua labbia si mova
un spirito soave pien d'amore,
che va dicendo a l'anima: «Sospira».

D ᴇʜ peregrini che pensosi andate,
forse di cosa che non v'è presente,
venite voi da sì lontana gente,
com'a la vista voi ne dimostrate,
che non piangete quando voi passate
per lo suo mezzo la città dolente,
come quelle persone che neente
par che intendesser la sua gravitate?

her. She passes, hearing herself praised, dressed most kindly with
humility; and it seems that she is a thing come upon earth from
heaven to show forth a miracle.

She shows herself so pleasant to whoever gazes at her, that
through the eyes she gives a sweetness to the heart which no one
can comprehend who has not known it: and it seems that from her
lips moves a sweet spirit full of love that goes to the soul with the
words: 'O sigh.'

O ᴘɪʟɢʀɪᴍs who go by thoughtful, perhaps because of something
that is not present to you here, do you come from so far a people as
by your look you show, that you do not weep as you pass through
the middle of the sorrowing city, like those who, it seems, do not
at all understand its heavy grief?

Se voi restate per volerlo audire,
certo lo cor de' sospir mi dice
che lagrimando n'uscirete pui.
Ell'ha perduta la sua beatrice;
e le parole ch'om di lei pò dire
hanno vertù di far piangere altrui.

Oltre la spera che più larga gira
passa 'l sospiro ch'esce del mio core;
intelligenza nova, che l'Amore
piangendo mette in lui, pur su lo tira.
Quand'elli è giunto là dove disira,
vede una donna, che riceve onore,
e luce sì, che per lo suo splendore
lo peregrino spirito la mira.

Vedela tal, che quando 'l mi ridice,
io no lo intendo, sì parla sottile
al cor dolente, che lo fa parlare.
So io che parla di quella gentile,
però che spesso ricorda Beatrice,
sì ch'io lo 'ntendo ben, donne mie care.

If you pause wishing to hear what it is, certainly, my heart of sighs tells me, you will leave it then in tears. It has lost its 'Blessed One'; and the things that men can say of her have the power to make everyone weep.

Beyond the sphere which most widely wheels, passes the sigh that comes from my heart; new understanding which Love weepingly instils into him, draws him upward still. When he has reached the place he wishes for, he sees a woman, who is visited with honour, and so shines, that this far-travelled spirit wonders at her brightness.

He sees her in such a guise that when he repeats this to me, I do not understand, he speaks so darkly to the sorrowing heart, which makes him speak. I know that he speaks of that gentle soul because often he recalls Beatrice, so that I understand him well, my dear ladies.

Guido, i' vorrei che tu e Lapo ed io
fossimo presi per incantamento
e messi in un vasel, ch'ad ogni vento
per mare andasse al voler vostro e mio;
sì che fortuna od altro tempo rio
non ci potesse dare impedimento,
anzi, vivendo sempre in un talento,
di stare insieme crescesse 'l disio.

E monna Vanna e monna Lagia poi
con quella ch'è sul numer de le trenta
con noi ponesse il buono incantatore:
e quivi ragionar sempre d'amore,
e ciascuna di lor fosse contenta,
sì come i' credo che saremmo noi.

Per una ghirlandetta
ch'io vidi, mi farà
sospirare ogni fiore.

Guido, I would that you and Lapo and I could be taken up by a
spell and put in a ship, that went through the sea with every wind,
as you and I wished; so that neither tempest nor other evil weather
could oppose us, but rather, living always in the one desire, the wish
to stay together would grow.

And then the good enchanter would put with us my lady Vanna
and my lady Lagia and the one who is to be found at the number
thirty: and then to converse always of love, and might each of
them be happy, as I believe we ourselves would be.

Because of a garland I have seen, every flower will make me sigh.

I' vidi a mia donna portare
ghirlandetta di fior gentile,
e sovr'a lei vidi volare
un angiolel d'amore umile;
e 'n suo cantar sottile
dicea: – Chi mi vedrà
lauderà 'l mio signore. –

Se io sarò là dove sia
Fioretta mia bella e gentile,
allor dirò a la donna mia
che port'in testa i miei sospire:
– Ma' per crescer disire
una donna verrà
coronata da Amore? –

Le parolette mie novelle
che di fiori fatto han ballata,
per leggiadria ci hanno tolt'elle
una vesta ch'altrui fu data.
Pero siate pregata,
qual uom la canterà,
che li facciate onore.

I saw my lady wearing a garland of gentle flowers, and above it
I saw a humble little angel of love flying: and in his fine singing he
said: 'He who sees me will praise my lord.'

If I am in some place and Fioretta, my gentle fair, is present, then
shall I say to my lady who bears my sighs upon her head: ' To
make desire grow, will a lady never come crowned with Love?'

These newborn words of mine which have made a song of
flowers, have stolen, out of gaiety, a dress that was given to others.
But you are desired to honour them whenever this song is heard.

— I' MI son pargoletta bella e nova,
che son venuta per mostrare altrui
de le bellezze del loco ond'io fui.

I' fui del cielo, e tornerovvi ancora
per dar de la mia luce altrui diletto;
e chi mi vede e non se ne innamora
d'amor non averà mai intelletto,
chè non mi fu in piacer alcun disdetto
quando natura mi chiese a Colui
che volle, donne, accompagnarmi a vui.

Ciascuna stella ne li occhi mi piove
del lume suo e de la sua vertute;
le mie bellezze sono al mondo nove,
però che di là su mi son venute:
le quai non posson esser canosciute
se non da canoscenza d'omo, in cui
Amor si metta per piacer altrui. —

'I AM a young girl, lovely and fresh, who have come to show people
the beauties of the place whence I am.
'I was in heaven, and I shall return there again to give others delight with my shining; and whoever sees me without falling in love
will never have an understanding of love, for no pleasantness was
denied me when nature asked for me from Him who wished, ladies,
to make me of your company.
'Every star rains its light upon my eyes and its influence; my
beauties are new to the world, because they have come to me from
on high: nor can they be known except to the discerning of a man
in whom Love resides at another's pleasure.'

Queste parole si leggon nel viso
d'un'angioletta che ci è apparita:
e io che per veder lei mirai fiso,
ne sono a rischio di perder la vita;
però ch'io ricevetti tal ferita
da un ch'io vidi dentro a li occhi sui,
ch'i' vo piangendo, e non m'achetai pui.

Io son venuto al punto de la rota
che l'orizzonte, quando il sol si corca,
ci partorisce il geminato cielo,
e la stella d'amor ci sta remota
per lo raggio lucente che la 'nforca
sì di traverso, che le si fa velo;
e quel pianeta che conforta il gelo
si mostra tutto a noi per lo grand'arco
nel qual ciascun di sette fa poca ombra:
e però non disgombra
un sol penser d'amore, ond'io son carco,
la mente mia, ch'è più dura che petra
in tener forte imagine di petra.

These words are to be read in the face of an angel who has appeared to us: and I, who gazed fixedly upon her, am in danger of losing my life; because I had such a wound from one whom I saw within her eyes, that I keep weeping and have not calmed myself since.

I HAVE come to the point of the circle where the horizon, when the sun goes to rest, gives birth to the Twin-governed sky, and the star of love is far from us because of the shining ray which crosses it, so as to make a veil; and that planet which cheers the frost appears to us through the great curve in which each of the Seven casts little shade: and yet my mind does not clear itself of a single thought of love, which presses upon me, for it is harder than a stone in firmly preserving an image of stone.

Levasi de la rena d'Etiopia
lo vento peregrin che l'aere turba,
per la spera del sol ch'ora la scalda;
e passa il mare, onde conduce copia
di nebbia tal, che, s'altro non la sturba,
questo emisperio chiude tutto e salda;
e poi si solve, e cade in bianca falda
di fredda neve ed in noiosa pioggia,
onda l'aere s'attrista tutto e piagne:
e Amor, che sue ragne
ritira in alto pel vento che poggia,
non m'abbandona; sì è bella donna
questa crudel che m'è data per donna.

Fuggito è ogne augel che 'l caldo segue
del paese d'Europa, che non perde
le sette stelle gelide unquemai;
e li altri han posto a le lor voci triegue
per non sonarle infino al tempo verde,
se ciò non fosse per cagion di guai;
e tutti li animali che son gai

The travelling wind which stirs the air rises from the Ethiopian
sand, heated now by the sun's sphere; and crosses the sea whence it
gathers such abundance of mist, that, if no other thing opposes, it
shuts off and binds this hemisphere; and then yields, and falls in
white drift of cold snow and in dreary rain, at which the air grows
altogether sad and weeps: and Love, who draws his nets on high
because of the powerful wind, does not leave me; so beautiful is this
cruel woman who has been given to me as mistress.

Every bird that follows the heat has fled from the land of Europe
which never once is rid of the seven frozen stars; the others have
imposed a truce upon their voices so that they will not ring out until
the green time, except for some grief; and all the animals that are

di lor natura, son d'amor disciolti,
però che 'l freddo lor spirito ammorta:
e 'l mio più d'amor porta;
chè li dolzi pensier' non mi son tolti
nè mi son dati per volta di tempo,
ma donna li mi dà c'ha picciol tempo.

Passato hanno lor termine le fronde
che trasse fuor la vertù d'Ariete
per ardonare il mondo, e morta è l'erba;
ramo di foglia verde a noi s'asconde
se non se in lauro, in pino o in abete
o in alcun che sua verdura serba;
e tanto è la stagion forte ed acerba,
c'ha morti li fioretti per le piagge,
li quai non poten tollerar la brina:
e la crudele spina
però Amor di cor non la mi tragge;
per ch'io son fermo di portarla sempre
ch'io sarò in vita, s'io vivesse sempre.

gay by nature are freed from loving because the cold deadens their
spirit: and mine bears greater love; for sweet thoughts are not
taken from me, nor are they given me by the changing of season,
but a woman who has been short time in the world gives them to
me.

Leaves which the power of the Ram brought forth to deck the
world have passed their date, and the grass is dead; every green-
leafed branch is hidden from us except in laurel, or in pine, or in fir,
or in other tree that keeps its greenness; and so strong and bitter is
the season, that it has killed the little flowers along the banks, which
cannot bear the frost: and yet Love does not draw the cruel thorn
from my heart; so I am determined to bear it for as long as there is
life in me, should I live for ever.

Versan le vene le fummifere acque
per li vapor' che la terra ha nel ventre,
che d'abisso li tira suso in alto;
onde cammino al bel giorno mi piacque
che ora è fatto rivo, e sarà mentre
che durerà del verno il grande assalto;
la terra fa un suol che par di smalto,
e l'acqua morta si converte in vetro
per la freddura che di fuor la serra:
e io de la mia guerra
non son però tornato un passo a retro,
nè vo' tornar; chè se 'l martiro è dolce,
la morte de' passar ogni altro dolce.

Canzone, or che sarà di me ne l'altro
dolce tempo novello, quando piove
amore in terra da tutti li cieli,
quando per questi geli
amore è solo in me, e non altrove?
Saranne quello ch'è d'un uom di marmo,
se in pargoletta fia per core un marmo.

The streams run with smoke-laden waters because of the steam the earth has in its bowels, which it draws out from the abyss into upper air; so that a path that I was glad to walk on when days were fair, has become a torrent, and will be one while the great onslaught of winter lasts; the earth has a surface that seems enamel, and the dead water changes to glass because of the cold which grips it from without: and I have not drawn back one step from this war of mine, nor want to draw back; for if suffering is sweet, death must surpass every other sweetness.

My song, what will become of me in the sweet new season when love rains upon the earth from every heaven, if love lives in me now, in spite of all these frosts, and nowhere else? I shall become a man of marble, if in a girl there is a heart of marble.

Aʟ poco giorno e al gran cerchio d'ombra
son giunto, lasso! ed al bianchir de' colli,
quando si perde lo color ne l'erba;
e 'l mio disio però non cangia 'l verde,
si è barbato ne la dura petra
che parla e sente come fosse donna.

Similmente questa nova donna
si sta gelata come neve a l'ombra;
che non la move, se non come petra,
il dolce tempo che riscalda i colli
e che li fa tornar di bianco in verde
perchè li copre di fioretti e d'erba.

Quand'ella ha in testa una ghirlanda d'erba
trae de la mente nostra ogn'altra donna;
perche si mischia il crespo giallo e l' verde
sì bel, ch'Amor lì viene a stare a l'ombra,
che m'ha serrato intra piccioli colli
più forte assai che la calcina petra.

I ʜᴀᴠᴇ come to a short day and a great arc of shadow, alas! and to the hill's whitening when colour vanishes from the grass; and my desire does not, for this, change its green, it is so rooted in the hard stone that speaks and hears as if it were a woman.

Likewise this heaven-born woman remains frozen like snow in the shade; for she is not moved, unless as a stone is, by the sweet time which warms the hills and makes them turn from white to green so that it may cover them with little flowers and plants.

When she has a grass garland upon her head, she draws our mind from every other woman, because she mingles the waving yellow and the green in such lovely wise that Love comes to stand in their shadow, he who has locked me between small hills much more firmly than lime locks stone.

La sua bellezza ha più vertù che petra,
e 'l colpo suo non può sanar per erba;
ch'io son fuggito per piani e per colli,
per poter scampar da cotal donna;
e dal suo lume non mi può far ombra
poggio nè muro mai, nè fronda verde.

Io l'ho veduta già vestita a verde
sì fatta, ch'ella avrebbe messo in petra
l'amor ch'io porto pur a la sua ombra;
ond'io l'ho chesta in un bel prato d'erba,
innamorata com'anco fu donna,
e chiuso intorno d'altissimi colli.

Ma ben ritorneranno i fiumi a' colli
prima che questo legno molle e verde
s'infiammi, come suol far bella donna,
di me; che mi torrei dormire in petra
tutto il mio tempo e gir pascendo l'erba,
sol per veder do' suoi panni fann'ombra.

Her beauty has more virtue than precious stones, and the wound
she gives is not to be cured by herb; for I have fled by plain and hill
to be able to escape from such a woman, and neither mound nor
wall nor green foliage can ever give me shade from her light.

I have seen her dressed in green, so fashioned that she would
have inspired a stone with the love I bear her very shadow; so that
I have wished her on a fair meadow of grass, surrounded by highest
hills, as much in love as ever woman was.

But well may the rivers return to the hills before this soft green
wood catches fire, as fair woman is wont to, for my sake; so that I
would choose to sleep out my life on hard stone and go about feeding on grass, only to look where her garments cast shade.

Quandunque i colli fanno più nera ombra,
sotto un bel verde la giovane donna
la fa sparer, com'uom petra sott'erba.

Così nel mio parlar voglio esser aspro
com'è ne li atti questa bella petra,
la qual ognora impetra
maggior durezza e più natura cruda,
e veste sua persona d'un diaspro
tal, che per lui, o perch'ella s'arretra,
non esce di faretra
saetta che già mai la colga ignuda:
ed ella ancide, e non val ch'om si chiuda
nè si dilunghi da' colpi mortali,
che, com'avesser alí,
giungono altrui e spezzan ciascun'arme;
sì ch'io non so da lei nè posso atarme.

Every time the hills cast blackest shade, it makes this young
woman disappear amid fair green, as a man hides a precious stone
in grass.

In my speech I wish to be as harsh as this lovely stone-girl is in her
actions, who every moment grows more stonelike in hardness and
rough nature, and clothes her person in adamant so that, because of
this, or because she makes away, no arrow ever comes from quiver
that can pierce her naked: and she kills, and it does not avail a man
to close himself in, or fly from the mortal blows, which, as if they
had wings, reach one and shatter every weapon; so that I know
nothing of her, nor can I help myself.

Non trovo scudo ch'ella non mi spezzi
nè loco che dal suo viso m'asconda;
chè, come fior di fronda,
così de la mia mente tien la cima:
cotanto del mio mal par che si prezzi,
quanto legno di mar che non lieva onda;
e 'l peso che m'affonda
è tal che non potrebbe adequar rima.
Ahi angosciosa e dispietata lima
che sordamente la mia vita scemi,
perchè non ti ritemi
sì di rodermi il core a scorza a scorza,
com'io di dire altrui chi ti dà forza?

Chè più mi triema il cor qualora io penso
di lei in parte ov'altri li occhi induca,
per tema non traluca
lo mio penser di fuor sì che si scopra,
ch'io non fo de le morte, che ogni senso
co li denti d'Amor già mi manduca;
ciò è che 'l pensier bruca
la lor vertù sì che n'allenta l'opra.
E m'ha percosso in terra, e stammi sopra

I find no shield which she does not shatter, nor place where I can
hide from her face; as, like the flower above the leaves, she holds
the topmost of my mind: she seems to heed my misfortune, as
much as a ship does a mild sea; and the weight which forces me
down is such that no rhyme could equal it. Ah agonizing and pitiless trap that deafly wears out my life, why do you not keep from
eating my heart skin by skin, as I refrain from telling anyone who
gives you power?

For my heart trembles more when I think of her, in a place where
I can be seen by others – for fear that my thought may shine
through and betray itself – than I tremble at death, which already
gnaws every nerve of mine with the teeth of Love; that is, the
thought devours their strength, so that their action falters. Love
has struck me to the ground and stands above me, holding the

con quella spada ond'elli ancise Dido,
Amore, a cui io grido
merzè chiamando, e umilmente il priego;
ed el d'ogni merzè par messo al niego.

Egli alza ad ora ad or la mano, e sfida
la debole mia vita, esto perverso,
che disteso a riverso
mi tiene in terra d'ogni guizzo stanco:
allor mi surgon ne la mente strida;
e 'l sangue, ch'è per le vene disperso,
fuggendo corre verso
lo cor, che 'l chiama: ond'io rimango bianco.
Elli mi fiede sotto il braccio manco
sì forte, che 'l dolor nel cor rimbalza:
allor dico: «S'elli alza
un'altra volta, Morte m'avrà chiuso
prima che 'l colpo sia disceso giuso.»

Così vedess'io lui fender per mezzo
lo core a la crudele che 'l mio squatra!
poi non mi sarebb'atra
la morte, ov'io per sua bellezza corro:

sword with which he slew Dido, and to him I cry for mercy, and
humbly pray; and he seems to be set on denying me every mercy.

Every now and then this perverse one, who keeps me on my
back upon the ground, too tired to twist, raises his hand, and chal-
lenges my weak life: then cries rise in my mind; and the blood
which is sent out through my veins comes in a rush to the heart,
which calls it; and I am left white. He wounds me under my left
arm so violently, that the pain starts up in my heart again: then I
say: 'If he raises his hand once more, Death will have gathered me
before the blow has descended.'

O might I see Love strike right through the heart of that cruel
one who quarters mine! then the death to which I run for sake of
her beauty would not be black to me: as she, that thieving, deadly

chè tanto dà nel sol quanto nel rezzo
questa scherana micidiale e latra.
Ohmè, perchè non latra
per me, com'io per lei, nel caldo borro?
chè tosto griderei: «Io vi soccorro»;
e fare' l volentier, sì come quelli
che ne' biondi capelli
ch'Amore per consumarmi increspe e dora
metterei mano, e piacere' le allora.

S'io avessi le belle trecce prese,
che fatte son per me scudiscio e ferza,
pigliandole anzi terza,
con esse passerei vespero e squille:
e non sarei pietoso nè cortese,
anzi farei com'orso quando scherza;
e se Amor me ne sferza,
io mi vendicherei di più di mille.
Ancor ne li occhi, ond'escon le faville
che m'infiammano il cor, ch'io porto anciso,
guarderei presso e fiso,
per vendicar lo fuggir che mi face;
e poi le renderei con amor pace.

murderess, inflicts as much by daylight as by dark. O, why does she
not yelp for me, as I for her, in the hot abyss? for I would quickly
shout: 'I'll help you'; and I'd do it willingly; as some men would,
so would I thrust my hand in the fair hair that Love has waved and
gilded to consume me, and then she would find me pleasant.

If I had once caught hold of the lovely locks which have become
both switch and whip for me, taking them before matins I would
spend evensong and midnight with them: and I would not be spar-
ing or kind, rather I would act like a bear when it is playful; and if
love now whips me with them, I would avenge myself more than a
thousand-fold. I would gaze, fixedly and close, into the eyes, from
which come the sparks that burn my heart, which I bear dead within
me, to avenge myself for her shunning me; and then with love I
would give her peace again.

Canzon, vattene dritto a quella donna
che m'ha ferito il core e che m'invola
quello ond'io ho più gola,
e dàlle per lo cor d'una saetta;
chè bell'onor s'acquista in far vendetta.

T RE donne intorno al cor mi son venute,
e seggonsi di fore;
chè dentro siede Amore,
lo quale è in segnoria de la mia vita.
Tanto son belle e di tanta vertute,
che 'l possente segnore,
dico quel ch'è nel core,
a pena del parlar di lor s'aita.
Ciascuna par dolente e sbigottita,
come persona discacciata e stanca,
cui tutta gente manca
e cui vertute nè beltà non vale.
Tempo fu già nel quale,
secondo il lor parlar, furon dilette;
or sono a tutti in ira ed in non cale.
Queste così solette

My song, go straight to that woman who has wounded my heart
and who robs me of what I most hunger for, and thrust an arrow
through her heart; for fine honour is won in taking revenge.

THREE women have come about my heart and sit outside it; for
Love sits within who has lordship of my life. The women are so
lovely and of such dignity, that the powerful lord, I mean he who
is in my heart, can scarcely bring himself to speak to them. Each
seems to be grieving and bewildered, like a hunted, weary person
who lacks all followers, and to whom worth and beauty are of no
avail. There was once a time when by their converse they were
found delightful; now they are scorned by everyone and dis-
regarded. So these women, deserted in this way, have come as if

venute son come a casa d'amico;
che sanno ben che dentro è quel ch'io dico.

Dolesi l'una con parole molto,
e 'n su la man si posa
come succisa rosa;
il nudo braccio, di dolor colonna,
sente l'oraggio che cade dal volto;
l'altra man tiene ascosa
la faccia lagrimosa:
discinta e scalza, e sol di sè par donna.
Come Amor prima per la rotta gonna
la vide in parte che il tacere è bello,
egli, pietoso e fello,
di lei e del dolor fece dimanda.
«Oh di pochi vivanda,»
rispose in voce con sospiri mista,
«nostra natura qui a te ci manda:
io, che son la più trista,
son suora a la tua madre, e son Drittura;
povera, vedi, a panni ed a cintura.»

to a friend's house; for they well know that he is within of whom I have spoken.

One sorrows much in her words, and rests her head upon her hand like a fresh-cut rose; the bare arm, column to grief, feels the downpour from her face; the other hand keeps her weeping face hidden: loosely girt and barefoot, and only in herself seeming woman. When Love first saw through her torn skirt that part of her that it is courteous to be silent about, he asked her, pitying and indignant, about herself and her grief. 'O food of the few,' she replied in a voice mixed with sighs, 'our nature brings us to you: I, who am the saddest, am sister to your mother, and am Right; poor, as you see, in dress and girdle.'

Poi che fatta si fu palese e conta,
doglia e vergogna prese
lo mio segnore, e chiese
chi fosser l'altre due ch'eran con lei.
E questa, ch'era sì di pianger pronta,
tosto che lui intese,
più nel dolor s'accese,
dicendo: «A te non duol de gli occhi miei?»
Poi cominciò: «Sì come saper dei,
di fonte nasce il Nilo picciol fiume
quivi dove 'l gran lume
toglie a la terra del vinco la fronda:
sovra la vergin onda
genera' io costei che m'è da lato
e che s'asciuga con la treccia bionda.
Questo mio bel portato
mirando sè ne la chiara fontana,
generò questa che m'è piu lontana.»

Fenno i sospiri Amore un poco tardo;
e poi con gli occhi molli,
che prima furon folli,
salutò le germane sconsolate.
E po' che prese l'uno e l'atro dardo,

When she had revealed and made herself known, my lord was seized by grief and shame, and asked who were the other two who were with her. And this woman, who was so possessed by weeping, as soon as she heard him, waxed angrier in sorrow, and said: 'Does it not hurt you to see me weep?' Then she began: 'As you must know, the Nile is born, as a little river, from a spring where the great light denies the earth the osier's leaf: by the virgin wave I gave birth to her who is by my side and who dries herself with her own fair hair. This lovely offspring of mine, gazing at herself in the clear fountain, begot her who is further away from me.'

Sighs made Love falter a little; and then with wet eyes, that first had been carefree, he greeted the disconsolate descendants. And when he had taken up one and the other dart he said: 'Raise up

disse: «Drizzate i colli;
ecco l'armi ch'io volli;
per non usar, vedete, son turbate.
Larghezza e Temperanza, e l'altre nate
del nostro sangue, mendicando vanno.
Però, se questo è danno,
piangano gli occhi e dolgasi la bocca
de li uomini a cui tocca,
che sono a' raggi di cotal ciel giunti;
non noi, che semo de l'eterna rocca:
chè, se noi siamo or punti,
noi pur saremo, e pur tornerà gente,
che questo dardo farà star lucente.»

E io, che ascolto nel parlar divino
consolarsi e dolersi
così alti dispersi
l'esiglio che m'è dato onor mi tegno:
chè, se giudizio o forza di destino
vuol pur che 'l mondo versi
i bianchi fiori in persi,
cader co' buoni è pur di lode degno.
E se non che de gli occhi miei 'l bel segno

your heads: here are the weapons that I wanted; they are in dis-
order, you see, for lack of use. Liberality and Temperance, and the
others born of our blood, go about begging. But, if this is harmful,
let the men weep and speak sadly whom it concerns, who have seen
the light of such a day; we need not grieve who are of the eternal
rock: for, if we are now afflicted, we shall still live on, and people
will be found again who will make this dart shine.'
And I, who listen to such noble refugees, lamenting and consoling themselves, hold the banishment that has been meted to me,
an honour: for, if judgement or the power of fate is still to make
the world turn its white flowers to red, to fall with the good is still
worthy of praise. And if it were not that my eyes are denied their

per lontananza m'è tolto dal viso
che m'have in foco miso,
lieve mi conterei ciò che m'è grave.
Ma questo foco m'have
già consumato sì l'ossa e la polpa,
che Morte al petto m'ha posto la chiave.
Onde, s'io ebbi colpa,
più lune ha volto il sol poi che fu spenta,
se colpa muore perchè l'uom si penta.

Canzone, a' panni tuoi non ponga uom mano,
per veder quel che bella donna chiude:
bastin le parti nude;
lo dolce pome a tutta gente niega,
per cui ciascun man piega.
Ma s'elli avvien che tu alcun mai trovi
amico di virtù, ed e' ti priega,
fatti di color novi,
poi li ti mostra; e 'l fior, ch'è bel di fori,
fa disiar ne li amorosi cori.

fair mark by distance, and this puts me in the fire, I would consider
what is grievous something slight. But this fire has already so de-
voured my flesh and bones, that Death has put its key to my breast.
So that, if I had a share of blame, the sun has brought on many
moons since it was expiated, if blame dies because a man repents.

My song, let no man lay a hand on your clothes, to see what
lovely woman hides: let the bare parts suffice; the sweet apple to
which every hand stretches, deny to every one. But if it chance that
you ever find one who is a friend to virtue, and he begs you, put
on new colours, and show yourself to him; and make the flower,
which is the beauty of flowers, be desired in loving hearts.

Canzone, uccella con le bianche penne;
canzone, caccia con li neri veltri,
che fuggir mi convenne,
ma far mi poterian di pace dono.
però nol fan che non san quel che sono:
camera di perdon savio uom non serra,
che 'l perdonare è bel vincer di guerra.

FRANCESCO PETRARCA

Voi ch'ascoltate in rime sparse il suono
di quei sospiri ond'io nudriva il core
in sul mio primo giovenile errore,
quand'era in parte altr'uom da quel ch'i' sono;
del vario stile in ch'io piango e ragiono
fra le vane speranze e 'l van dolore,
ove sia chi per prova intenda amore,
spero trovar pietà, non che perdono.

My song, bird with the white feathers, song, hunt with the black
harehounds whom I should rather flee, but they could make me a
gift of peace. But they do not do it, for they do not know what
manner of man I am: a wise man does not lock the door of pardon,
for to pardon is a fine victory in war.

You who hear in my scattered rhymes the sound of those sighs
on which I fed my heart in my first youthful mistake, when I was
in part another man from the one I am now; for the varied manner
in which I weep and reflect there, amid vain hopes and vain grief,
I hope to have pity, not only pardon, from whosoever by experience knows love.

Ma ben veggio or sì come al popol tutto
favola fui gran tempo: onde sovente
di me medesmo meco mi vergogno:
e del mio vaneggiar vergogna è 'l frutto,
e 'l pentirsi, e 'l conoscer chiaramente
che quanto piace al mondo è breve sogno.

LA gola e 'l sonno e l'oziose piume
hanno del mondo ogni vertù sbandita;
ond'è dal corso suo quasi smarrita
nostra natura, vinta dal costume.
Ed è sì spento ogni benigno lume
del ciel, per cui s'informa umana vita,
che per cosa mirabile s'addita
chi vol far d'Elicona nascer fiume.

Qual vaghezza di lauro? qual di mirto?
«Povera e nuda vai, Filosofia,»
dice la turba al vil guadagno intesa.
Pochi compagni avrai per l'altra via;
tanto ti prego più, gentile spirto:
non lassar la magnanima tua impresa.

But I see clearly today how I was the talk of everyone for a long time, and for this often, within me, I grow ashamed of myself: and I see how shame is the fruit of my having strayed, and repentance, and the clear knowledge that whatever the world loves is a brief dream.

GLUTTONY and dullness and slothful couches have banished every virtue from the world; so that our nature, overcome by habit, has all but lost the way. And all the kindly lights, by which human life is quickened, are so extinguished in heaven, that he who wishes to lead a stream from Helicon is pointed out as a marvel.

Such desire for laurels? such desire for myrtle? 'Philosophy, you go along poor and naked,' say the crowd, bent on vile gain. You will have few companions on the other road; I beg you so much the more, gentle spirit, not to turn from your great-hearted undertaking.

Movesi il vecchierel canuto e bianco
del dolce loco ov'ha sua età fornita,
e da la famigliuola sbigottita
che vede il caro padre venir manco
indi traendo poi l'antiquo fianco
per l'estreme giornate di sua vita,
quanto più pò col buon voler s'aita,
rotto da gli anni e dal camino stanco:

e viene a Roma, seguendo 'l desio,
per mirar la sembianza di Colui
ch'ancor lassù nel ciel vedere spera.
Così, lasso! talor vo cercand'io,
donna, quanto è possibile, in altrui
la disiata vostra forma vera.

Mille fiate, o dolce mia guerrera,
per aver co' begli occhi vostri pace,
v'aggio profferto il cor; ma a voi non piace
mirar sì basso con la mente altera:

The poor old man, grizzled and white, leaves the sweet place where he has always kept himself, and leaves his frightened family who see their dear father failing. Then dragging his aged limbs through the last days of life, broken by the years and weary of journeying, he takes what help he can from a good will;

and comes to Rome, pursuing his desire, to see the likeness of Him whom he hopes to see above in heaven once more. So, alas! do I sometimes go seeking, my lady, as far as I may, your desired true form in others.

A thousand times, o my sweet warrior, to have peace with your lovely eyes, I have offered you my heart; but you do not care, with your proud mind, to look so low: and if perchance some other

e se di lui fors'altra donna spera,
vive in speranza debile e fallace:
mio, perchè sdegno ciò ch'a voi dispiace,
esser non può giammai così com'era.

Or s'io lo scaccio, ed e' non trova in voi
nell'esilio infelice alcun soccorso,
nè sa star sol, nè gire ov'altri 'l chiama
poria smarrire il suo natural corso;
che grave colpa fia d'ambeduo noi,
e tanto più di voi, quanto più v'ama.

Solo e pensoso i più deserti campi
vo mesurando a passi tardi e lenti,
e gli occhi porto per fuggire intenti
ove vestigio uman l'arena stampi.
Altro schermo non trovo che mi scampi
dal manifesto accorger de le genti;
perchè ne gli atti d'allegrezza spenti
di fuor si legge com'io dentro avampi:

woman should hope for that heart of mine, she lives in hope that is
weak and false: it can never be as it was, since I despise what you
dislike.

Now if I expel my heart, and it does not find any refuge in its
unhappy exile in you, nor knows how to live alone, nor to go
where others call, it might wander from its natural course; which
will be a grave offence in both of us, and more so in you, since it
loves you the more.

Alone and thoughtful, I go pacing the most deserted fields with
slow hesitant steps, and I am watchful so as to flee from any
place where human traces mark the sand. I find no other defence
that protects me from known gatherings of people; because they
can see from without, in my actions bereft of joy, how I inwardly
flame:

sì ch'io mi credo omai che monti e piagge,
e fiumi e selve sappian di che tempre
sia la mia vita, ch'è celata altrui.
Ma pur sì aspre vie nè sì selvagge
cercar non so ch'Amor non venga sempre
ragionando con meco, ed io con lui.

NON al suo amante più Diana piacque
quando, per tal ventura, tutta ignuda
la vide in mezzo delle gelid'acque;
ch'a me la pastorella alpestra e cruda,
posta a bagnar un leggiadretto velo,
ch'a l'aura il vago e biondo capel chiuda;
tal che mi fece or quand'egli arde il cielo,
tutto tremar d'un amoroso gelo.

PADRE del Ciel, dopo i perduti giorni,
dopo le notti vaneggiando spese
con quel fero desio ch'al cor s'accese
mirando gli atti per mio mal sì adorni;

so that now I believe that mountains and banks, and rivers and woods know what the tenour of my life is, which is hidden from others. And yet I cannot find any paths so harsh or wild that Love will not always come, talking with me the while, and I with him.

DIANA did not please her lover more when, by such a chance, he saw her naked in the midst of icy waters, than I was pleased by the hard mountain shepherdess, set there to wash a graceful veil that binds that lovely fair hair from the breeze; such that she made me tremble with an amorous chill, now when the heavens burn.

FATHER of Heaven, after the lost days, after the nights spent in straying with that fierce desire that burned in my heart when I looked upon those lineaments so lovely to my harm, may it please

piacciati omai, col tuo lume, ch'io torni
ad altra vita ed a più belle imprese;
sì ch'avendo le reti indarno tese,
il mio duro avversario se ne scorni.

Or volga, Signor mio, l'undecim'anno
ch'i' fui sommesso al dispietato giogo,
che sopra i più soggetti è più feroce.
Miserere del mio non degno affanno;
riduci i pensier vaghi a miglior luogo;
rammenta lor com'oggi fosti in croce.

Nova angeletta sovra l'ale accorta
scese dal cielo in sulla fresca riva
là ond'io passava sol per mio destino.
Poi che senza compagna e senza scorta
mi vide, un laccio che di seta ordiva,
tese fra l'erba ond'è verde il camino.
Allor fui preso; e non mi spiacque poi;
sì dolce lume uscìa degli occhi suoi.

you now, by your light, that I should turn to another life and
nobler endeavours; so that my hard adversary, having stretched his
nets in vain, may be discomfited.

Now the eleventh year comes round, my Lord, since I was bent
under the pitiless yoke which is crueller to the more submissive.
Have mercy on my unworthy suffering; bring back my wandering
thoughts to a better place; remind them how today you were on
the cross.

A wondrous angel borne on rapid wing came down from heaven
upon the fresh bank where I was passing alone, to my fate. When
she saw I was without fair companion or guide, she stretched a
noose she had wound of silk, in the grass with which the path was
green. Then was I taken; nor did it displease me after; so sweet a
light issued from her eyes.

Chiare, fresche e dolci acque,
ove le belle membra
pose colei che sola a me par donna;
gentil ramo, ove piacque
(con sospir mi rimembra)
a lei di fare al bel fianco colonna;
erba e fior, che la gonna
leggiadra ricoverse
con l'angelico seno;
aer sacro sereno,
ov'Amor co' begli occhi il cor m'aperse:
date udienzia insieme
alle dolenti mie parole estreme.

S'egli è pur mio destino
(e il cielo in ciò s'adopra)
ch'Amor quest'occhi lagrimando chiuda,
qualche grazia il meschino
corpo fra voi ricopra,
e torni l'alma al proprio albergo ignuda.
La morte fia men cruda

CLEAR, fresh, and sweet waters, where she who alone to me seems woman rested her lovely limbs; gentle trunk, of which she liked (as I remember with sighs) to make a column for her lovely side; grass and flower, which the gay dress covered as well as the heavenly bosom; holy calm air, where Love opened my heart with those lovely eyes: give hearing all together to my last grieving words.

If it is my destiny (and heaven works for this) that Love should close these eyes even while they weep, may some kindness inter my miserable body in your midst, and may my soul return naked to its own abode. Death will be less cruel if I can go forward with

se questa spene porto
a quel dubbioso passo;
che lo spirito lasso
non poria mai in più riposato porto
nè 'n più tranquilla fossa
fuggir la carne travagliata e l'ossa.

Tempo verrà ancor forse,
ch'all'usato soggiorno
torni la fera bella e mansueta;
e là 'v'ella mi scorse
nel bendetto giorno,
volga la vista desiosa e lieta,
cercandomi; et, o pietà!
già terra infra le pietre
vedendo, Amor l'inspiri
in guisa che sospiri
sì dolcemente che mercè m'impetre,
e faccia forza al Cielo,
asciugandosi gli occhi col bel velo.

this hope to that uncertain pass; as my weary spirit could never fly from my troubled flesh and bones to a more restful haven or a quieter grave.

Perhaps a time will still come when this mild and lovely fierce one may come back to her accustomed haunt; and there, where she noticed me upon that blessed day, may turn her happy eager face to look for me; and, o pity! seeing me already earth among the stones, Love may inspire her to sigh so softly that she will obtain mercy for me, and have her way with Heaven, drying those eyes with that lovely veil.

Da' be' rami scendea   1
(dolce nella memoria)
una pioggia di fior sovra 'l suo grembo;
ed ella si sedea
umile in tanta gloria,
coverta già dell'amoroso nembo.
Qual fior cadea sul lembo,
qual su le trecce bionde,
ch'oro forbito e perle
eran quel dì a vederle;
qual si posava in terra, e qual su l'onde;
qual con un vago errore
girando, parea dir: qui regna Amore.

Quante volte diss'io
allor pien di spavento:
costei per fermo nacque in Paradiso!
Così carco d'obblio
il divin portamento
e 'l volto e le parole e 'l dolce riso
m'aveano, e sì diviso

From the lovely branches there came down (sweet in memory)
a rain of flowers into her lap, and she sat modest amid so great glory,
covered now by the loving shower. A flower fell upon her hem,
another on her fair hair which seemed polished gold and pearl that
day; one rested on the ground, and another upon the wave; one,
in charmed flight, turning as it fell, seemed to say: here Love
reigns.

How many times did I say then full of fear: she was born, for
certain, in Paradise! Her divine bearing and face and words had
so weighted me with forgetfulness and cut me off from the true

dall'immagine vera,
ch'i' dicea sospirando:
qui come venn'io, o quando?
credendo esser in Ciel, non là dov'era.
Da indi in qua mi piace
quest'erba sì, ch'altrove non ho pace.

Se tu avessi ornamenti quant' hai voglia,
potresti arditamente
uscir del bosco e gir infra la gente.

ITALIA mia, benchè 'l parlar sia indarno
alle piaghe mortali
che nel bel corpo tuo sì spesse veggio,
piacemi almen ch'e' miei sospir sian quali
spera 'l Tevero e l'Arno,
e 'l Po, dove doglioso e grave or seggio.
Rettor del ciel, io cheggio
che la pietà che ti condusse in terra,
ti volga al tuo diletto almo paese:
vedi, Signor cortese,
di che lievi cagion che crudel guerra;
e i cor, che 'ndura e serra

image of things that I said sighing: how did I come here, or when?
believing myself in Heaven, not where I really was. From that time
forth this grass has so pleased me that I find peace in no other
place.

[Song], if you had as much ornament as you have desire, you
could leave the wood boldly and go among people.

My Italy, although talking cannot heal the mortal wounds that I
see so frequent in your fair body, I am glad that at least my sighs
are such as Tiber and the Arno and the Po (where I now sit sorrowful and heavy) hope for. Governor of Heaven, I ask that the pity
which brought you upon earth may turn you now to your beloved
kindly country. See, gracious Lord, how cruel a war from how

Marte superbo e fero,
apri tu, Padre, e 'ntenerisci e snoda;
ivi fa che 'l tuo vero
(qual io mi sia) per la mia lingua s'oda.

Voi, cui Fortuna ha posto in mano il freno
delle belle contrade,
di che nulla pietà par che vi stringa,
che fan qui tante pellegrine spade?
Perchè 'l verde terreno
del barbarico sangue si depinga?
Vano error vi lusinga;
poco vedete, e parvi veder molto;
che 'n cor venale amor cercate o fede.
Qual più gente possede,
colui è più da' suoi nemici avvolto.
O diluvio raccolto
di che deserti strani
per inondar i nostri dolci campi!
Se dalle proprie mani
questo n'avven, or che fia che ne scampi?

slight causes: and do you open, Father, and soften and free the hearts that proud, fierce Mars hardens and holds fast: there let your truth be heard (whatever I may be) from my tongue.

O you, in whose hands Fortune has put the bridle of the fair regions, no pity of which seems to restrain you, what are so many alien swords doing here? Why is the green earth painted with barbarian blood? A vain mistake is deluding you; little you see and think you see a lot; since you look for love and faith in mercenary hearts. He who possesses most people is most surrounded by his enemies. O deluge borne here from what foreign deserts to flood our pleasant fields! If this comes about by our own hands, who will there be, then, to save us?

Ben provide Natura al nostro stato
quando dell'Alpi schermo
pose fra noi e la tedesca rabbia;
ma 'l desir cieco e 'ncontra 'l suo ben fermo
s'è poi tanto ingegnato,
ch'al corpo sano ha procurato scabbia.
Or dentro ad una gabbia
fere selvagge e mansuete gregge
s'annidan sì che sempre il miglior geme:
ed è questo del seme,
per più dolor, del popol senza legge,
al qual, come si legge,
Mario aperse sì 'l fianco,
che memoria dell'opra anco non langue,
quando, assetato e stanco,
non più bevve del fiume acqua, che sangue.

Nature provided excellently for our state when she placed the shield of the Alps between us and the German rage: but blind desire, set against its own good, has now devised so well that it has brought sores to the healthy body. Now, in the one cage, wild beasts and submissive flocks couch, so that the better has always to weep: and this is the doing, to our greater grief, of the descendants of that lawless people * whose side was laid open by Marius so savagely that the memory of the deed has not languished, when, tired and thirsty, he did not drink water from the river so much as blood.

---

* The Teutones.

Cesare taccio, che per ogni piaggia
fece l'erba sanguigne
di lor vene, ove 'l nostro ferro mise.
Or par, non so per che stelle maligne,
che 'l Cielo in odio n'aggia:
vostra mercè cui tanto si commise:
vostre voglie divise
guastan del mondo la più bella parte.
Qual colpa, qual giudicio o qual destino,
fastidire il vicino
povero; e le fortune afflitte e sparte
perseguire; e 'n disparte
cercar gente, e gradire
che sparga 'l sangue e venda l'alma a prezzo?
Io parlo per ver dire,
non per odio d'altrui nè per disprezzo.

I keep silent about Caesar who, on every shore where he took our arms, made the grass bloody from their veins. Now it seems, I know not by what evil stars, that Heaven hates us: thanks to you to whom so much has been committed: your divided wills lay waste the fairest part of the world. What guilt, what judgement, or what destiny, drives you to worry your poor neighbour, and to hunt out his threatened and scattered goods, and recruit your soldiers from foreign countries, and be glad that blood should be shed, and the soul traded for a price? I talk to speak the truth, and not from hate or contempt of others.

Nè v'accorgete ancor, per tante prove,
del bavarico inganno,
che, alzando 'l dito, con la morte scherza?
Peggio è lo strazio, al mio parer, che 'l danno.
Ma 'l vostro sangue piove
più largamente; ch'altr'ira vi sferza.
Dalla mattina a terza
di voi pensate, e vedrete come
tien caro altrui chi tien sè così vile.
Latin sangue gentile,
sgombra da te queste dannose some:
non far idolo un nome
vano, senza soggetto:
che 'l furor di lassù, gente ritrosa,
vincerne d'intelletto,
peccato è nostro e non natural cosa.

And are you not yet made aware, by such repeated experience,
of the deceit of the Bavarians who raise a finger and toy with death?
The dishonour, as I see it, is worse than the harm. But your blood
rains more widely; as a different anger whips you on. Take thought
of yourselves from matins to the third hour, and you will see how
dear the man holds others who holds himself so vile. Noble Latin
blood, shake from yourself these hurtful burdens: do not make an
idol of an empty, groundless name: that the fury from up there, a
backward people, overcomes us in intelligence is our failing and
nothing natural.

Non è questo 'l terren ch'i' toccai pria?
Non è questo 'l mio nido,
ove nudrito fui sì dolcemente?
Non è questa la patria in ch'io mi fido,
madre benigna e pia,
che copre l'uno e l'altro mio parente?
Per Dio, questo la mente
talor vi mova; e con pietà guardate
le lagrime del popol doloroso,
che sol da voi riposo,
dopo Dio, spera: e, pur che voi mostriate
segno alcun di pietate,
virtù contra furore
prenderà l'arme; e fia 'l combatter corto;
che l'antico valore
nell'italici cor non è ancor morto.

Signor, mirate come 'l tempo vola,
e sì come la vita
fugge, e la morte n'è sovra le spalle.
Voi siete or qui: pensate alla partita;
chè l'alma ignuda e sola
conven ch'arrive a quel dubbioso calle.
Al passar questa valle,

Is this not the ground I first touched? Is not this my nest, where
I was so sweetly nurtured? Is this not the native land in which I
trust, kind, devout mother, who covers both parents of mine? In
God's name, let this sometimes move your minds; look with pity
upon the tears of the sorrowful people who, after God, hope for
rest from you alone: and, as long as you show some sign of pity,
virtue will take arms against fury; and the fighting shall be brief;
for the ancient valour is not yet dead in Italian hearts.

My Lords, see how time is winging, and how life flies, and death
is at our shoulders. You are now here: think of your leave-taking;
for the soul must needs reach that uncertain pass, naked and alone.

piacciavi porre giù l'odio e lo sdegno,
venti contrari alla vita serena;
e quel che 'n altrui pena
tempo si spende, in qualche atto più degno,
o di mano o d'ingegno,
in qualche bella lode,
in qualche onesto studio si converta:
così quaggiù si gode,
e la strada del ciel si trova aperta.

Canzone, io t'ammonisco
che tua ragion cortesemente dica;
perchè fra gente altera ir ti conviene,
e le voglie son piene
già dell'usanza pessima ed antica
del ver sempre nemica.
Proverai tua ventura
fra magnanimi pochi, a chi 'l ben piace:
di' lor: chi m'assicura?
I 'vo gridando: pace, pace, pace.

To go through that valley, may it please you to lay down hate and
disdain, adverse winds for the life of calm; and let the time which is
being spent in causing others pain be turned to some worthier deed
of hand or mind, to some fine, praiseworthy thing, to some just
endeavour; in this way one rejoices here below, and finds the way
to heaven open.

My song, I charge you that you give out your meaning courteously, because you must go among proud people; and minds are
now full of the worst old prejudices, always the enemy of truth.
You will take your chance among the magnanimous few, who will
be well pleased with you. Say to them: Who will champion me?
I keep crying: peace, peace, peace.

Di pensier in pensier, di monte in monte
mi guida Amor; ch'ogni segnato calle
provo contrario alla tranquilla vita.
Se 'n solitaria piaggia, rivo o fonte,
se 'n fra duo poggi siede ombrosa valle,
ivi s'acqueta l'alma sbigottita;
e, com'Amor la 'nvita,
or ride or piagne or teme or s'assicura:
e 'l volto che lei segue, ov'ella il mena,
si turba e rasserena,
ed in un esser picciol tempo dura;
onde alla vista uom di tal vita esperto
diria: questi arde, e di suo stato è incerto.

Per alti monti e per selve aspre trovo
qualche riposo; ogni abitato loco
è nemico mortal degli occhi miei.
A ciascun passo nasce un pensier novo
della mia donna, che sovente in gioco
gira il tormento ch'i' porto per lei;
et appena vorrei

FROM thought to thought, from mountain to mountain Love leads me; since I find every marked path hostile to the life of quiet. If there is a stream or fountain on a lonely slope, if, between two hills, lies a shady vale, there the frightened soul calms itself: and, as Love bids, now laughs, now weeps, now fears, now is assured: and my face which follows the soul, wherever it leads, is disturbed and clears, and stays little time in the one state; so that a man learned in such a life would say on seeing me: This one burns, and is uncertain of his fortune.

In high mountains and in wild woods I find some rest; each inhabited place is the mortal enemy of my eyes. With each pace some new thought of my mistress is born, as the torment I bear for her often comes into play; and as soon as I would change my sweet and

cangiar questo mio viver dolce amaro,
ch'i' dico: forse ancor ti serva Amore
ad un tempo migliore;
forse a te stesso vile, altrui se' caro:
et in questa trapasso sospirando:
Or potrebb'esser vero? or come? or quando?

Ove porge ombra un pino alto od un colle,
talor m'arresto, e pur nel primo sasso
disegno con la mente il suo bel viso.
Poi ch'a me torno, trovo il petto molle
della pietate; ed allor dico: ahi lasso,
dove se' giunto; ed onde se' diviso!
Ma mentre tener fiso
posso al primo pensier la mente vaga,
e mirar lei, ed obbliar me stesso,
sento Amor sì da presso
che del suo proprio error l'alma s'appaga:
in tante parti e sì bella la veggio,
che se l'error durasse, altro non cheggio.

bitter life, then I say: perhaps Love is still preserving you for a
better time; perhaps, though hateful to yourself, you are dear to
another: and, sighing the while, I go on: But could this be true?
but how? but when?

Where a tall pine tree or a hill offers shade, sometimes I stop, and
on the nearest stone trace mentally her lovely face. When I come to
myself again, I find my breast wet from tenderness; and then I say:
Alas, what have you come to, and what have you left behind? But as
long as I can keep my mind steadily upon that first thought, and
gaze on her and forget myself, I feel Love so closely that my mind
is ravished by its own delusion. I see her in so many places and her
so lovely, that were the deception to last, I ask nothing more.

I' l'ho più volte (or chi fia che mel creda?)
nell'acqua chiara e sopra l'erba verde
veduta viva, e nel troncon d'un faggio,
e 'n bianca nube sì fatta che Leda
avria ben detto che sua figlia perde,
come stella che 'l Sol copre col raggio:
e quanto in più selvaggio
loco mi trovo e 'n più deserto lido,
tanto più bella il mio pensier l'adombra.
Poi quando il vero sgombra
quel dolce error, pur lì medesmo assido
me freddo, pietra morta in pietra viva,
in guisa d'uom che pensi e pianga e scriva.

Ove d'altra montagna ombra non tocchi,
verso 'l maggior e 'l più spedito giogo,
tirar mi suol un desiderio intenso:
indi i miei danni a misurar con gli occhi
comincio, e 'ntanto lagrimando sfogo
di dolorosa nebbia il cor condenso,
allor ch'i miro e penso,

I have many times (now who will believe me?) seen her vividly
in clear water or on green grass, and in the trunk of a beech tree
and on a white cloud, so fashioned that Leda would have surely
said that her daughter is eclipsed, like a star that the Sun obscures
with its rays: and the wilder the place, the lonelier the strand where
I happen to be, so much the lovelier does my thought shadow her
forth. Then when the truth clears away that sweet deception, still I
sit there the same, sit cold, dead stone on living stone, like a man
who thinks and weeps and writes.

An intense desire continually draws me to the loftiest, most
advantageous crest which the shadow of other mountains does not
touch. From there I begin to judge my sufferings with my eyes,
and weep then, and ease the heart, oppressed by a sorrowful mist,
when I see and think what a space separates me from that lovely

quanta aria dal bel viso mi diparte,
che sempre m'è sì presso e sì lontano.
Poscia fra me pian piano:
Che fai tu lasso? forse in quella parte
or di tua lontananza si sospira:
ed in questo pensier l'alma respira.

Canzone, oltra quell'alpe,
là dove 'l ciel è più sereno e lieto,
mi revedrai sovr'un ruscel corrente,
ove l'aura si sente
d'un fresco ed odorifero laureto.
Ivi è 'l mio cor, e quella che 'l m'invola:
qui veder puoi l'immagine mia sola.

IN qual parte del ciel, in qual idea
era l'esempio, onde Natura tolse
quel bel viso leggiadro, in ch'ella volse
mostrar qua giù quanto lassù potea?
Qual ninfa in fonti, in selve mai qual dea,
chiome d'oro sì fino a l'aura sciolse?
Quando un cor tante in sè vertuti accolse?
Ben che la somma è di mia morte rea.

face, which is always so near to me and so far. Then softly to myself: What are you doing, wretch? Perhaps over there she sighs for
your being far away: and in this thought the soul breathes.

My song, beyond that mount, where the sky is clearer and more
glad, you will see me again by a running stream where the breeze
smells of a fresh and fragrant laurel grove. There is my heart, and
she who steals it from me: here you can see only my effigy.

IN what part of heaven, in what celestial form was the original
from which Nature took that glad, lovely face by which it wanted to
show down here how much on high could be created? What nymph
in fountain, or in the woods what goddess, ever loosed to the breeze
hair of such fine gold? When did a heart gather into itself so many
virtues? Although the sum of this evilly becomes my death.

Per divina bellezza indarno mira
chi gli occhi de costei già mai non vide
come soavemente ella gli gira;
non sa come Amor sana, e come ancide,
chi non sa come dolce ella sospira,
e come dolce parla, e dolce ride.

Or che 'l ciel e la terra e 'l vento tace,
e le fere e gli augelli il sonno affrena,
notte 'l carro stellato in giro mena,
e nel suo letto il mar senz'onda giace;
veggio, penso, ardo, piango; e chi mi sface
sempre m'è innanzi per mia dolce pena:
guerra è 'l mio stato, d'ira e di duol piena;
e sol di lei pensando ho qualche pace.

Così sol d'una chiara fonte viva
move 'l dolce e l'amaro ond'io mi pasco;
una man sola mi risana e punge.
E perchè 'l mio martir non giunga a riva,
mille volte il dì moro e mille nasco;
tanto dalla salute mia son lunge.

He looks in vain for divine beauty who never saw the eyes of this fair as she gently turns them; nor does he know how Love heals and kills who does not know how sweetly she sighs, and how sweetly talks, and sweetly laughs.

Now that the heavens and the earth and the wind is silent, and the wild beasts and the birds are bridled by sleep, night leads its starry car upon its round, and, without one wave, the sea lies in its bed; I see, think, burn, and weep; and she who is my undoing is always before me to my sweet pain: my state is one of war, full of rage and grief; and only in thinking of her do I have some peace.

So from one clear and living fountain the sweet and the bitter move upon which I feed; one single hand heals and pierces me. And so that my suffering may not come to shore, I die a thousand times each day, a thousand I am born; so far am I from my salvation.

Pien d'un vago pensier, che mi desvia
da tutti gli altri, e fammi al mondo ir solo,
ad or ad or a me stesso m'involo,
pur lei cercando che fuggir devria:
e veggiola passar sì dolce e ria,
che l'alma trema per levarsi a volo;
tal d'armati sospir conduce stuolo
questa bella d'Amor nemica e mia.

Ben, s'io non erro, di pietate un raggio
scorgo fra 'l nubiloso altero ciglio,
che 'n parte rasserena il cor doglioso:
allor raccolgo l'alma, e poi ch'i' aggio
di scovrirle il mio mal preso consiglio,
tanto le ho a dir che 'ncominciar non oso.

Per mezz'i boschi inospiti e selvaggi
onde vanno a gran rischio uomini et arme,
vo securo io; chè non pò spaventarme
altri che 'l Sol ch'à d'Amor vivo i raggi.

FULL of one fond thought that separates me from all other men,
and makes me go through the world alone, from time to time I am
rapt out of myself, while I look for her whom I should fly from.
And I see her go by so sweet and deadly that my soul trembles to
take flight, she leads such a troop of armed sighs with her, this
beautiful enemy of Love and mine.

Truly, if I am not mistaken, I make out a ray of pity coming
from that high cloudy brow which in part brightens my sad heart.
Then I summon up my soul again, and when I am about to reveal
my ill-advised choice to her, I have so much to tell her that I do not
dare begin.

THROUGH the heart of inhospitable, wild woods where men with
arms go at great risk, I go secure; for nothing can frighten me but
that Sun which draws its living rays from Love. And I go singing

E vo cantando (o penser miei non saggi!)
lei che 'l ciel non poria lontana farme;
ch'i' l'ho negli occhi; e veder seco parme
donne e donzelle, e sono abeti e faggi!

Parme d'udirla, udendo i rami e l'ôre
e le frondi e gli augei lagnarsi, e l'acque
mormorando fuggir per l'erba verde.
Raro un silenzio, un solitario orrore
d'ombrosa selva mai tanto mi piacque;
se non che dal mio Sol troppo si perde.

O CAMERETTA, che già fosti un porto
a le gravi tempeste mie diurne,
fonte se' or di lagrime notturne,
che 'l dì celate per vergogna porto.
O letticciuol, che requie eri e conforto
in tanti affanni, di che dogliose urne
ti bagna Amor, con quelle mani eburne,
sol ver' me crudeli a sì gran torto!

(o my foolish thoughts!) her whom heaven cannot make distant
from me; for I have her in my eyes; and seem to see women and
girls with her, and they are firs and beech-trees!

I seem to hear her, hearing the branches and the breeze and the
leaves and the birds complaining, and the waters murmuring as they
flee through the green grass. Rarely did a silence, a lonely awfulness
of shady woodland so please me; except that too much of my Sun
is meanwhile lost.

O LITTLE room that were once a harbour from those severe daily
tempests of mine, you are now a fount of nightly tears which by
day I bear hid for shame. O little bed that were repose and comfort
in so many torments, from what sorrowful urns does Love bathe
you, with those ivory hands that are cruel to me alone – so wrongly!

Nè pur il mio secreto, e 'l mio riposo
fuggo, ma più me stesso, e 'l mio pensèro,
che, seguendol talor, levommi a volo;
e 'l vulgo, a me nemico, et odioso
(chi 'l pensò mai?), per mio refugio chero:
tal paura ho di ritrovarmi solo.

Rotta è l'alta Colonna e 'l verde Lauro
che facean ombra al mio stanco pensero;
perdut'ho quel che ritrovar non spero
dal borea all'austro, o dal mar indo al mauro.
Tolto m'hai, Morte, il mio doppio tesauro,
che mi fea viver lieto e gire altero;
e ristorar nol può terra nè impero,
nè gemma oriental nè forza d'auro.

I do not flee from privacy and rest, but rather from myself and
my own thoughts which, when I used to follow them, sometimes
raised me to flight; and I desire the crowd, hostile and hateful to me
(who would ever have thought it?), for my refuge: so great a fear
have I of being alone again.

Shattered is the high column * and the green Laurel † which
cast shade for my tired thoughts; I have lost what I do not hope to
find again from Boreas to Auster, from the Indian sea to the
Mauritanian. You have taken my double treasure from me, Death,
which made me go about so lightsome and proud; and the earth
cannot, nor empire, nor eastern gem, nor power of gold, make good
my loss.

------

* his protector, Colonna; † his lady, Laura
(who had both died shortly before)

Ma se consentimento è di destino,
che poss'io più se no aver l'alma trista,
umidi gli occhi sempre e 'l viso chino?
O nostra vita, ch'è sì bella in vista,
com' perde agevolmente in un mattino
quel che 'n molt'anni a gran pena s'acquista!

GLI occhi di ch'io parlai sì caldamente,
e le braccia e le mani e i piedi e 'l viso
che m'avean sì da me stesso diviso
e fatto singular dall'altra gente;
le crespe chiome d'or puro lucente,
e 'l lampeggiar dell'angelico riso
che solean far in terra un paradiso,
poca polvere son, che nulla sente.

Ed io pur vivo; onde mi doglio e sdegno,
rimaso senza 'l lume ch'amai tanto,
in gran fortuna e 'n disarmato legno.
Or sia qui fine al mio amoroso canto:
secca è la vena dell'usato ingegno,
e la cetera mia rivolta in pianto.

But if this is with the consent of fate, what can I do but bear a sad soul, wet eyes and bent head for ever? O our life which is so fair outwardly, how easily does it lose in a morning what in many years with great struggling is gained!

THE eyes of which I so warmly spoke, and the arms and the hands and the feet and the face which had so separated me from myself, and marked me out from other people; the waving hair of pure and shining gold, and the flashing of the angelic smile which used to make a paradise on earth, are now a little dust which feels no mortal thing.

And yet I live; at which I grieve and despise myself, left as I am without the light I so loved, in a great storm, in a disabled ship. Now let there be here an end to my loving song: dry is the vein of accustomed skill, and my lyre all turned to weeping.

Levommi il mio pensèr in parte ov'era
quella ch'io cerco, e non ritrovo in terra:
ivi, fra lor che 'l terzo cerchio serra,
la rividi più bella, e meno altera.
Per man mi prese, e disse: in questa spera
sarai ancor meco, se 'l desir non erra;
i' so' colei che ti die' tanta guerra,
e compie' mia giornata inanzi sera.

Mio ben non cape in intelletto umano:
te solo aspetto, e quel che tanto amasti
e là giuso è rimaso, il mio bel velo.
Deh, perchè tacque ed allargò la mano?
Ch'al suon de' detti sì pietosi e casti
poco mancò ch'io non rimasi in cielo.

Quel rosignuol che sì soave piagne
forse suoi figli o sua cara consorte,
di dolcezza empie il cielo e le campagne
con tante note sì pietose e scorte;

My thoughts raised me to a place where was she whom I seek and find no more on earth: there, among those whom the third circle encloses, I saw her again, more lovely and less proud. She took me by the hand, and said: you will be with me again in this sphere, if your desire does not go astray; I am she who inflicted such war upon you, and who completed my day before evening.

My goodness is not compassed by human understanding: you alone I wait for, and, what you so much loved that stays below, my lovely veil. O, why did she go silent and open her hand? For at the sound of words so pitying and pure little more was wanted for me to have stayed in heaven.

That nightingale that is so softly weeping perhaps for its children or its dear mate, fills the heavens and the fields with the sweetness of so many pitiful and brilliant notes, and all night, it seems, accom-

e tutta notte par che m'accompagne
e mi rammente la mia dura sorte:
ch'altri che me non ho di cui mi lagne;
che 'n Dee non credev'io regnasse Morte.

O che lieve è ingannar chi s'assecura!
Que' duo bei lumi, assai più che 'l Sol chiari,
chi pensò mai veder far terra oscura?
Or conosch'io che mia fera ventura
vuol che vivendo e lagrimando impari
come nulla quaggiù diletta e dura.

Lɪ angeli eletti e l'anime beate
cittadine del cielo, il primo giorno
che Madonna passò, le fur intorno
piene di maraviglia e di pietate.
Che luce è questa, qual nova beltate?
dicean tra lor; perch'abito sì adorno
dal mondo errante a quest'alto soggiorno
non salì mai in tutta questa etate.

panies me, and reminds me of my hard fate: for I have none for
whom to grieve but myself; because I did not believe that Death
could reign in Goddesses.

O how easy it is, the deceiving of one who feels secure! Who
would ever have thought to see two lovely lights, clearer far than
the sun, become dark earth? Now I know that my savage fate is to
make me learn, living and weeping, that nothing here below delights and lasts.

Tʜᴇ chosen angels and the blessed souls, citizens of heaven, on
the first day that my lady passed, gathered about her full of wonder
and deference. What light is this, and what new beauty? they said
to one another: since never in this age did so fair a form mount
from the wandering earth to this high rest.

Ella contenta aver cangiato albergo,
si paragona pur coi più perfetti;
e parte ad or ad or si volge a tergo
mirando s'io la seguo, e par ch'aspetti:
ond'io voglie e pensier tutti al ciel ergo;
perch'io l'odo pregar pur ch'i' m'affretti.

I' vo piangendo i miei passati tempi
i quai posi in amar cosa mortale,
senza levarmi a volo, avend'io l'ale
per dare forse di me non bassi esempi.
Tu, che vedi i miei mali indegni ed empi,
re del cielo, invisibile, immortale,
soccorri all'alma disviata e frale,
e 'l suo difetto di tua grazia adempi:

sì che, s'io vissi in guerra ed in tempesta,
mora in pace et in porto; e se la stanza
fu vana, almen sia la partita onesta.
A quel poco di viver che m'avanza
ed al morir degni esser tua man presta.
Tu sai ben che 'n altrui non ho speranza.

She, happy to have changed her abode, stands equal with the
most perfect; and meanwhile, from time to time, she turns and
looks back to see if I am following her, and it seems that she is waiting: so that I raise all my thoughts and wishes heavenwards; because I hear her praying that I should hasten.

I KEEP weeping over my past which I spent in loving a mortal
thing, without lifting myself to flight, although I had wings to give
perhaps no mean proof of myself. You, who see my unworthy and
wicked ills, king of heaven, unseen, everlasting, help this soul, lost
and frail, and make good its infirmity with your grace:
  so that, if I have lived in war and tempest, I may die in peace and
in port; and, if my sojourn was vain, my leave taking at least may
be just. May your hand deign to be near in that little of life which is
left to me and in my death. You know full well that I place no hope
in any other being.

FAZIO DEGLI UBERTI

Io guardo i crespi e li biondi capelli,
de' quali ha fatto per me rete Amore;
d'un fil di perle e quando d'un bel fiore
per me' pigliare i' trovo che gli adesca.
E poi riguardo dentro gli occhi belli,
che passan per li miei dentro dal core
con tanto vivo e lucente splendore,
che propriamente par che d'un sol esca.
Virtù mostra che in lor ognor più cresca,
ond'io, che sì leggiadri star gli veggio,
così fra me sospirando ragiono:
– Ohmè! perchè non sono
a solo a sol con lei ov'io la cheggio?
sì ch'io potessi quella treccia bionda
disfarla a onda a onda
e far de' suoi begli occhi a miei due specchi,
che lucon sì che non trovan parecchi.

I LOOK upon her fair and waving locks, of which Love has made
a net for me; I find that to catch me more easily he sometimes
baits it with a string of pearls and sometimes with a fine flower.
And then I look into her lovely eyes, which pass through mine into
my heart, with a splendour so bright and vivid that it really seems
to come from a sun. They show a goodness that grows in them constantly, so that I, to whom they are so comely, say to myself with
sighs: 'Oh! why am I not alone with her, alone where I wish to be?
so that I may undo that fair head of hair wave by wave, and make
her eyes two mirrors to mine, so shining as not to meet their
equal.'

Poi guardo l'amorosa e bella bocca,
la spaziosa fronte e 'l vago piglio
e i bianchi denti, il dritto naso e 'l ciglio
pulito e brun, tal che dipinto pare.
E 'l vago mio pensier allor mi tocca
dicendo: – Vedi allegro dar di piglio
dentro a quel labbro sottile e vermiglio,
dov'ogni dolce e saporito pare!
E odi suo vezzoso ragionare
quanto ben mostra, morbida e pietosa,
e come 'l suo parlar parte e divide.
Vedi, quand'ella ride
che passa per diletto ogn'altra cosa! –
Così di quella bocca il pensier mio
mi sprona, perchè io
non ho nel mondo cosa ch'io non desse
a tal ch'un sì con buon voler dicesse.

Poi guardo la sua svelta e bianca gola
com'esce ben delle spalle e del petto;
il mento tondo, fesso, piccioletto,
tal che più bel con l'occhio non disegno.

Then I look at her beautiful loving mouth, her broad forehead
and fond expression, white teeth, straight nose, and comely brown
eyebrows, such that they seem painted. And an amorous thought
then recurs to me with these words: 'Think how gladdening it
would be to catch fast within that fine, scarlet lip, where every
sweetness and savour seems to be. And listen to her charming
speech, how well it sounds, soft and compassionate, and how she
breaks and orders her talk. See, when she laughs, how she surpasses
every other thing in delight!' In this way my thought, playing
about her mouth, spurs me on, for I possess nothing in this world
that I would not give so that it might say 'yes' with a good will.

Then I look at her slender, white throat and the exquisite way it
rises from her shoulders and her bosom; her round chin, small and
dimpled, such that the eye can discern no better. And that thought

E quel pensier che sol per lei m'invola
mi dice: – Vedi allegro e bel diletto
aver quel collo fra le braccia stretto
e fare in quella gola un picciol segno! –
Poi soppragiunge e dice: – Apri lo ingegno;
se le parti di fuor son così belle,
l'altre che den valer che dentro copre!
chè sol per le belle opre,
che fanno in ciel il sole e l'altre stelle
dentro da lor si crede 'l paradiso.
Dunque, se miri fiso
pensar ben dei ch'ogni terren piacere
si trova dove tu non puoi vedere.

Poi guardo i bracci suoi distesi e grossi,
la bianca mano morbida e pulita,
le belle lunghe e sottilette dita
vaghe di quello anel che l'un tien cinto.
E 'l mio pensier mi dice: – Or se tu fossi
dentro a que' bracci, fra quella partita,
tanto diletto avrebbe la tua vita,
che dir per me non si potrebbe il quinto.
Vedi ch'ogni suo membro par dipinto,

which puts me in ecstasy for her sake alone says to me: – Think of
the fine, gay delight of having that neck tight in your arms and of
making a little mark on that throat! Then it goes on and says:
'Stir your imagination; if the outward parts are so lovely, how rare
must be the others which she hides! for paradise is believed to be
beyond the sun and others stars simply because of the lovely effect
that these have in heaven. So, if you gaze steadily, you will think
that every earthly bliss lies where your eye cannot go.'

Then I look at her full and shapely arms, the hand, white, soft,
and neat, the lovely, long slender fingers heightened by the ring
which holds one of them in its circlet. And my thought says: 'Now
if you were in those arms, in their embrace, your life would know
such joy that I could not express the hundredth part of it. See how
every one of her limbs seems painted ample and large as is right for

formoso e grande quanto a lei s'avviene,
con un colore angelico di perla;
graziosa a vederla
e disdegnosa dove si convene,
umile e vergognosa e temperata;
e sempre a virtù guata,
e in fra' suoi be' costumi un atto regna
che d'ogni riverenza la fa degna.

Soave va a guisa di pavone,
diritta sopra sè com'una grua;
guarda che propriamente ben par sua
quant'esser può donnesca leggiadria.
– E se ne vuoi veder viva ragione, –
dice il pensier – guardi la mente tua
ben fissamente allor ch'ella s'indua
con donna che leggiadra e bella sia:
chè, come par che fugga e vada via
dinanzi al sole ogni altra chiarezza,
così costei ogni adornezza isface.
Vedi se ella piace
ch'amore è tanto quanto sua bellezza

her, with an angelic hue of pearl; pleasant in her bearing and scorn-
ful when it is seemly, humble and shy and mild; and she looks constantly to virtue, and a grace reigns in her fine ways that makes her
worthy of every deference.'

Soft she walks in the manner of a peacock, holding herself upright as the crane does; see how everything of womanly gaiety
seems hers by right. 'And if you wish to see the living proof of this,'
my thought says, 'keep your attention on her when she is with a
woman who is beautiful and gay: for, as every other brightness
seems to fly and vanish before the sun, so does this fair vanquish
every other beauty. Judge if she is pleasant when love is no more

e la somma bontà che in lei si trova.
Quel ch'a lei piace e giova
è sol d'onesta e di gentil usanza,
chè sol in suo ben far prende speranza.

Canzon, tu puoi ben dir sicuramente
che, poi ch'al mondo bella donna nacque,
nessun mai non piacque
generalmente quanto fa costei;
perchè si trova in lei
biltà di corpo e d'anima bontade,
fuor che le manca un poco di pietade.

GIOVANNI BOCCACCIO

Vetro son fatti i fiumi, ed i ruscelli
gli serra di fuor ora la freddura;
vestiti son i monti e la pianura
di bianca neve e nudi gli arbuscelli,
l'erbette morte, e non cantan gli uccelli
per la stagion contraria a lor natura;
borea soffia, ed ogni creatura
sta chiusa per lo freddo ne' sua ostelli.

than her beauty and the excelling good which is in her. What she likes and indulges is always honest and seemly, and she puts her hope solely in acting rightly.'

My song, you can say with certainty that since beautiful woman was born into the world, none has found such universal favour as this one has, because in her there is both beauty of body and goodness of soul, only she somewhat lacks sympathy.

The rivers have turned to glass, and the cold now locks the streams from without; the mountains and the plains are clad in white snow, and the trees are bare, the grass dead, and the birds do not sing because of the season inimical to their nature; the north wind blows, and every creature stays, because of the cold, shut fast in its abode.

Ed io, dolente, solo ardo ed incendo
in tanto foco, che quel di Vulcano
a rispetto non è una favilla;
e giorno e notte chiero, a giunta mano,
alquanto d'acqua il mio signor, piangendo,
nè posso impetrar sol una stilla.

In morte del Petrarca

O R sei salito, caro signor mio,
nel regno, al quale ancor salire aspetta
ogn'anima da Dio a quell'eletta,
nel suo partir di questo mondo rio;
or se' colà, dove spesso il desio
ti tirò già per veder Lauretta,
or sei dove la mia bella Fiammetta
siede con lei nel cospetto di Dio.

Or con Sennuccio e con Cino e con Dante
vivi, sicuro d'eterno riposo,
mirando cose da noi non intese.
Deh, s'a grado ti fui nel mondo errante,
tirami drieto a te, dove gioioso
veggia colei che pria d'amor m'accese.

And I alone, grieving, burn and flame so fiercely, that Vulcan's fire was not a spark to this one of mine; and day and night I beg, with joined hands, weeping the while, for a little water from my lord, nor can I procure one single drop.

Upon the Death of Petrarch

Now have you gone up, my dear lord, to the realm whither every soul chosen by God for that honour, trusts to ascend on leaving this wicked world: now you are where your desire drew you frequently in the past, to see Laura, now you are where my lovely Fiammetta sits with her in the sight of God.

Now you live with Sennuccio and Cino and Dante, sure of eternal rest, looking on things not comprehended by us. O, if I was pleasant to you in the wandering world, draw me after you, where, glad, I might see her who first fired me with love.

Dal «Decameron»

(Giornata II)

AMOR, s'io posso uscir de' tuoi artigli,
appena creder posso
che alcuno altro uncin mai più mi pigli.

Io entrai giovanetta en la tua guerra,
quella credendo somma e dolce pace,
e ciascuna mia arme posi in terra,
come sicuro chi si fida face;
tu, disleal tiranno aspro e rapace,
tosto mi fosti addosso
con le tue armi e co' crudel roncigli.

Poi, circondata dalle tue catene,
a quel che nacque per la morte mia,
piena d'amare lagrime e di pene
presa mi desti, ed hammi in sua balìa;
ed è sì cruda la sua signoria,
che già mai non l'ha mosso
sospir nè pianto alcun che m'assottigli.

From the 'Decameron'

(The Second Day)

LOVE, if I can get free from your claws, I can hardly imagine any other hook will ever take me.

I went into your war when young, thinking it would be the highest peace and sweet, and laid every one of my arms on the ground, as confidently as one who trusts; dishonourable, harsh, and thieving tyrant, you seized upon me immediately with your arms and cruel hooks.

Then, wound in your chains, you gave me captive, full of tears and griefs, to him who was born for my death, and he has me in thrall; and his lordship is so brutal that he has never once been moved by any of the sighing or weeping that wastes me.

Li prieghi miei tutti glien porta il vento:
nullo n'ascolta nè ne vuole udire;
per che ognora cresce il mio tormento,
onde 'l viver m'è noi' nè so morire;
deh! dolgati, signor, del mio languire;
fa' tu quel ch'io non posso:
dalmi legato dentro a' tuoi vincigli.

Se questo far non vuogli, almeno sciogli
i legami annodati da speranza;
deh! io ti priego, signor, che tu vogli:
chè, se tu 'l fai, ancor porto fidanza
di tornar bella qual fu mia usanza,
ed il dolor rimosso,
di bianchi fiori ornarmi e di vermigli.

FRANCO SACCHETTI

Di poggio in poggio e di selva in foresta,
come falcon che da signor villano
di man si leva e fugge di lontano,

The wind bears all my prayers to him: he will not hear or consider them; thus my anguish increases all the time, so that to live is tedious, nor can I die; o grieve, my lord, for my languishing; effect what I cannot: deliver him to me in your bonds.

If you will not do this, at least free me from the ties knotted by hope; oh I beg you, my lord, be pleased to: for, if you do, I feel sure I shall become beautiful again, as I used to be, and when sorrow has been taken from me, I shall deck myself with white flowers and with crimson ones.

From hill to hill and from wood to forest, like a falcon which springs up from the hand of an uncouth master and flees far,

lasso, men vo, ben ch'io non sia disciolto,
donne, partir volendo da colui
che vi dà forza sovra i cor altrui.

Ma, quando pelegrina esser più crede
da lui mia vita, più presa si vede.

La neve e 'l ghiaccio e' venti d'oriente,
la fredda brina e l'alta tramontana
cacciata hanno de' boschi suo' Diana.

Perch'ella vide secche l'erbe e' fiori,
volar le fronde e spogliar la foresta,
coverta s'ha col vel la bionda testa,

ed è venuta al loco ov'ella nacque,
dove più ch'altra donna sempre piacque.

– O vaghe montanine pasturelle,
donde venite sì legiadre e belle?

wearied, I go on, though I am not freed, ladies, even while I wish to leave him who gives you power over the hearts of men.

But when my life believes itself most remote from him, it sees it is most taken.

The snow and the ice and the east winds, the cold hoar-frost and the high north wind have chased Diana from her woods.

Because she sees the grass withered, and withered the flowers, the leaves flying and the forest bared, she has covered her fair head with a veil,

and she has come to the place where she was born, where she always delighted more than other woman.

'O delighting mountain shepherdesses, whence do you come so gay and fair?

Qual'è il paese dove nate sète,
che sì bel frutto più che gli altri aduce?
Creature d'Amor vo' mi parete,
tanto la vostra vista addorna luce!
Nè oro nè argento in voi riluce,
e, mal vestite, parete angiolelle. –

– No' stiamo in alpe, presso ad un boschetto;
povera capannetta è 'l nostro sito:
col padre e con la madre in picciol letto
torniam la sera dal prato fiorito,
dove natura si ha sempre nodrito,
guardando il dì le nostre peccorelle. –

– Assa' si de' doler vostra bellezza,
quando tra monti e valli la mostrate;
chè non è terra di sì grande altezza
dove non foste degne ed onorate.
Deh ditemi se voi vi contentate
di star ne' boschi così poverelle. –

'What country were you born in, that brings forth fruit so much lovelier than the others? You seem to me creatures of love, your aspect is so enhanced with light. No gold or silver shines on you, and, poorly dressed, you seem angels.'

'We stay in the mountains, near a little wood; our dwelling is a poor hut: in the evening we go back to our father and mother to share a little bed, from the flowering meadow where Nature has ever cared for us, while we watch our sheep by day.'

'Much is your beauty to be lamented, when you show it amid mountains and valleys; for there is no earthly place of so great height but you would be worthy and honoured there. O tell me if you are content to stay so poor in the woods.'

– Più si contenta ciascuna di noi
andar drieto le mandre a la pastura
che non farebbe qual fosse di voi
d'andar a feste dentro a vostre mura.
Richezza non cerchiam, nè più ventura
che balli e canti e fiori e ghirlandelle. –

Ballata, s'i' fosse come già fui,
diventerei pastore e montanino;
e prima ch'io il dicesse altrui,
sarei al loco di costor vicino;
ed or direi – Biondella! – ed or – Martino! –
seguendo sempre dove andasson elle.

MATTEO BOIARDO

Nè più dolce a' nostri ochi il ciel sfavilla
de luci adorno che la notte inchina,
nè il vago tremolar de la marina
al sol nascente lucida e tranquilla;
nè quella stella che de su ne stilla
fresca rogiada a l'ora matutina,
nè in giazio terso nè in candida brina
ragio di sol che sparso resintilla;

'Each of us is happier following the flocks to pasture than anyone of you would be to go to a feast within your walls. We do not
look for riches, nor other excitement than dances and songs and
flowers and garlands.'

Song, if I were as once I was, I would become a shepherd and a
highlander, and before I told anyone of it, I would be living near
their place; and now I would say – Whitey! – and now – Martin! –
always following where they went.

HEAVEN does not sparkle more sweetly to our eyes when it is fair
with lights that the night brings low, nor the charmed trembling of
the waves, clear and calm in the rising sun; nor that star which
drops the fresh dew at the morning hour, nor a ray from the sun
that, refracted, dazzles on gleaming ice or white hoar-frost;

nè tanto el veder nostro a sè retira
qual cosa più gentile et amorosa
su nel ciel splende, on qua giù in terra spira:
quanto la dolce vista e graziosa
de quei begli occhi che Amor volve e gira;
e chi no il crede, de mirar non li osa.

G I À vidi uscir di l'onde una matina
il sol di ragi d'òr tutto iubato,
e di tal luce in facia colorato,
che ne incendeva tutta la marina.
E vidi la rogiada matutina
la rosa aprir d'un color sì infiamato,
che ogni luntan aspetto avria stimato
che un foco ardesse ne la verde spina.

E vidi a la stagion prima e novella
uscir la molle erbetta, come sòle
aprir le foglie ne la prima etate.
E vidi una ligiadra donna e bella
su l'erba coglier rose al primo sole
e vincer queste cose di beltate.

nor does anything more gracious and enamouring shine in
heaven or breathe upon earth that draws our gaze as does the sweet
and blissful look of those lovely eyes which Love turns this way
and that; and whoever doubts this, has not dared to look upon
them.

I HAVE seen the sun rising from the waves one morning, maned all
with gold, and complexioned with such light that he set all the
waves on fire. And I have seen the morning dew bring the rose to
open with so flaming a colour that any distant eye would have
judged a fire to be burning upon the green thorn.

And I have seen the soft grass spring in the new and early season,
as it is wont to open its blades in its first days. And I saw a woman,
gay and fair, going over the grass, gathering roses in the first sunlight and overcoming all these things in beauty.

Ecco la pastorella mena al piano
la bianca torma ch'è sotto sua guarda,
vegendo il Sol calare, e l'ora tarda,
e fumar l'alte ville di luntano.
Erto se leva lo aratore insano,
e il giorno fugitivo intorno guarda,
e scioglie il iugo a' bovi, che non tarda,
per gire al suo riposo a mano a mano.

Et io soletto, sanza alcun sogiorno,
de' mei pensier co' il Sol sosta non have,
e con le stelle a sospirar ritorno.
Dolce affanno d'amor, quanto èi suave:
chè io non poso la notte e non al giorno,
e la fatica eterna non me è grave!

LORENZO DE MEDICI

Donne belle, io ho cercato
lungo tempo del mio core.
Ringraziato sie tu, Amore,
ch'io l'ho pure alfin trovato.

Now the shepherdess leads the white troop that is in her keeping down to the plain, for she sees the sun declining, and the hour late, and the high country-houses sending up their smoke in the disance. The bent ploughman lifts himself straight and tall, and looks about at the day that flees, and frees his oxen from the yoke that he may not be late in returning to his rest.

And I alone, without any refuge, have no respite from my thoughts with the sun, and come to sigh again with the stars. Sweet unrest of love, how mild you are: for I rest neither by night nor by day, and the eternal travail does not weigh on me!

Fair ladies, I have searched a long time for my heart. You are to be thanked, Love, for my finding it at long last.

Egli è forse in questo ballo
chi il mio cor furato avìa:
hallo seco, e sempre arallo,
mentre fia la vita mia:
ella è sì benigna e pia,
ch'ella arà sempre il mio core.
Ringraziato sie tu, Amore,
ch'io l'ho pure alfin trovato.

Donne belle, io v'ho da dire
come il mio cor ritrovai:
quand'io me 'l sentii fuggire,
in più luoghi ricercai:
poi duo begli occhi guardai,
dove ascoso era il mio core.
Ringraziato sie tu, Amore,
ch'io l'ho pure alfin trovato.

Che si viene a questa ladra,
che il mio cor m'ha così tolto?
Com'ell'è bella e leggiadra,
come porta amor nel volto!

Perhaps the one who had stolen my heart is in this dance: she
has it with her and will have it as long as my life lasts: she is so
kindly and tender, that she will always have my heart. You are to
be thanked, Love, for my finding it at long last.

Fair ladies, I must tell you how I found my heart again: when I
felt it escaping from me, I search for it in many places: then I looked
into two lovely eyes where my heart was hidden. You are to be
thanked, Love, for my finding it at long last.

What does this fair thief deserve, who has taken my heart like
this? How fair and gay she is, and how love shows in her face!

Non sia mai il suo cor sciolto,
ma sempre arda col mio core,
Ringraziato sie tu, Amore,
ch'io l'ho pure alfin trovato.

Questa ladra, o Amore, lega,
o col furto insieme l'ardi:
non udir s'ella ti priega;
fa' che gli occhi no li guardi:
ma, se hai saette e dardi,
fa' vendetta del mio core.
Ringraziato sie tu, Amore,
ch'io l'ho pure alfin trovato.

Canzona di Bacco

QUANT'È bella giovinezza,
che si fugge tuttavia!
Chi vuol esser lieto, sia:
di doman non c'è certezza.

Quest'è Bacco e Arianna
belli, e l'un dell'altro ardenti:
perchè 'l tempo fugge e 'nganna,
sempre insieme stan contenti.

Never let her heart be freed, but let it always burn with mine. You are to be thanked, Love, for my finding it at long last.

Bind this fair thief, o Love, and let her burn with what she has stolen: don't listen if she pleads; watch you do not look into her eyes: but if you have arrows and darts, avenge my heart. You are to be thanked, Love, for my finding it at last.

Song for Bacchus

How lovely youth is that flies us ever! Let him be glad who will be: there is no certainty in tomorrow.

This is Bacchus and Ariadne, fair, and each burning for the other: because time flies and deceives, they always stay together in

Queste ninfe ed altre genti
sono allegre tuttavia.
Chi vuol esser lieto, sia:
di doman non c'è certezza.

Questi lieti satiretti
delle ninfe innamorati,
per caverne e per boschetti
han lor posto cento agguati:
or da Bacco riscaldati,
ballon, salton tuttavia.
Chi vuol esser lieto, sia:
di doman non c'è certezza.

Queste ninfe hanno anco caro
da lor essere ingannate:
non può fare a Amor riparo
se non gente rozze e 'ngrate:
ora insieme mescolate
suonon, canton tuttavia.
Chi vuol esser lieto, sia:
di doman non c'è certezza.

happiness. These nymphs and other people are always merry. Let
him be glad who will be: there is no certainty in tomorrow.

These glad little satyrs are in love with the nymphs, and have
laid a hundred ambushes for them in caves and woods: now, heated
by Bacchus, they keep up their dancing and their leaping. Let him
be glad who will be: there is no certainty in tomorrow.

These nymphs would fain be tricked by them: no one can guard
against Love but uncouth, ungrateful people: now mingling together, they play instruments and sing always. Let him be glad who
will be: there is no certainty in tomorrow.

Questa soma che vien drieto
sopra l'asino, è Sileno:
così vecchio è ebbro e lieto,
già di carne e d'anni pieno:
se non può star ritto, almeno
ride e gode tuttavia.
Chi vuol esser lieto, sia:
di doman non c'è certezza.

Mida vien dopo costoro:
ciò che tocca, oro diventa.
E che giova aver tesoro,
s'altri poi non si contenta?
Che dolcezza vuoi che senta
chi ha sete tuttavia?
Chi vuol esser lieto, sia:
di doman non c'è certezza.

Ciascun apra ben gli orecchi:
di doman nessun si paschi;
oggi sian, giovani e vecchi,
lieti ognun, femmine e maschi;
ogni tristo pensier caschi,
facciam festa tuttavia.
Chi vuol esser lieto, sia:
di doman non c'è certezza.

This load who comes behind them upon an ass is Silenus: so old
and drunk and glad, and full, by now, of years and meat: if he cannot stand upright, at least he laughs and has enjoyment still. Let
him be glad who will be: there is no certainty in tomorrow.

Midas comes after these: whatever he touches turns to gold.
What point is there in having treasure, if it does not make you
happy? What sweet pleasure do you imagine a man has who is
always thirsty? Let him be glad who will be: there is no certainty in
tomorrow.

Let every one open their ears wide: let no one feed on tomorrow;
let every one, young and old, women and men, be glad this very
day; banish every sad thought, let us keep perpetual holiday. Let
him be glad who will be: there is no certainty in tomorrow.

Donne e giovinetti amanti,
viva Bacco e viva Amore!
Ciascun suoni, balli e canti!
Arda di dolcezza il core!
Non fatica, non dolore!
Quel c'ha esser, convien sia.
Chi vuol esser lieto, sia;
di doman non c'è certezza.

ANGELO POLIZIANO

Canzona

Udite, selve, mie dolce parole,
poi che la ninfa mia udir non vole.

La bella ninfa è sorda al mio lamento
e 'l suon di nostra fistula non cura:
di ciò si lagna il mio cornuto armento,
nè vuol bagnare il grifo in acqua pura,
nè vuol toccar la tenera verdura;
tanto del suo pastor gl'incresce e dole.
Udite, selve, mie dolce parole.

Woman and young lovers, long live Bacchus and long live Love!
Let each one play, and dance, and sing! Let the heart burn with
sweetness! Neither labour, nor grief! What is to happen needs must
be. Let him be glad who will be; there is no certainty in tomorrow.

Song

Hear, woods, my sweet words, since my nymph will not hear
them.

The lovely nymph is deaf to my lament and does not care for the
sound of our pipe: and so my horned flock languishes, nor will
they put their mouths to pure water, nor wish to touch the tender
grass; so do they suffer and grieve for their shepherd.

Hear, woods, my sweet words.

Ben si cura l'armento del pastore:
la ninfa non si cura dello amante;
la bella ninfa che di sasso ha il core,
anzi di ferro, anzi l'ha di diamante:
ella fugge da me sempre d'avante,
come agnella dal lupo fuggir sòle.
Udite, selve, mie dolce parole.

Digli, zampogna mia, come via fugge
cogli anni insieme la bellezza snella;
e digli come il tempo ne distrugge,
nè l'età persa mai si rinnovella:
digli che sappi usar suo' forma bella,
chè sempre mai non son rose e viole.
Udite, selve, mie dolce parole.

Portate, venti, questi dolci versi
dentro all'orecchie della ninfa mia:
dite quant'io per lei lacrime versi,
e lei pregate che crudel non sia:
dite che la mia vita fugge via
e si consuma come brina al sole.

The flock feels deeply for the shepherd: the nymph does not feel
for her lover; the lovely nymph who has a heart of stone, of iron
rather, no, rather of diamond: she always runs from before me, as
lamb is wont to run from wolf.
Hear, woods, my sweet words.
Tell her, my pipe, that slim loveliness flies with the years; and
tell her how time destroys us, and a lost time of life is never renewed: tell her that she should know how to use her lovely form,
for roses and violets are not for eternity.
Hear, woods, my sweet words.
Bear, winds, these sweet numbers to the ears of my nymph: tell
her how many tears I shed for her, and beg her not to be cruel: tell
her my life flies from me and is consumed like hoar-frost in the sun.

Udite, selve, mie dolce parole;
poichè la ninfa mia udir non vole.

Baccanale

Ognun segua, Bacco, te!
Bacco Bacco, eù oè!

Chi vuol bever, chi vuol bevere,
vegna a bever, vegna qui.
Voi imbottate come pevere.
Io vo' bever ancor mì.
Gli è del vino ancor per tì.
Lassa bever prima a me.
Ognun segua, Bacco, te.

Io ho vòto già il mio corno:
dammi un po' il bottazo in qua.
Questo monte gira intorno,
e 'l cervello a spasso va.
Ognun corra in qua e in là,
come vede fare a me;
ognun segua, Bacco, te.

Hear, woods, my sweet words; since my nymph will not hear them.

Bacchanal

Let each one follow you, Bacchus! Bacchus Bacchus, yuh yeh!
    Whoever wants to drink, whoever wants to drink, let him come and drink, let him come here. You swallow like big funnels. I want to drink, me as well. There is wine for you as well. Let me drink first. Let each one follow you, Bacchus.
    I have already emptied my horn: give me the flask over here for a moment. This mountain is wheeling round, and my brain has gone for a spin. Everyone run here and there, as you see me doing; let each one follow you, Bacchus.

I' mi moro già di sonno.
Son io ebra, o sì o no?
Star più ritti i piè non ponno.
Voi siet'ebrie, ch'io lo so.
Ognun facci com'io fo:
ognun succi come me:
ognun segua, Bacco, te.

Ognun gridi Bacco Bacco,
e pur cacci del vin giù:
poi con suoni farem fiacco.
Bevi tu, e tu, e tu.
I' non posso ballar più.
Ognun gridi eù, oè;
ognun segua, Bacco, te.
Bacco Bacco, eù oè!

I' MI trovai, fanciulle, un bel mattino
di mezo maggio in un verde giardino.

I am already dying of tiredness. Am I drunk, say yes or no? My feet cannot hold me upright any longer. You are drunk, that I know. Everyone do as I do: everyone swill like me: everyone follow you, Bacchus.

Everyone cry Bacchus, Bacchus, and still toss the wine back. Then we will get feebler and feebler with our noise. You drink, and you, and you. I can dance no longer. Everyone shout yuh yeh! everyone follow you, Bacchus. Bacchus Bacchus, yuh yeh!

I FOUND myself, maidens, one fine morning in the middle of May, in a green garden.

Eran d'intorno violette e gigli
fra l'erbe verde, e vaghi fior novelli
ond'io porsi la mano a côr di quelli
per adornar e' mie' biondi capelli
e cinger di grillanda el vago crino.
I' mi trovai, fanciulle ...

Ma poi ch'i' ebbi pien di fiori un lembo,
vidi le rose e non pur d'un colore:
io corsi allor per empier tutto el grembo,
perch'era sì soave il loro odore
che tutto mi senti' destar el core
di dolce voglia e d'un piacer divino.
I' mi trovai, fanciulle ...

I' posi mente: quelle rose allora
mai non vi potre' dir quant'eran belle:
quale scoppiava della boccia ancora;
qual'erano un po' passe e qual novelle.
Amor mi disse allor: – Va', cô' di quelle
che più vedi fiorite in sullo spino. –
I' mi trovai, fanciulle ...

Around me in the green grass were violets and lilies and other
lovely new flowers, blue, yellow, white, and crimson: so that I
stretched out my hand to pluck them to deck my fair hair and to
crown my beloved's locks with a garland. I found myself,
maidens. ...

But when I had a skirt-fold full of flowers, I saw roses, and not
of a single colour: I ran then to fill all my lap, because they smelt so
sweetly that my heart came quite awake with soft desire and a
divine pleasure. I found myself, maidens. ...

I took thought: I could never tell you how lovely those roses
were then: some were still bursting from the bud; others were
slightly overblown, and some, quite new. Love said to me then:
'Go, gather those which you see flowering most perfectly upon the
thorn.' I found myself, maidens. ...

Quando la rosa ogni suo' foglia spande,
quando è più bella, quando è più gradita;
allora è buona a mettere in ghirlande,
prima che sua belleza sia fuggita:
sicchè, fanciulle, mentre è più fiorita,
coglian la bella rosa del giardino.
I' mi trovai, fanciulle ...

Io ti ringrazio, Amore,
d'ogni pena e tormento,
e son contento · omai d'ogni dolore.

Contento son di quanto ho mai sofferto,
Signor, nel tuo bel regno;
poi che per tua merzè sanza mio merto
m'hai dato un sì gran pegno,
poi che m'hai fatto degno
d'un sì beato riso,
che 'n paradiso · n'ha portato il core.
Io ti ringrazio, Amore.

When the rose stretches every petal, when it is most lovely,
when it is most pleasant; then is it good for putting in a garland,
before its beauty be fled: so, maidens, let us gather the fair rose of
the garden while its bloom is perfect. I found myself, maidens. ...

I THANK you, Love, for every pain and torment, and am happy
now for your every sorrow.

I am happy for what I have suffered, Lord, in your fine kingdom;
since in your generosity, without my deserving it, you have given
me so great a pledge, since you have made me worthy of so blessed
a smile that it has carried my heart away to paradise. I thank you,
Love.

In paradiso el cor n'hanno portato
que' begli occhi ridenti,
ov'io ti vidi, Amore, star celato
con le tue fiamme ardenti.
O vaghi occhi lucenti
che 'l cor tolto m'avete,
onde traete · sì dolce valore?
Io ti ringrazio, Amore.

I' ero già della mia vita in forse:
madonna in bianca vesta
con un riso amoroso mi soccorse,
lieta bella et onesta:
dipinta avea la testa
di rose e di viole,
gli occhi che 'l sole · avanzan di splendore.
Io ti ringrazio, Amore.

Those lovely eyes have carried my heart away to paradise, where
I saw you, Love, hidden in your glowing flames. O shining eyes
that have taken my heart, whence do you draw such sweet power?
I thank you, Love.

I doubted for my life: my lady dressed in white saved me with a
loving smile, happy, fair, and modest, she: her hair was decked
with roses and violets, her eyes surpassed the sun in brightness. I
thank you, Love.

Ben venga maggio
e 'l gonfalon selvaggio:

Ben venga primavera
che vuol l'uom s'innamori.
E voi, donzelle, a schiera
con li vostri amadori,
che di rose e di fiori
vi fate belle il maggio,

venite alla frescura
delli verdi arbuscelli.
Ogni bella è sicura
fra tanti damigelli;
chè le fiere e gli uccelli
ardon d'amore il maggio.

Chi è giovane e bella
deh non sie punto acerba,
chè non si rinnovella
l'età, come fa l'erba:
nessuna stia superba
all'amadore il maggio.

Welcome May and its wild banner.
Welcome spring that desires man to fall in love. And you, maidens, in a crowd with your lovers, who make yourselves lovely with roses and other flowers in May, come to the cool shade of the green bushes. Every fair is safe among so many youths; for beasts and birds burn with love in May.

She who is young and beautiful, oh do not let her be harsh, for this age does not renew itself as does the grass: let none be proud with her lover in May.

Ciascuna balli e canti
di questa schiera nostra.
Ecco che i dolci amanti
van per voi, belle, in giostra:
qual dura a lor si mostra
farà sfiorire il maggio.

Per prender le donzelle
si son gli amanti armati.
Arrendetevi, belle,
a' vostri innamorati;
rendete e' cuor furati,
non fate guerra il maggio.

Chi l'altrui core invola
ad altrui doni el core.
Ma chi è quel che vola?
È l'angiolel d'amore,
che viene a fare onore
con voi, donzelle, al maggio.

Let each one of this our band sing and dance. See, your sweet lovers go to the joust for your sakes, you fair: she who shows herself hard to them makes the May shed its bloom.

The loving youths are armed to win the maidens. Surrender yourselves, you fair, to your lovers. Give back the hearts you have robbed, do not wage war in May.

Let the one who has stolen a heart from another give hers in exchange. But who is that flying there? It is the angel of love who comes to do honour with you, my maidens, to the May.

Amor ne vien ridendo
con rose e gigli in testa,
e vien di voi caendo.
Fategli, o belle, festa.
Qual sarà la più presta
a dargli e' fior del maggio?

Ben venga il peregrino.
Amor, che ne comandi?
Che al suo amante il crino
ogni bella ingrillandi;
chè le zitelle e grandi
s'innamoran di maggio.

LUDOVICO ARIOSTO

Capitolo VIII

O PIÙ che 'l giorno a me lucida e chiara,
dolce, gioconda, aventurosa notte,
quanto men ti sperai tanto più cara.

Stelle a furti d'amor soccorrer dotte,
che minuisti il lume, nè per vui
mi fur l'amiche tenebre interrotte.

Love comes here laughing, crowned with roses and lilies, and comes seeking you. Celebrate in his honour, you fair. Who will be quickest to give him the May-flower?

Welcome to the traveller. Love, what is your bidding? That every fair put a garland about the head of her love; that girls and grown women fall in love in May.

Poem in Terza Rima – VIII

O NIGHT, more shining and clear, sweeter, gladder, more fortunate than the day to me, so much the dearer as I little expected you.

Stars learned in helping love's own thefts that dimmed your light, not by you were the friendly shades broken.

Sonno propizio, che lasciando dui
vigili amanti soli, così oppresso
avevi ogn'altro, che invisibil fui.

Benigna porta, che con sì sommesso
e con sì basso suon mi fusti aperta,
ch'a pena ti sentì chi t'era presso.

O mente ancor di non sognar incerta,
quando abbracciar da la mia dea mi vidi,
e fu la mia con la sua bocca inserta.

O benedetta man, ch'indi mi guidi;
o cheti passi che m'andate inanti;
o camera, che poi così m'affidi.

O complessi iterati, che con tanti
nodi cingete i fianchi, il petto, il collo,
che non ne fan più l'edere o li acanti.

Bocca ove ambrosia libo nè satollo
mai ne ritorno; o dolce lingua, o umore,
per cui l'arso mio cor bagno e rimollo.

Timely sleep, that leaving two wide-awake lovers alone, had so overcome everyone else, that I was invisible.

Kindly door, that were opened with so subdued and low a sound, that he who was close to you hardly heard.

O mind still uncertain if it dreamed or not, when I saw myself clasped by my goddess, and my mouth was enclosed in hers.

O blessed hand, that next lead me; o quiet steps that proceed me, o room, that then so secure me.

O repeated embraces, that bind hips, breast, neck, with so many twinings that ivy or acanthus have fewer.

Mouth, whence I sup ambrosia, nor ever come away satiate; o soft tongue, o dewiness, in which I bathe and soften my burnt heart again.

Fiato, che spiri assai più grato odore
che non porta da l'indi o da sabei
fenice al rogo, in che s'incende e more.

O letto, testimon de' piacer miei;
letto cagion ch'una dolcezza io gusti,
che non invidio il lor nettare ai dèi.

O letto donator de' premi giusti,
letto, che spesso in l'amoroso assalto
mosso, distratto ed agitato fusti.

Voi tutti ad un ad un, ch'ebbi de l'alto
piacer ministri, avrò in memoria eterna,
e quanto è il mio poter, sempre vi esalto.

Nè piu debb'io tacer di te, lucerna,
che con noi vigilando, il ben ch'io sento
vuoi che con gli occhi ancor tutto discerna.

Per te fu dupplicato il mio contento;
nè veramente si può dire perfetto
uno amoroso gaudio a lume spento.

Breath, that inhale far more pleasant fragrance than the phoenix
on his pyre, on which he flames and dies, yields among Indians or
Sabaeans.

O bed, witness to my pleasures; bed, cause of my tasting a
sweetness such that I do not envy the gods their nectar.

O bed, giver of just rewards, bed, which was often moved,
ruffled, and shaken by the loving tussle.

All of you, one by one, shall I keep in everlasting memory as
ministers of my high pleasure, and I praise you as much as in my
power.

Nor should I keep more silent about you, lantern, that, staying
awake with us, desire that my eyes should perceive the good I
know.

My happiness was doubled through you; nor can love enjoyed
by extinguished light be truly said to be perfect.

Quanto più giova in sì suave effetto,
pascer la vista or de li occhi divini,
or de la fronte, or de l'eburneo petto;

mirar le ciglia e l'aurei crespi crini,
mirar le rose in su le labbra sparse,
porvi la bocca e non temer de' spini;

mirar le membra, a cui non può uguagliarse
altro candor e giudicar mirando
che le grazie del ciel non vi fur scarse,

e quando a un senso satisfar, e quando
all'altro e sì che ne fruiscan tutti,
e pur un sol non ne lasciar in bando!

Deh! perche son d'amor sì rari i frutti?
deh! perche del gioir sì brieve il tempo?
perche sì lunghi e senza fine i lutti?

Perchè lasciasti, ohimè, così per tempo
invida Aurora, il tuo Titone antico,
e del partir m'accelerasti il tempo?

How much more it adds, to such sweet consequence, to feed the
gaze upon the divine eyes, her forehead, her ivory bosom;
    look upon her eyelids and hair of curling gold, look on the roses
shed upon her lips, put your mouth there, and fear no thorns;
    look upon her limbs, which no other whiteness can equal and
think as you look that heaven's graces were never wanting there,
    and now indulge one sense, and now another and in such a style
that all have play, and not even one stays banished!
    O why are the fruits of love so rare? o why the time for enjoy-
ing them so short? why so long and endless are our griefs?
    Why, envious Dawn, ah me! did you leave your ancient
Tithonus so promptly, and speed my time of parting?

Ti potess'io, come ti son nemico,
nocer così! Se 'l tuo vecchio t'annoia,
chè non ti cerchi un più giovane amico?

e vivi, e lascia altrui viver in gioia!

MICHELANGELO BUONARROTI

(Su di uno schizzo del David al Louvre – 1502)

DAVITTE colla fromba
e io coll'arco
Michelagniolo.
Rott'è l'alta colonna.

QUANTO si gode, lieta e ben contesta
di fior, sopra crin d'or d'una, ghirlanda,
che l'altro innanzi l'uno all'altro manda,
come che 'l primo sia a baciar la testa!
Contenta è tutto il giorno quella vesta
che serra 'l petto e poi par che si spanda,
e quel d'oro filato si domanda
le guance e 'l collo di toccar non resta.

If only I could hurt you like that, for I am your enemy! If your old man bores you, why not find a younger lover?
and live, and let live in joy!

(On a sketch for his 'David' in the Louvre, dated 1502)

DAVID with the sling and I with the bow, Michelangelo. Broken is the high column.

HOW the garland rejoices, happy and finely woven with flowers, on the golden hair of this woman, as it puts another flower forward, then one before that, as if all might be first to kiss her head. That dress is contented all the day, binding that bosom and, lower, spreading out, and that lace of gold asks for those cheeks and does not cease to touch the neck.

Ma più lieto quel nastro par che goda,
dorato in punta, con sì fatte tempre,
che preme e tocca il petto, ch'egli allaccia.
E la schietta cintura, che s'annoda,
mi par dir seco: qui vo' stringer sempre!
Or che farebber dunque le mie braccia!

Qua si fa elmi di calici e spade,
e 'l sangue di Cristo si vend'a giumelle,
e croce e spine son lance e rotelle,
e pur da Cristo pazienza cade.
Ma non c'arrivi più 'n queste contrade,
che n'andre' 'l sangue suo 'nsin alle stelle,
poscia ch'a Roma gli vendon la pelle,
e ecci d'ogni ben chiuse le strade.

But happier still that ribbon, gilded at the edge, so finely tempered, that presses and touches the bosom which it entwines. And the shapely girdle which, fastened, seems to say to itself: here would I clasp for ever! Then what would my arms do!

HERE they make helmets and swords from chalices, and sell the blood of Christ by the cup-full, and cross and thorns are lances and shields, and still patience descends on us from Christ. But let him come no more in these parts, for his blood would spurt up to the stars, since at Rome they sell his skin, and the ways to every good are closed to us.

S'i' ebbi ma' voglia a perder tesauro,
per ciò che qua opra da me è partita,
e puo' quel nel manto che Medusa in Mauro;
ma se alto in cielo è povertà gradita,
qual fia di nostro stato il gran restauro,
s'un altro segno ammorza l'altra vita?

finis.

Vostro Miccelangniolo in Turchia

DIMMI, di grazia, Amor, se gli occhi mei
veggono 'l ver della beltà, c'aspiro,
o s'io ho dentro, allor che, dov'io miro,
veggo scolpito il viso di costei.
Tu 'l de' saper, po' che tu vien con lei
a torm'ogni mia pace, ond'io m'adiro;
nè vorre' manco un minimo sospiro
nè men ardente foco chiederei.

If ever I had the desire to lose what is precious, for all work has
gone from me here, he in the mantle can do what the Medusa did
in Mauritania; but if poverty finds favour in high heaven, what will
be the great remedy for our state, if this other ensign smothers the
other life?

finish.

Your Michelangelo in Turkey

TELL me, Love, I pray, if my eyes see the truth of the beauty to
which I aspire, or if I have it within me, since, where I look, I see
her face engraved. You must know, because you come with her to
rob me of every moment of peace, at which I rage; not that I
would want one sigh the less, nor would ask for a less blazing fire.

La beltà, che tu vedi, è ben da quella,
ma cresce, poi c'a miglior loco sale,
se per gli occhi mortali all'alma corre.
Quivi si fa divina, onesta e bella,
com'a sè simil vuol cosa immortale.
Questa e non quella a gli occhi tuo' precorre.

OHIMÈ, ohimè, ch'i' son tradito
da' giorni mie' fugaci e dallo specchio,
che 'l ver dice a ciascun, che fiso 'l guarda!
Così n'avvien, chi troppo al fin ritarda,
com'ho fatt'io, che 'l tempo m'è fuggito,
si trova come me 'n un giorno vecchio.
Nè mi posso pentir, nè m'apparecchio,
nè mi consiglio con la morte appresso.
Nemico di me stesso,
inutilmente i pianti e sospir verso,
che non è danno pari al tempo perso.

The beauty which you see comes really from her, but grows
when it ascends to a higher place – if it should pass through mortal
eyes to the soul. There it becomes divine, pure, and lovely in the
likeness of the immortal part that wishes it so. This latter is the
beauty that goes before your eyes, not the first one.

ALAS, alas, for I am betrayed by my fleeting days and by the mirror, that tells the truth to each one who looks on it fixedly! So does
it befall whoever puts off too much to the end, as I have done, for
my time has flown, he finds himself, like me, old in a day. Nor can I
repent, nor make ready, nor can I take counsel of myself with death
near. My own self's enemy, I uselessly pour forth tears and sighs,
for there is no harm like time lost.

Ohimè, Ohimè, pur reiterando
vo 'l mio passato tempo e non ritrovo
in tutto un giorno che sia stato mio!
Le fallaci speranza e 'l van desio,
piangendo, amando, ardendo e sospirando
(c'affetto alcun mortal non mi è più nuovo)
m'hanno tenuto, ond'il conosco e provo:
lontan certo dal vero,
or con periglio pero;
chè 'l breve tempo m'è venuto manco,
nè saria ancor, se s'allungasse, stanco.

I' vo lasso, ahimè, nè so ben dove;
anzi temo, ch'il veggio, e 'l tempo andato
me 'l mostra, nè mi val che gli occhi chiuda.
Or che 'l tempo la scorza cangia e muda,
la morte e l'almà insieme ognor fan prove,
la prima e la seconda, del mio stato.
E s'io non sono errato
(che Dio 'l voglia ch'io sia!)
l'eterna pena mia
nel mal libero inteso oprato vero
veggio, Signor, nè so quel ch'io mi spero.

Alas, Alas, I keep going over my past time and do not find in the whole of it one day that has been mine! False hopes and empty desire, weeping, loving, longing, and sighing (for no human feeling is any longer new to me) have possessed me, so that I know and feel this: certainly far from truth, I perish now in danger; for our short time of life has dwindled for me, nor would I weary of those things, if it could be prolonged.

I go on wearily, alas, nor do I well know where; rather I am afraid for I see it, and departed time points it, nor does it serve for me to close my eyes. Now that time has changed and transformed its bark, death, the first and second, and the soul struggle together constantly for my being. And if I am not in error (God grant that I am), I see eternal suffering for me in the truth I understood and wantonly abused, nor do I know what I have to hope for.

SE nel volto per gli occhi il cor si vede,
altro segno non ho più manifesto
della mia fiamma; adunque basti or questo,
Signor mio caro, a domandar mercede.
Forse lo spirto tuo, con maggior fede
ch'i' non credo, che sguarda il foco onesto,
che m'arde, fia di me pietoso e presto,
come grazia c'abbonda a chi ben chiede.

O felice quel dì, se questo è certo!
Fermisi in un momento il tempo e l'ore,
il giorno e 'l sol nella su' antica traccia,
acciò ch'i' abbi, e non già per mio merto,
il desiato mio dolce signore
per sempre nell'indegne e pronte braccia.

IF the heart is seen in one's face, in one's eyes, I have no more evident sign of my heart's flame; therefore let this suffice you now,
my dear Lord, as a request for recompense. Perhaps your spirit,
with greater faith than I think, looking on the pure fire which burns
me, will be pitying, and speedily, towards me, as grace abounds to
him who prays earnestly.

O happy that day, if this is certain! Let time and the hours stop
in one moment, day and the sun in his ancient track, so that I may
have, and not, certainly, for my worthiness, my sweet longed-for
lord for ever in my unworthy and ready arms.

I' t'ho comprato, ancor che molto caro,
un po' di non so che, che sa di buono,
perc'a l'odor la strada spesso imparo.
Ovunque tu ti sia, dovunqu'i' sono,
senz'alcun dubbio ne son certo e chiaro.
Se da me ti nascondi, i' tel perdono.
Portando 'l, dove vai, sempre con teco,
ti troverei, quand'io fossi ben cieco.

In me la morte, in te la vita mia.
Tu distingui e concedi e parti il tempo;
quanto vuo', breve e lungo è il viver mio.

Felice son nella tua cortesia.
Beata l'alma, ove non corre tempo,
per te s'è fatta a contemplare Dio.

I have bought you, at great expense, it is true, a little something,
which smells sweetly, because I often come to know a street by its
scent. Wherever you may be, wherever I am, I am certain and clear
about that now, without one doubt. If you hide from me, I forgive
you. Carrying this with you always, as you go about, I would find
you if I were quite blind.

In me death, in you my life. You mark and grant and separate time;
as you wish, short or long is the pace of my life.
   Happy am I in your courtesy. Blessed the soul in which time
does not run. By you, it is made to look upon God.

Veggio nel tuo bel viso, Signor mio,
quel che narrar mal puossi in questa vita.
L'anima della carne ancor vestita,
con esso è già più volte ascesa a Dio.
E se 'l vulgo malvagio, isciocco e rio
di quel che sente altrui segna e addita,
non è l'intensa voglia men gradita,
l'amor, la fede e l'onesto desio.

A quel pietoso fonte, onde siam tutti,
s'assembra ogni beltà che qua si vede,
più c'altra cosa alle persone accorte;
nè altro saggio abbiam, nè altri frutti
del cielo in terra; e chi v'ama con fede
trascende a Dio, e fa dolce la morte.

O nott', o dolce tempo, benchè nero,
con pace ogn'opra sempr'al fin assalta.
Ben ved'e ben intende chi t'esalta,
e chi t'onor', ha l'intellett'intero.

I see in your fair face, my Lord, what can ill be told in this life.
Your soul has already ascended many times to God, still clothed in
the flesh, and with that face. And if the malicious, foolish, evil
throng marks and points out what others feel, the burning will is
not less pleasing, nor the love, the faith, the honest desire.

Every beauty that is seen here recalls, more than other things,
that fount of pity, whence we all come, to feeling people; nor do
we have other earnest, nor other fruit of heaven upon this earth;
and he who loves you with faith ascends to God, and sees death as
sweet.

O night, o sweet time, in spite of blackness, you overcome each
labour with peace in the end. He who praises you sees and under-
stands clearly, and he has a sound judgement who does you

Tu mozzi e tronchi ogni stanco pensiero,
che l'umid'ombra et ogni quiet'appalta,
e dall'infima parte alla più alta
in sogno spesso porti, ov'ire spero.

O ombra del morir, per cui si ferma
ogni miser', a l'alma, al cor nemica,
ultimo degli afflitti e buon rimedio;
tu rendi sana nostra carn'inferma,
rasciugh'i pianti, e posi ogni fatica,
e furi a chi ben vive ogn'ir'e tedio.

Non vider gli occhi miei cosa mortale,
allor che ne' bei vostri intera pace
trovai, ma dentro, ov'ogni mal dispiace,
chi d'amor l'alma a sè simil m'assale:
e se creata a Dio non fosse eguale,
altro che 'l bel di fuor, c'agli occhi piace,
più non vorria; ma perch'è si fallace,
trascende nella forma universale.

honour. You break and cut short every tired thought, which is licensed by dank shade and every quiet; and often in dream you bear us from the lowest part to the highest, where I hope to go.

O shadow of dying, for whom each affliction, the enemy of soul and heart, is suspended, last and good remedy of the miserable; you make our weak flesh whole, dry our tears, and lay every effort to rest, and steal anger and tedium from him who lives well.

My eyes saw no mortal thing, when I found utter peace in your fine eyes, but saw within, where every evil is unwelcome, him who attacks my soul – his likeness – with love: and if that were not created in the image of God, I would no longer desire other than the outward beauty which pleases the eye; but because this is fallacious, it loses itself in the form of universal beauty.

Io dico, c'a chi vive quel che muore
quetar non può desir, nè par s'aspetti
l'eterno al tempo, ove altri cangia il pelo.
Voglia sfrenata il senso è, non amore,
che l'alma uccide; e 'l nostro fa perfetti
gl'amici qui, ma più per morte in cielo.

N on ha l'ottimo artista alcun concetto
c'un marmo solo in sè non circoscriva
col suo soverchio; e solo a quello arriva
la man che ubbidisce all'intelletto.
Il mal ch'io fuggo, e 'l ben ch'io mi prometto,
in te, Donna leggiadra, altera e diva,
tal si nasconde; e perch'io più non viva,
contraria ho l'arte al disiato effetto.

Amor dunque non ha, nè tua beltate,
o durezza, o fortuna, o gran disdegno,
del mio mal colpa, o mio destino o sorte,
se dentro del tuo cor morte e pietate
porti in un tempo, e che 'l mio basso ingegno
non sappia, ardendo, trarne altro che morte.

I say that what dies cannot still the desire of him who is living,
nor does eternity appear to wait upon time, where the skin of
beings changes. The senses lead, not to love, but to unbridled desire
that kills the soul; and our love makes perfect friendships here, but
more perfect still, through death, in heaven.

The best artist has not one idea that a piece of marble, still unworked, does not contain within itself; and that potential form is
realized only by the hand that obeys the judgement. The evil I fly
from, and the good I promise myself are likewise hid in you, gay,
proud, divine Lady; and, to my life's impoverishing, my art is opposed to the desired result.

So Love is not to blame for my plight, nor your beauty, nor the
hardness of things, nor chance, nor great scorn, nor is my destiny
or fate, if within your heart you bear at the one time death and pity,
and my miserable wit does not know, though daring, how to draw
anything from you but death.

Sì come per levar, Donna, si pone
in pietra alpestra e dura
una viva figura,
che là più cresce, u' più la pietra scema;
tal alcun'opre buone,
per l'alma, che pur trema,
cela il soverchio della propria carne
con l'inculta sua cruda e dura scorza.
Tu pur dalle mie streme
parti puo' sol levarne,
ch'in me non è di me voler nè forza.

Ben può talor col mio 'rdente desio
salir la speme, e non essere fallace;
chè s'ogni nostro affetto al ciel dispiace,
a che fin fatto avrebbe il mondo Iddio?
Qual più giusta cagion dell'amart'io
è, che dar gloria a quella eterna pace,
onde pende il divin, che di te piace,
e c'ogni cor gentil fa casto e pio?

LADY, just as one supposes a living figure to be in hard alpine
stone, so as to draw it out, and it gradually grows as the stone flakes
away; so the surface of our own flesh with its unworked, rough,
hard skin, hides deeds worthy of the soul that trembles the while.
And you can draw these from my outward parts, you alone, as in
me there is neither will nor strength of mine.

My hope can sometimes ascend with my burning desire, and not be
false; for if every one of our desires is unacceptable to heaven, to
what end did God make the world? What more righteous cause
have I for loving you, than to glorify that eternal peace (from which
what is divine and pleases in you comes) that makes every heart
chaste and holy?

Fallace speme ha sol l'amor, che muore
con la belta, c' ogni momento scema,
ond'è soggetta al variar d'un bel viso.
Dolce è ben quella in un pudico core
che per cangiar di scorza o d'ora strema
non manca, e qui caparra il paradiso.

I' FU', già son molt'anni, mille volte
ferito e morto, non che vinto e stanco,
da te, mia colpa; e or col capo bianco,
riprenderò le tue promesse stolte?
Quante volte ha' legate, e quant'isciolte
le triste membra, e sì spronato il fianco,
c'appena posso ritornar meco, anco,
bagnando il petto con lacrime molte!

Di te mi dolgo, Amor, con teco parlo,
sciolto da tue lusinghe, a che bisogna
prender l' arco crudel, tirare a voto?
Al legno incenerato sega o tarlo
o dietro a un corrĕdo è gran vergogna
c'ha perso e ferma ogni destrezza e moto.

Only that love is tainted with false hope that dies with beauty which lessens every moment, for, in this way, it is subject to the changing of a fair face. Sweet is that love in an innocent heart which does not fail for altering of feature or the last hour, and it savours paradise here.

I WAS, many years since, wounded and annihilated a thousand times, not simply conquered and wearied, by you, my failing; and now when I have white hairs, shall I take up your promises again? How many times have you bound, and how many, freed these sad limbs, and so spurred this side, that I can scarce come to myself yet, though bathing my breast with many tears!

I complain of you, Love, I am talking to you, freed as I am from your lures: Why must you take up your cruel bow and shoot wildly? For saw or wood-worm to attack burnt wood, or work upon cloth which has lost all suppleness and resilience, is a most shameful thing.

Dᴇʜ fàmmiti vedere in ogni loco!
Se da mortal bellezza arder mi sento,
appresso al tuo mi sarà foco ispento,
e io nel tuo sarò, com'ero, in foco.
Signor mio caro, i' te sol chiamo e 'nvoco
contro l'inutil mio cieco tormento:
tu sol puo' rinnovarmi fuora e drento
le voglie, e 'l senno, e 'l valor lento e poco;

tu desti al tempo ancor quest'alma diva,
e 'n questa spoglia ancor fragil' e stanca
l'incarcerasti, e con fiero destino.
Che poss'io altro, che così non viva?
Ogni ben senza te, Signor, mi manca;
il cangiar sorte è sol poter divino.

Pᴀssᴀ per gli occhi al core in un momento
qualunque obbietto di beltà lor sia,
e per sì larga e sì capace via,
c'a mille non si chiude, non c'a cento,

Oᴍᴀᴋᴇ me see you in every place! If I feel myself burn for mortal beauty, mine will be a dead fire when yours approaches, and in yours I will be, as I have been, on fire. Dear my Lord, I call and invoke you alone against my fruitless, blind torment: you alone can renew for me, without and within, my desires and judgement and my little tardy worth;

you gave to time this soul, though divine, and imprisoned it in this form, though frail and tired, with a savage destiny. What more can I do, so that I may not live like this? Every good without you, Lord, is held from me; to change fate is a power solely divine.

Aɴʏ feature of beauty that comes before my eyes passes through them in an instant to my heart, and by so broad and capacious a way, that it is not closed to a thousand, far less a hundred, of every

d'ogni età, d'ogni sesso: ond'io pavento,
carco d'affanni, e più di gelosia;
nè fra sì vari volti so qual sia
c'anzi morte mi die 'ntero contento.

S'un ardente desir mortal bellezza
ferma del tutto, non discese insieme
dal ciel con l'alma; è dunque umana voglia.
Ma se pass'oltre, Amor, tuo nome sprezza,
c'altro die cerca; e di quel più non teme
c'a lato vien contro sì bassa spoglia.

La forza d'un bel viso a che mi sprona?
C'altro non è c'al mondo mi diletti:
ascender vivo fra gli spirti eletti,
per grazia tal, c'ogn'altra par men buona.
Se ben col fattor l'opra sua consuona,
che colpa vuol giustizia ch'io n'aspetti,
s'i' amo, anz'ardo, e per divin concetti,
onoro e stimo ogni gentil persona?
....

age, each sex: so that I am afraid, burdened with weariness and
more with jealousy, nor do I know which might be the face among
so many different ones that would give me complete happiness
before death.

If mortal beauty quite arrests a burning desire, that beauty did
not come down from heaven with the soul; the desire is therefore
human. But if it goes beyond, then, Love, it scorns your name,
since it seeks another day; and does not fear what comes at its side
for so base a prize.

What does the power of a beautiful face spur me to? For there is
nothing else in the world that delights me: to ascend living among
the blessed spirits, by such access of grace, that every other seems
less good. If the work is in harmony with its maker, what blame
does justice keep in store for me, if I love, no, burn, and honour
and value every gentle being, for divine thoughts?

L'ALMA, inquieta e confusa, in sè non trova
altra cagion c'alcun grave peccato
mal conosciuto, onde non è celato
all'immensa pietà, c'a' miser giova.
I' parlo a te, Signor, c'ogni mia prova,
fuor del tuo sangue, non fa l'uom beato:
miserere di me, da ch'io son nato
a la tua legge; e non fia cosa nuova.

Non può, Signor mio car, la fresca e verde
età sentir, quant'a l'ultimo passo
si cangia gusto, amor, voglie e pensieri.
Più l'alma acquista, ove più 'l mondo perde;
l'arte e la morte non van bene insieme:
che convien più, che di me dunque speri?

Giunto è già 'l corso della vita mia,
con tempestoso mar per fragil barca,
al comun porto, ov'a render si varca
conto e ragion d'ogn'opra trista e pia.

THE uneasy, troubled soul finds no cause for its state but some
heavy sin, ill recognized, though not for that concealed from the
immense Pity that the miserable need.

I speak to you, Lord, – no experience of mine can attain bliss,
without your blood: have mercy upon me, since I am born to your
law; and there is to be no new way.

OUR fresh, green age cannot, my dear Lord, know how much
taste, love, wishes, and thoughts change at our final step. The soul
gains more, the more it loses the world; art and death do not go
well together: what else is needed, what then do you hope from
me?

THE course of my life has now brought me, through a stormy sea,
in a frail ship, to the common port, where one crosses over to
account for every miserable and every holy work. So that I now

Onde l'affettuosa fantasia,
che l'arte mi fece idol'e monarca,
conosco or ben, com'era d'error carca,
e quel c'a mal suo grado ogn'uom desia.

Gli amorosi pensier, già vani e lieti,
che fien'or, s'a due morti m'avvicino?
D'una so 'l certo, e l'altra mi minaccia.
Nè pinger nè scolpir fia più che quieti
l'anima volta a quell'Amor divino
c'aperse, a prender noi, 'n croce le braccia.

GL'INFINITI pensier mie', d'error pieni,
ne gli ultim'anni della vita mia
restringer si dovrien 'n un sol, che sia
guida agli eterni suo' giorni sereni.
Ma che poss'io, Signor, s'a me non vieni
con l'usata ineffabil cortesia?
....

see how utterly mistaken was the fond imagining that made art an
idol and a king for me, and know what, to his own harm, each man
desires.

What will become, now, of thoughts of love, once light and gay,
if I draw near to two deaths? I know the certainty of one, and the
other threatens me. There shall be no more painting, no more
making sculpture to calm the soul turned to that divine Love that
opened arms upon the cross, to take us.

MY infinite thoughts, full of confusion, should be narrowed down
to one in the last years of my life, one which can be my guide to
eternal, unclouded days.

But what can I do, Lord, if you do not come to me with your
familiar ineffable courtesy?

L<small>E</small> favole del mondo m'hanno tolto
il tempo dato a contemplare Iddio,
nè sol le grazie sue poste in oblio,
ma con lor, più che senza, a peccar volto.
Quel c'altri saggio, me fa cieco e stolto,
e tardi a riconoscer l'error mio.
Manca la speme, e pur cresce 'l desio,
che da te sia dal proprio amor disciolto.

Ammezzami la strada c'al ciel sale,
Signor mio caro, e a quel mezzo solo
salir m'è di bisogno la tua 'ita.
Mettimi in odio quante 'l mondo vale,
e quante sue bellezze onoro e colo,
c'anzi morte caparri eterna vita.

S<small>CARCO</small> d'un'importuna e greve salma,
Signor mio caro, e dal mondo disciolto,
qual fragil legno a te stanco rivolto
da l'orribil procella in dolce calma.

T<small>HE</small> idle tales of the world have robbed me of the time I was given
to know God, nor have they only thrust his gracious gifts into
oblivion, but, with them, rather than without, have turned me to
sinning. What makes others wise makes me blind and stupid, and
slow to acknowledge my error. Hope fails me, and yet the desire
to be freed from self-love by you, God, grows.

Cut by half for me the road that climbs to heaven, my dear Lord,
and for that half alone I shall need your help to climb. Make me
hate what has value in the world, and those of its beauties that I
honour and serve, so that before death I may have earnest of
eternal life.

R<small>ELIEVED</small> of a demanding and heavy burden, my dear Lord, and
freed from the world, I turn to you, wearied, like a frail ship from
the fearful storm, towards sweet calm. The thorns and the nails and

Le spine e i chiodi, e l'una e l'altra palma
col tuo benigno, umil, pietoso volto
prometton grazia di pentirsi molto,
e speme di salute a la trist'alma.

Non mirin con giustizia i tuo' sant'occhi
il mio passato, e 'l castigato orecchio
non tenda a quello il tuo braccio severo.
Tuo sangue sol mie colpe lavi e tocchi,
e più affondi, quant'i' sono più vecchio,
di pronta aita e di perdono intero.

VITTORIA COLONNA

Vivo su questo scoglio orrido e solo,
quasi dolente augel che 'l verde ramo
e l'acqua pura abborre; e a quelli ch'amo
nel mondo ed a me stessa ancor m'involo,
perchè espedito al sol che adoro e colo
vada il pensiero. E sebben quanto bramo
l'ali non spiega, pur quando io 'l richiamo
volge dall'altre strade a questa il volo.

the palm of one and the other hand, with your kindly, humble,
pitying face, promise the grace of great repentance, and hope of
salvation to the sad soul.

Do not let your holy eyes look upon my past in judgement, and
do not let your cruelly offended ear make you stretch an arm in
anger against me. Let your blood only wash and touch upon my
faults, and let it go the deeper, bringing ready aid and complete
pardon, as I am so much the older.

I LIVE upon this fearful, lonely rock, like a sorrowing bird that
shuns green branch and clear water; and I take myself away from
those I love in this world and from my very self, so that my thoughts
may go speedily to him, the sun I adore and worship. And although
they do not try their wings as much as I wish, yet when I call them
back, they turn their flight from other paths to this one.

E 'n quel punto che giunge lieto e ardente
là 've l'invio, sì breve gioia avanza
qui di gran lunga ogni mondan diletto.
Ma se potesse l'alta sua sembianza
formar, quant'ella vuol, l'accesa mente,
parte avrei forse qui del ben perfetto.

QUAL digiuno augellin, che vede ed ode
batter l'ali alla madre intorno, quando
gli reca il nutrimento, ond'egli, amando
il cibo e quella, si rallegra e gode,
e dentro al nido suo si strugge e rode
per desio di seguirla anch'ei volando,
e la ringrazia in tal modo cantando
che par ch'oltre 'l poter la lingua snode;

tal io qualor il caldo raggio e vivo
del divin sole, onde nutrisco il core,
più dell'usato lucido lampeggia,
muovo la penna spinta dall'amore
interno; e senza ch'io stessa m'avveggia
di quel ch'io dico, le sue lodi scrivo.

And at the instant they reach, glad and fervent, the place I send
them to, their joy, so brief, greatly surpasses any worldly delight.
But if they could recreate his high aspect, as the kindled mind
desires, I would perhaps here have a part in perfect good.

LIKE a hungry fledgling, who sees and hears his mother beating her
wings about her, when she brings him back nourishment, so that
he, who loves the food and her, rejoices and is glad, and, confined
in his nest, chafes and rages with the desire to follow her, flying
himself, and thanks her by singing in such style that his tongue
seems loosened beyond its power;
so do I sometimes, when the warm and living ray of the divine
sun whence I nourish my heart flashes with more than usual clearness, move my pen urged by inward love; and write his praises
without noting myself what I say.

GASPARA STAMPA

Io non v'invidio punto, angeli santi,
le vostre tante glorie e tanti beni,
e que' disir di ciò che braman pieni,
stando voi sempre a l'alto Sire avanti;
perchè i delitti miei son tali e tanti,
che non posson capire in cor terreni,
mentr'ho davanti i lumi almi e sereni,
di cui conven che sempre scriva e canti.

E come in ciel gran refrigerio e vita
dal volto Suo solete voi fruire,
tal io qua giù da la beltà infinita.
In questo sol vincete il mio gioire,
che la vostra è eterna e stabilita,
e la mia gloria può tosto finire.

Per le saette tue, Amor, ti giuro,
e per la tua possente e sacra face,
che, se ben questa m'arde e 'l cor mi sface,
e quelle mi feriscon, non mi curo;

I don't envy you in the least, holy angels, your so many glories
and blessings, and those longings for what, fully enjoyed, is still
desired, you being always in the presence of our exalted Lord; because my joys are of such a kind and so numerous, as not to be
compassed by earthly hearts, while I have before me those kindly,
serene eyes, of which I must needs write and sing always.

And as you are wont to cull great refreshment and life from His
face in heaven, so do I here below, from his infinite beauty. In this
alone do you surpass my delight, that your glory is eternal and
fixed, and mine can speedily end.

By your arrows, Love, I swear, and by your mighty, sacred torch,
that, although the one burn me and waste my heart, and the others
wound, I do not mind; however far you go into the past or the

quantunque nel passato e nel futuro
qual l'une acute, e qual l'altra vivace,
donne amorose, e prendi qual ti piace,
che sentisser giamai nè fian, nè furo;

perchè nasce virtù da questa pena,
che 'l senso del dolor vince ed abbaglia,
sì che o non duole, o non si sente appena.
Quel, che l'anima e 'l corpo mi travaglia,
è la temenza ch'a morir mi mena,
che 'l foco mio non sia foco di paglia.

Io son da l'aspettar ormai sì stanca,
sì vinta dal dolor e dal disio,
per la sì poca fede e molto oblio
di chi del suo tornar, lassa, mi manca,
che lei, che 'l mondo impalidisce e 'mbianca
con la sua falce e dà l'ultimo fio,
chiamo talor per refrigerio mio,
sì 'l dolor del mio petto si rinfranca.

future, there never was, nor will be, loving women, and take which-
ever one you will, to feel the first sharp, and the second devouring,
as I do;
    for a virtue is born of this pain of mine that overcomes and dazes
the sense of suffering, so that it does not hurt, or is hardly felt.
That – and it tortures soul and body – is the fear which leads me
towards death, lest my fire should be a blaze of straw.

I AM by now so tired from waiting, so beaten by grief and desire, because of the so little faith and great forgetfulness of him who denies
me, weary as I am, his return, that I call on the presence, who makes
the world pale and whiten with her sickle, and extorts the last
penalty, to relieve me, so strongly does the grief wake in my
bosom.

Ed ella si fa sorda al mio chiamare
schernendo i miei pensier fallaci e folli,
come sta sordo anch'egli al suo tornare.
Così col pianto, ond'ho gli occhi miei molli,
fo pietose quest'onde e questo mare;
ed ei si vive lieto ne' suoi colli.

O GRAN valor d'un cavalier cortese,
d'aver portato fin in Francia il core
d'una giovane incauta, ch'Amore
a lo splendor de' suoi begli occhi prese!
Almen m'aveste le promesse attese
di temprar con due versi il mio dolore,
mentre, signor, a procacciarvi onore
tutte le voglie avete ad una intese.

I' ho pur letto ne l'antiche carte
che non ebber a sdegno i grandi eroi
parimenti seguir Venere e Marte.
E del re, che seguite, udito ho poi
che queste cure altamente comparte,
ond'è chiar dagli espèri ai lidi eoi.

And she becomes deaf to my cries, despising my fond and foolish
thoughts, as he stays deaf to the thought of his returning. So with
tears which keep my eyes wet, I make these waves and this sea pitiful; and he lives happy among his hills.

O RARE bravery of a gentle knight to have carried away, right
into France, the heart of an unwary young woman whom Love
took with the shining of his fine eyes! If you had only kept your
promises to mitigate my grief with two lines, while, sir, you keep
all your desires bent to one, to win honour for yourself.

I have, however, read in antique pages that the great heroes did
not scorn to follow Venus and Mars equally. And I have since heard
of the king whom you follow, that he divides his cares between
these in exalted style, for which he is renowned from the western to
the eastern world.

O NOTTE, a me più chiara e più beata
che i più beati giorni ed i più chiari,
notte degna da' primi e da' più rari
ingegni esser, non pur de ma, lodata;
tu de le gioie mie sola sei stata
fida ministra; tu tutti gli amari
de la mia vita hai fatto dolci e cari,
resomi in braccio lui che m'ha legata.

Sol mi mancò che non divenni allora
la fortunata Alcmena, a cui stè tanto
più de l'usato a ritornar l'aurora.
Pur così bene io non potrò mai tanto
dir di te, notte candida, ch'ancora
da la materia non sia vinto il canto.

O TANTE indarno mie fatiche sparse,
o tanti indarno miei sparsi sospiri,
o vivo foco, o fè, che, se ben miri,
di tal null'altra mai non alse ed arse,

O NIGHT, more clear and blest for me than the clearest, most blessed days, night worthy to be praised by the first, the finest wits, not only by me; you alone have been the trustful minister of my joys; you have made all the bitters of my life sweet and dear, giving me into the arms of him who has bound me.

All that was lacking was for me then to have become lucky Alcmena, for whom the dawn delayed to return so much longer than its wont. Yet I can never speak so much good of you, fair night, that my song would not be surpassed by its theme.

O MY labours poured out in vain, o my so many vainly poured out sighs, o living fire, o faith, which, if I see aright, never chilled, nor

o carte invan vergate e da vergarse
per lodar quegli ardenti amati giri,
o speranze ministre de' disiri,
a cui premio più degno dovea darse,

tutte ad un tratto ve ne porta il vento,
poi che da l'empio mio signore stesso
con queste proprie orecchie dir mi sento
che tanto pensa a me, quanto m'è presso,
e partendo, si parte in un momento
ogni membranza del mio amor da esso.

Rimandatemi il cor, empio tiranno,
ch'a sì gran torto avete ed istraziate,
e di lui e di me quel proprio fate,
che le tigri e i leon di cerva fanno.
Son passati otto giorni, a me un anno,
ch'io non ho vostre lettere od imbasciate,
contra le fè che voi m'avete date,
o fonte di valor, conte, e d'inganno.

burned any other woman in such a way, o papers vainly scored,
and to be scored, in praise of those burning, beloved charms, o
hopes ministering to desires, to which a worthy prize should have
been given,
    all of you are carried away in a moment by the wind, since I have
heard with these ears of mine my wicked lord himself say that he
thinks of me, being near, and when he leaves, every memory of
my love leaves him in an instant.

Send back my heart, wicked tyrant, which you have and tear so
wrongly, and do to it and me just what tigers and lions do to hinds.
Eight days have passed, a year to me, in which I have had no letters
or messages from you, contrary to the vow you made me, o count,
spring of valour and deceit.

Credete ch'io sia Ercol o Sansone
a poter sostener tanto dolore,
giovane e donna e fuor d'ogni ragione,
massime essendo qui senza 'l mio core
e senza voi a mia difensione,
onde mi suol venir forza e vigore?

Io non veggio giamai giunger quel giorno,
ove nacque Colui che carne prese,
essendo Dio, per scancellar l'offese
del nostro padre al suo Fattor ritorno,
che non mi risovenga il modo adorno,
col quale, avendo Amor le reti tese
fra due begli occhi ed un riso, mi prese:
occhi, ch'or fan da me lunge soggiorno;

e de l'antico amor qualche puntura
io non senta al desire ed al cor darmi,
sì fu la piaga mia profonda e dura.
E, se non che ragion pur prende l'armi
e vince il senso, questa acerba cura
sarebbe or tal che non potrebbe aitarmi.

Do you think I am Hercules or Samson to bear so much grief, I,
young and a woman and out of my wits, above all since I am here
without my heart and without you to defend me, you, from whom
strength and vigour are wont to reach me?

I NEVER see that day return when He was born, who put on flesh,
although God, come to us again to wipe away our father's wicked
acts against his Maker, without remembering the compelling way
in which Love, spreading his net between two fine eyes and a smile,
caught me: eyes that now sojourn far from me;
    and without feeling the old love give some prick to my desires
and my heart, so deep and severe was my wound. And, if reason did
not take up arms and conquer feeling, that bitter care would even
now be such that reasoning could not help me.

La piaga, ch'io credea che fosse salda
per la omai molta assenzia e poco amore
di quell'alpestro ed indurato core,
freddo più che di neve fredda falda,
si desta ad or ad ora e si riscalda,
e gitta ad or ad or sangue ed umore;
sì che l'alma si vive anco in timore,
ch'esser devrebbe omai sicura e balda.

Nè, perchè cerchi aggiunger novi lacci
al collo mio, so far che molto o poco
quell'antico mio nodo non m'impacci.
Si suol pur dir che foco scaccia foco;
ma tu, Amor, che 'l mio martir procacci,
fai che questo in me, lassa, or non ha loco.

TORQUATO TASSO

Ecco mormorar l'onde
e tremolar le fronde
a l'aura mattutina e gli arboscelli,
e sovra i' verdi rami i vaghi augelli
cantar soavemente
e rider l'oriente:

The wound, which I believed to be healed by the now continued absence and slight love of that flinty, hardened heart, colder than cold sheet of snow, wakes from time to time, and grows warm, and spurts, from time to time, with blood and moistness; so that my soul still lives in fear, when it should now be safe and confident.

Nor can I in any way put new bonds to my neck, without that early knot's hindering me more or less. They often say that fire drives away fire; but you, Love, who seek my martyrdom, prevent this happening in me, weary though I be.

Now the waves murmur and leaves and bushes tremble in the morning breeze, and above the green branches enamoured birds sing softly and the east smiles: now the dawn already shows and is

ecco già l'alba appare
e si specchia nel mare,
e rasserena il cielo
e le campagne imperla il dolce gelo,
e gli alti monti indora.
O bella e vaga Aurora.
L'aura è tua messaggera, e tu de l'aura
ch'ogni arso cor ristaura.

ORE, fermate il volo
nel lucido oriente,
mentre se 'n vola il ciel rapidamente;
e, carolando intorno
a l'alba mattutina
ch'esce da la marina,
l'umana vita ritardate e 'l giorno.
E voi, Aure veloci,
portate i miei sospiri
là dove Laura spiri
e riportate a me sue chiare voci,
sì che l'ascolti io solo,
sol voi presenti e 'l signor nostro Amore.
Aure soavi ed Ore.

mirrored in the sea, and the sky grows clear and the mild frost decks
the fields with pearls and the high mountains with gold. O lovely,
eager Dawn. The breeze is your messenger, and you are hers,
who freshens every parched heart.

HOURS, halt your flight in the shining east, while heaven flies
quickly on; and, dancing about the first light, as it comes up from
the waves, slow human life and the day. And you, swift Breezes,
bear my sighs where Laura breathes and carry back to me her own
clear words, so that I may listen to them alone, with only you
present and our lord Love, sweet Breezes and Hours.

LA giovinetta scorza,
ch'involge il tronco e i rami
d'un verde lauro, Amor vuol ch'io sempre ami;
e le tenere fronde,
fra cui vaghi concenti
fan gli augelletti al mormorar de' venti;
e l'ombra fresca e lieta
che da le foglie acerbe
cade co' dolci sonni in grembo a l'erbe.
Quivi le rete asconde,
nè 'n parte più secreta,
stanco di saettare, Amor s'acqueta.

GIAMMAI più dolce raggio
non spiega il sole in un fiorito maggio
di quel che le tue rose e i tuoi ligustri
fa sì chiari ed illustri;
nè caggiono giammai la state e 'l verno,
tal c'hai l'aprile eterno:
perpetua primavera hai nel bel viso
e 'l sol è il dolce riso.

LOVE invites me to love for ever the tender bark that enwraps a
green laurel's trunk and branches; and the young foliage from
which the birds make harmony to the wind's murmuring; and the
fresh and happy shade that falls from the unripened leaves upon the
grass's lap with soft slumbers. There Love hides his nets, nor is
there a more secluded place where, tired of shooting his arrows, he
is soothed.

THE sun in a flowering May never shed a sweeter light than the
one which makes your roses and may-flowers so clear and brilliant;
nor do they ever fall in summer or winter, so that you have an
eternal April: you have perpetual spring in your face and your soft
smile is the sun.

VITA de la mia vita,
tu mi somigli pallidetta oliva
o rosa scolorita;
nè di beltà sei priva,
ma in ogni aspetto tu mi sei gradita,
o lusinghiera o schiva;
e se mi segui o fuggi
soavemente mi consumi e struggi.

O VIA più bianca e fredda
di lei che spesso fa parer men belle
col suo splendor le stelle;
turba il suo puro argento
o nube o pioggia o vento,
nulla il tuo bel candore e i vaghi giri.
S'in me tu lieta giri
sia la mia vita un sogno ed io contento.

LIFE of my life, you seem like the pallid olive to me, or the faded rose; nor are you charmless, but you are pleasant to me, however you appear, flattering or shy; and whether you follow or fly, softly you consume and unmake me.

O WHITER and colder far than her who often makes the stars less fair with her shining; a cloud or rain or wind dims her pure silver, nothing, your lovely whiteness and your charming movements. If you turn glad to me, my life can be a dream and I be happy.

SIEPE, che gli orti vaghi
e me da me dividi,
sì bella rosa in te giammai non vidi
com'è la donna mia
bella, amorosa e pia;
e mentr'io stendo sovra te la mano
la mi stringe pian piano.

MENTRE angoscia e dolore
e spavento e timore
sono intorno al mio core afflitto e stanco,
vestitevi di bianco,
o miei negri pensieri:
del candor de la fede,
ch'ove s'uccide più forte rinasce,
siano le vostre fasce.
O miei fidi guerrieri,
su, su, veloci e pronti
prendete i passi ed ingombrate i monti.

HEDGE, that separate the fair orchards and me from myself, I never saw so lovely a rose in you, as lovely, fond, and holy as my lady is; and while I stretch my hand over you, she presses it softly.

WHILE anguish and grief and terror and doubting are about my tired afflicted heart, clothe yourselves in white, o black thoughts of mine: let your robes be of the whiteness of the faith, which with killing is more strongly reborn. O my trusty warriors, up, up, quick and ready, take the passes and throng the mountains.

QUAL rugiada o qual pianto
quai lacrime eran quelle
che sparger vidi dal notturno manto
e dal candido volto de le stelle?
E perchè seminò la bianca luna
di cristalline stelle un puro nembo
a l'erba fresca in grembo?
Perchè ne l'aria bruna
s'udian, quasi dolendo, intorno intorno
gir l'aure insino al giorno?
Fur segni forse de la tua partita,
vita de la mia vita?

IO v'amo sol perchè voi siete bella,
e perchè vuol mia stella,
non ch'io speri da voi, dolce mio bene,
altro che pene.

E se talor de gli occhi miei mostrate
aver qualche pietate,
io non spero da voi del pianger tanto
altro che pianto.

WHAT dew or what weeping, what tears were those that I saw
scattered from night's mantle and the pallid face of the stars? And
why did the white moon sow a pure cloud of crystalline stars in the
lap of the fresh grass? Why were the breezes heard swirling around
in the dusky air, as if complaining, until daylight? Were they signs
perhaps of your leaving, life of my very life?

I LOVE you simply because you are fair, and my star wishes it,
not that I hope for anything from you, my sweet life, but woes.
    And if you show pity sometimes for my eyes, I do not hope for
anything but weeping for so much weeping.

Nè, perchè udite i miei sospiri ardenti
che per voi spargo a i venti,
altro spera da voi questo mio core
se non dolore.

Lasciate pur ch'io v'ami e ch'io vi miri
e che per voi sospiri,
chè pene pianto e doglia è sol mercede
de la mia fede.

Fummo un tempo felici
io amante ed amato,
voi amata ed amante in dolce stato.
Poi d'amante nemica
voi diveniste, ed io
volsi in disdegno il giovanil desio.
Sdegno vuol ch'io ve'l dica,
sdegno che nel mio petto
tien viva l'onta del mio don negletto;
e le fronde ne svelle
del vostro lauro; or secche e già sì belle.

Nor, because you hear my burning sighs, that for you I give out to the winds, does this heart of mine hope for anything from you but sorrow.

Let me still love you and look on you and sigh for you, since woes, weeping, and sorrow is all the reward I have for loyalty.

We were once happy, I loving and beloved, you beloved and loving, in a sweet state. Then you became love's enemy, and I changed my youthful passion into scorn. Scorn demands that I tell you this, scorn that in my breast keeps fresh the shame of my neglected offering; and tears the leaves from your laurel; now dry and once so beautiful.

A la Signora Duchessa di Ferrara

Sposa regal, già la stagion ne viene
che gli accorti amatori a' balli invita,
e ch'essi a' rai di luce alma gradita
vegghian le notti gelide e serene.
Del suo fedel già le secrete pene
ne' casti orecchi è di raccorre ardita
la verginella, e lui tra morte e vita
soave inforsa e 'n dolce guerra il tiene.
Suonano i gran palagi e i tetti adorni
di canto; io sol di pianto il carcer tetro
fo risonar. Questa è la data fede?
Son questi i miei bramati alti ritorni?
Lasso! dunque prigion, dunque ferètro
chiamate voi pietà, Donna, e mercede?

To Her Grace the Duchess of Ferrara

Royal bride, now the season is coming round which invites attentive lovers to dances, and in which they charm the chill, clear nights in the rays of kindly, pleasing light. The young virgin dares to tell now the secret pangs of her lover to chaste ears, and softly leaves him doubtful between life and death and keeps him in sweet warfare.

The great palaces, the ornamented roofs resound with song; alone I make this dark prison echo with weeping. Is this the faith you plighted? Are these my longed-for, high deserts? Alas! then, Lady, you call a prison, pity, a coffin, then, recompense?

A Guglielmo Gonzaga, Duca di Mantova

SIGNOR, nel precipizio ove mi spinse
Fortuna, ognor più caggio in ver' gli abissi,
nè quinci ancora alcun mio prego udissi,
nè volto di pietà per me si pinse.
Ben veggio il sol, ma qual talora il cinse
oscuro velo in tenebroso eclissi;
e veggio in cielo i lumi erranti e fissi:
ma chi d'atro pallor così li tinse?
Or dal profond oscuro a te mi volgo
e grido: – A me, nel mio gran caso indegno,
dammi, che puoi, la destra e mi solleva;
ed a quel peso vil che sì l'aggreva
sottraggi l'ale del veloce ingegno,
e volar mi vedrai lunge dal volgo. –

To Guglielmo Gonzaga, Duke of Mantua

SIR, down the precipice over which Fortune thrust me, I fall and
deeper fall towards the abyss, nor has anyone hearkened to my
prayer up till now, nor has a face coloured with pity for me. Indeed I see the sun, but as he is when a dark veil wraps him in
shadowy eclipse; and I see the fixed and wandering stars in heaven:
but who has stained them like that with gloomy pallor?

Now from the dark depths I turn to you and cry: Give me,
you who can, your right hand in my great, unworthy plight, and
raise me; and draw the wing of swift invention from under the vile
weight that crushes it, and you will see me fly far from the crowd.

In morte di Margherita Bentivoglio

Non è questo un morire,
immortal Margherita,
ma un passar anzi tempo a l'altra vita;
nè de l'ignota via
duol ti scolori o tema,
ma sol pietà per la partenza estrema.
Di noi penosa e pia,
di te lieta e sicura,
t'accommiati dal mondo, anima pura.

Al Signor Gaspare Micinelli

Quando fioriva io già di fama e d'anni,
scriver bramai con sì purgati inchiostri
ne l'alta patria tua, fra pompe ed ostri
che ristorasser d'aspro esilio i danni;
or, perch'uom cinto di purpurei panni
lodi miei versi e li rilegga e mostri,
non me n'appago e bramo ombrosi chiostri
ov'io faccia a la morte illustri inganni.

On the Death of Margherita Bentivoglio

This is not a dying, immortal Margaret, but a passing before your time to another life; nor may grief or fear at the unknown way make you pale, but only pity for the final parting. Troubled and compassionate for our sake, happy and sure for your own, you bid the world good-bye, pure soul.

To Signor Gaspare Micinelli

When I flourished in fame and years, I longed to write with such purified inks in your exalted country, among the pomp and purple that might repay bitter exile's losses; now, I am not satisfied if a man clad in princely robes should praise my lines and read them again and show them, and I long for shady cloisters where I might cheat death in illustrious style.

Gasparro, oh foss'io pur ne' vostri monti
tra' novi alberghi e le memorie antiche
di color che gran pregio ebber ne l'armi,
che forse canterei sì gravi carmi
a me medesmo ed a le Muse amiche
che farei scorno a molti illustri e conti!

Al Padre Don Angelo Grillo

Io sparsi ed altri miete: io pur inondo
pianta gentil, cultor non forse indegno,
ed altri i frutti coglie, e me 'n disdegno,
ma per timore il duol nel petto ascondo.
Io porto il peso, io solco il mar profondo,
altri n'han la merce: chi giusto regno
così governa? o chi sarà sostegno
s'in terra caggio o tra gli scogli affondo?

O that I were, Gasparro, among your mountains, among new
abodes and the old memories of those who were greatly skilled in
arms, for I should perhaps utter, then, songs of such weight to myself and the befriending Muses that I would shame many high and
renowned ones!

To Father Don Angelo Grillo

I SOWED and others reap: I still water a gentle plant, a perhaps not
unworthy husbandman, and others seize on the fruit, myself dis-
daining, but for fear I hide my grief within my bosom. I bear the
weight, I furrow the deep sea, others have the merchandise: who
governs a lawful kingdom so? or who will be my prop if I fall to
the ground or sink among rocks?

E mentre pur m'attempo e d'anno in anno
sento le forze in me più stanche e dome,
non sono eguali al dolor mio le glorie,
nè verdeggia in Parnaso a queste chiome
sacrato lauro: e, perchè arroge al danno,
son tromba muta a mille altrui vittorie.

Ad un buffone del Duca Alfonso II

SIGNOR, storta di Palla e tremebondo
cannon di Marte e turbine e tempesta,
di cui temendo di tremar non resta
Tifeo là sotto, onde ne squassa il pondo,
così armatura senza pari al mondo
il zoppo fabro di sua man ti vesta,
e la sua moglie un par di corna in testa
gli ponga, accesa del tuo amor giocondo:

And while still I age, and from year to year feel the powers in me more weary and more subdued, glories are not equal to my sorrow, nor does a consecrated laurel spring green upon Parnassus for these locks: and, to aggravate the harm, I am the mute trumpet of a thousand victories by others.

To a Clown of Duke Alfonso II's

SIR, scimitar of Pallas and trembling cannon of Mars and whirl-wind and tempest, fearing which, Typheus does not stop quaking there below, so that his load shakes – may the limping smith clothe you in such armour, unparalleled in the world, and his wife, on fire with joyful love of you, place a pair of horns upon his head:

opra col tuo signor, che si disserri
la mia prigione, o tu con un fendente
manda in pezzi le porte e i catenacci:
così n'andremo in fra la Marzia gente,
tu tutto armato, io sol con gli spallacci,
fra noi le penne accomunando e i ferri.

*Loda il Signor Luigi Camoens, il Quale ha scritto un poema
in lingua Spagnola de' Viaggi del Vasco*

Vasco, le cui felici, ardite antenne
incontro al sol che ne riporta il giorno
spiegâr le vele e fêr colà ritorno
ov'egli par che di cader accenne,
non più di te per aspro mar sostenne
quel che fece al Ciclope oltraggio e scorno,
nè chi turbò l'Arpie nel suo soggiorno,
nè die più bel subietto a colte penne.

work upon your lord, that my prison be unbolted, or do you
with a downward cut send doors and horrid chains into pieces; so
we shall go among the Martian folk, you, completely armed, I with
shoulder-plates alone, sharing equally between us the feathers and
the irons.

*He Praises Signor Luigi Camoens, who Has Written a Long Poem
in Spanish about the Voyages of Vasco da Gama*

Vasco, whose happy, daring masts spread sails towards the sun
which brings us new day, and returned where it appears to hint
of falling, not more was borne on the harsh sea by him who insulted
and mocked the Cyclops, or who roused the Harpy in her den, nor
did this give fairer subject for learned quill.

Ed or quella del colto e buon Luigi
tant'oltre stende il glorioso volo,
ch'i tuoi spalmati legni andar men lunge:
ond'a quelli a cui s'alza il nostro polo
ed a chi ferma in contra i suoi vestigi
per lui del corse tuo la fama aggiunge.

O BELLA età de l'oro,
non già perchè di latte
se 'n corse il fiume e stillò mèle il bosco;
non perchè i frutti loro
diêr da l'aratro intatte
le terre, e gli angui errâr senz'ira o tosco;
non perchè nuvol fosco
non spiegò allor suo velo,
ma in primavera eterna
ch'ora s'accende e verna,
rise di luce e di sereno il cielo;
nè portò peregrino
o merce o guerra a gli altrui lidi il pino.

And now that of learned, good Luigi draws out its glorious
flight so surpassingly, that your caulked hulls did not go as far:
so that the fame of your journey reaches, through him, both those
above whom our pole is raised and those who gaze on the signs of
the opposite one.

O LOVELY age of Gold, not because the river ran with milk and
the wood dripped honey; not because the earth, untouched by the
plough, gave forth its fruits, and the snakes came and went without
hate or poison; nor because dark cloud did not spread its veil, but
the sky, which now burns and freezes, laughed with light and clearness; nor bark bore pilgrim or goods or war to foreign strands.

Mal sol perchè quel vano
nome senza soggetto,
quell'idolo d'errori, idol d'inganno,
quel che da 'l volgo insano
onor poscia fu detto,
che di nostra natura il feo tiranno,
non mischiava il suo affanno
fra le liete dolcezze
de l'amoroso gregge;
nè fu sua dura legge
nota a quell'alme in libertate avvezze;
ma legge aurea e felice
che Natura scolpì: *S'ei piace, ei lice.*

Allor tra fiori e linfe
traen dolci carole
gli Amoretti senz'archi e senza faci;
sedean pastori e ninfe,
meschiando a le parole
vezzi e susurri, ed a i susurri i baci
strettamente tenaci;

But only because that vain name without substance, that idol of
errors, idol of deception (what was later called honour by the sense-
less crowd, which made it the tyrant of our nature) did not mingle
its wearisomeness with the gay pleasures of the amorous flock; nor
was its hard law known to those souls charmed with liberty; only
a golden, happy law that Nature engraved: *What you desire to do,
you may.*

Then Cupids, without bows or torches, carolled softly among
flowers and plants; shepherds and nymphs sat mixing caresses and
whispers with their words, and kisses with their whispers, tightly

la verginella ignude
scopria le fresche rose,
ch'or tien ne 'l velo ascose,
e le poma de 'l seno acerbe e crude;
e spesso in fiume o in lago
scherzar si vide con l'amata il vago.

Tu prima, Onor, velasti
la fonte de i diletti,
negando l'onde a l'amorosa sete:
tu a' begli occhi insegnasti
di starne in sè ristretti,
e tener lor bellezze altrui secrete:
tu raccogliesti in rete
le chiome a l'aura sparte:
tu i dolci atti lascivi
festi ritrosi e schivi,
a i detti il fren ponesti, a i passi l'arte:
opra è tua sola, o Onore,
che furto sia quel che fu don d'Amore.

clinging; the young virgin displayed her fresh roses nakedly which
she now keeps hidden by a veil, and the small, unsweetened apples
of her breasts; and often was the lover seen to play with the beloved
in river or in lake.

You first, Honour, veiled the fountain of delights, denying its
waves to amorous thirst; you taught lovely eyes to stay contracted
to themselves, and keep their beauties concealed from others, you
gathered in a net the tresses scattered to the wind: you made the
sweet, lascivious acts, shy and shameful, and forced a bridle upon
words, and art on simple walking: this work is yours alone, o
Honour, that what was Love's gift should become robbery.

E son tuoi fatti egregi
le pene e i pianti nostri.
Ma tu, d'Amore e di Natura donno,
tu domator de' regi,
che fai tra questi chiostri
che la grandezza tua capir non ponno?
Vattene, e turba il sonno
a gl'illustri e potenti:
noi qui negletta e bassa
turba, senza te lassa
viver ne l'uso de l'antiche genti.
Amiam, chè non ha tregua
con gli anni umana vita, e si dilegua.

Amiam: chè 'l Sol si muore e poi rinasce;
a noi sua breve luce
s'asconde, e 'l sonno eterna notte adduce.

And your boasted deeds are our pains and tears. But you, lord of Love and Nature, you governor of kings, what are you doing in these alleys that cannot contain your greatness? Be gone, and trouble the sleep of the famous and the powerful: leave us here, a low, neglected crowd, to live without you, in the manner of ancient peoples. Let us love, for human life makes no truce with the years, and dwindles away.

Let us love: for the sun dies and then is born again; from us he hides his brief light, and eternal night brings sleep.

GIORDANO BRUNO

Amor, per cui tant'alto il ver discerno,
ch'apre le porte di diamante e nere,
per gli occhi entra il mio nume; e per vedere
nasce, vive, si nutre, ha regno eterno.
Fa scorger quanto ha il ciel, terra ed inferno,
fa presenti d'assenti effigie vere,
repiglia forze, e, trando dritto, fere,
e impiaga sempre il cuor, scopre ogni interno.

Adunque, volgo vile, al vero attendi;
porgi l'orecchio al mio dir non fallace;
apri, apri, se puoi, gli occhi, insano e bieco.
Fanciullo il credi, perchè poco intendi;
perchè ratto ti cangi, ei par fugace;
per esser orbo tu, lo chiami cieco.

E chi m'impenna, e chi mi scalda il core,
chi non mi fa temer fortuna o morte,
chi le catene ruppe e quelle porte,
onde rari son sciolti ed escon fore?

Love, by whom I distinguish the truth so remote and high, who opens the black and diamond-set gates, enters my spirit through my eyes; and is born to see; lives, is fed, has eternal reign for this. He calls into being all that heaven, earth, and hell contain, he causes true copies of the absent to be present, summons up powers and, hurling straight, strikes, wounds the heart ever, and discovers every inward.

Therefore, base throng, look to the truth; incline you ears to my not false speech; open, open, if you can, you ears, cross-grained and mad as you are. You believe him a child, because you understand so little; because you change rapidly, he seems elusive; as you are eyeless, you call him blind.

And who is to fledge me, and who warm my heart, who not make me fear chance or death, who break the chains and those gates, whence few are freed and go forth? Ages, years, months, days, and

L'etadi, gli anni, i mesi, i giorni e l'ore,
figlie ed armi del tempo, e quella corte
a cui nè ferro, nè diamante è forte,
assicurato m'han dal suo furore.

Quindi l'ali sicure a l'aria porgo,
ne temo intoppo di cristallo o vetro;
ma fendo i cieli, e a l'infinito m'ergo.
E mentre dal mio globo agli altri sorgo,
e per l'eterio campo oltre penetro,
quel ch'altri lungi vede, lascio al tergo.

MAI fia che de l'amor io mi lamente
senza del qual non voglio esser felice;
sia pur ver che per lui penoso stente,
non vo' non voler quel che sì me lice.
Sia chiar o fosco il ciel, fredd' o ardente,
sempr'un sarò ver l'unica fenice.
Mal può disfar altro destin o sorte
quel nodo che non può sciorre la morte.

hours, daughters and weapons of time, and that assembly for whom
not iron or diamond is durable, have made me safe from his fury.
   So that I stretch my wings to the air, nor fear barrier of crystal or
glass; but cut the heavens, and rise to the infinite. And as from my
globe I ascend to others, and penetrate higher into the ethereal field,
what others see as distant I leave behind my back.

NEVER shall it come about that I complain of love without which
I do not wish to be happy; it may be true that for its sake I struggle
painfully, I still do not want not to want what is granted me thus.
Let the heavens be clear or dark, cold or burning, I shall always be
the same towards the only phoenix. Ill can any other destiny or fate
undo that knot which death itself cannot loose.

Al cor, al spirto, a l'alma
non è piacer, o libertade, o vita,
qual tanto arrida, giove e sia gradita,
qual più sia dolce, graziosa ed alma,
ch'il stento, giogo e morte,
ch'ho per natura, voluntade e sorte.

Unico augel del sol, vaga Fenice,
ch'appareggi col mondo gli anni tui
quai colmi ne l'Arabia felice,
tu sei che fuste, io son quel che non fui.
Io per caldo d'amor muoio infelice,
me te ravviv' il sol co' raggi sui.
Tu bruggi 'n un, ed io in ogni loco;
io da Cupido, hai tu da Febo il foco.

Hai termini prefissi
di lunga vita, e io ho breve fine,
che pronto s'offre per mille ruine;
nè so quel che vivrò, nè quel che vissi:
me cieco fato adduce,
tu certo torni a riveder tua luce.

There is no pleasure, liberty, life, that so smiles on, serves and is pleasant, that is sweeter, comelier, and kinder, to my heart, my spirit, my soul, than the hardship, yoke, and death, that I have by nature, will, and fate.

Only bird of the sun, fair Phoenix, who equal the world's years with your own, which you live out in Araby the blest, you are what you were, I am what I was not. I die unhappy from heat of love, but the sun revives you with his rays. You burn in one, and I, in every place; I have my fire from Cupid, you from Phoebus.

You have fixed term of long life, and I have a short course which readily yields itself in a thousand different ruinings; nor do I know what I shall live out, nor what I have lived: blind fate leads me, you return surely to see your light again.

ANNOSA quercia, che gli rami spandi
a l'aria, e fermi le radici 'n terra;
nè terra smossa, nè gli spirti grandi
che da l'aspro Aquilon il ciel disserra,
nè quanto fia ch'il vern' orrido mandi,
dal luogo ove stai salda, mai ti sferra;
mostri della mia fè ritratto vero,
qual smossa mai strani accidenti fero.

Tu medesmo terreno
mai sempre abbracci, fai colto e comprendi,
e di lui per le viscere distendi
radici grate al generoso seno:
i' ad un solo oggetto
ho fisso il spirto, il senso e l'intelletto.

TOMMASO CAMPANELLA

Modo di filosofare

IL mondo è il libro dove il Senno eterno
scrisse i propri concetti, e vivo tempio
dove, pingendo i gesti e 'l proprio esempio,
di statue vive ornò l'imo e 'l superno;

AGED oak, who spread your branches to the air, and set your roots
in earth; neither tremor of earth, nor the great powers which the
North wind looses from the skies, nor whatever the hateful winter
sends, ever dislodges you from the spot where you rise firm; you
stand as the true image of my faith.

You ever and always embrace the same soil, make it fruitful and
bind it, and through its bowels thrust roots welcome to the generous breast: I have spirit, senses, and intellect constant to one end.

The Way of Progressing in Philosophy

THE world is the book where eternal Wisdom wrote its own ideas,
and the living temple where, depicting its own acts and likeness, it
decorated the height and the depth with living statues; so that every

perch'ogni spirto qui l'arte e 'l governo
leggere e contemplar, per non farsi empio,
debba, e dir possa: – Io l'universo adempio,
Dio contemplando a tutte cose interno. –

Ma noi, strette alme a' libri e tempii morti,
copiati dal vivo con più errori,
gli anteponghiamo a magistero tale.
O pene, del fallir fatene accorti,
liti, ignoranze, fatiche e dolori:
deh torniamo, per Dio, all'originale!

Gli uomini son giuoco di Dio e degli Angeli

Nel teatro del mondo ammascherate
l'alme da' corpi e dagli effetti loro,
spettacolo al supremo consistoro
da natura, divina arte, apprestate,
fan gli atti e detti tutte a chi son nate;
di scena in scena van, di coro in coro;
si veston di letizia e di martòro,
dal comico fatal libro ordinate.

spirit, to guard against profanity, should read and contemplate here art and government, and each should say: 'I fill the universe, seeing God in all things.'

But we, souls bound to books and dead temples, copied with many mistakes from the living, place these things before such instruction. O ills, quarrels, ignorance, labours, pains, make us aware of our falling away: o, let us, in God's name, return to the original!

Men Are the Sport of God and His Angels

Masked upon the stage of the world by bodies and their properties, our souls, prepared by nature, divine art, for their performance before the highest council, go through the actions and pronounce the words which they were born to; from scene to scene, from interlude to interlude, clothe themselves in gladness and suffering, as ordained by the fateful comedy-book.

Nè san, nè ponno, nè vogliono fare,
nè patir altro che 'l gran Senno scrisse,
di tutte lieto, per tutte allegrare;
quando, rendendo, al fin di giuochi e risse,
le maschere alla terra, al cielo, al mare,
in Dio vedrem chi meglio fece e disse.

Contro Cupido

So n tremila anni omai che 'l mondo cole
un cieco Amore, c'ha la faretra e l'ale;
ch'or di più è fatto sordo, e l'altrui male,
privo di caritate, udir non vuole.
D'argento è ingordo, e a brun vestirsi suole,
non più nudo fanciul schietto e leale,
ma vecchio astuto; e non usa aureo strale,
poichè fur ritrovate le pistole,

Nor do they know, nor can they, nor wish to do, or suffer other
than what great Wisdom, pleased with all, has written to make all
glad; when, at the end of games and disputes, their masks restored
to earth, sky, sea, we shall see in God who best wrought and who
best spoke.

Against Cupid

It is now three thousand years since the world first worshipped
Love that is blind, with his arrows and his wings; who now, in
addition, has been made deaf, and will not, in his lack of all charity,
hear of another's misfortune. He is gluttonous of silver, and accustomed to dress in brown, no longer a plain and loyal naked child,
but a cunning old man; and he does not use a golden arrow, since
pistols were contrived,

ma carbon, solfo, vampa, tuono e piombo,
che di piaghe infernali i corpi ammorba,
e sorde e losche fa l'avide menti.
Pur dalla squilla mia sento un rimbombo:
– Cedi, bestia impiagata, sorda ed orba,
al saggio Amor dell'anime innocenti –

Al carcere

COME va al centro ogni cosa pesante
dalla circonferenza, e come ancora
in bocca al mostro che poi la devora,
donnola incorre timente e scherzante;
così di gran scienza ognuno amante,
che audace passa dalla morta gora
al mar del vero, di cui s'innamora,
nel nostro ospizio alfin ferma le piante.

but coal, sulphur, flame, thunder, and lead, which infects bodies with hellish wounds, and makes greedy minds deaf and unseeing. Yet I hear an echo to my alarm: 'Yield, beast, scarred, deaf, and blind, to the wise Love of innocent souls.'

To His Prison

As every heavy thing travels from circumference to centre, and as, too, the timorous and playful weasel runs into the mouth of the monster that then devours it, so every lover of great knowledge, who boldly passes from the dead pond to the sea of truth, with which he falls in love, fixes his feet at last in our abode.

Ch'altri l'appelli antro di Polifemo,
palazzo altri d'Atlante, e chi di Creta
il laberinto, e chi l'inferno estremo,
che qui non val favor, saper, nè pietà,
io ti so dir; del resto, tutto tremo,
ch'è rocca sacra a tirannia segreta.

Di sè etesso

Sciolto e legato, accompagnato e solo,
gridando cheto, il fiero stuol confondo:
folle all'occhio mortal del basso mondo,
saggio al Senno divin dell'altro polo.
Con vanni in terra oppressi al ciel men volo,
in mesta carne d'animo giocondo;
e, se talor m'abbassa il grave pondo,
l'ale pur m'alzan sopra il duro suolo.

Which some call Polyphemus's cavern, others, Atlas's palace, and some, the Cretan labyrinth, and some, uttermost hell – I can tell you that here favour, knowledge or piety have no power; for the rest, I tremble utterly, for this is a citadel sacred to hidden tyranny.

On Himself

Freed and bound, accompanied and alone, quiet and shouting, I confound the savage throng: mad to the mortal eye of this low world, wise to the divine Wisdom of the other pole. With my pinions crushed to earth I fly to heaven, a joyful spirit in sad flesh; and, if at times the heavy burden bows me, my wings still raise me above the hard ground.

La dubbia guerra fa le virtù conte.
Breve è verso l'eterno ogn'altro tempo,
e nulla è più leggier ch'un grato peso.
Porto dell'amor mio l'imago in fronte,
sicuro d'arrivar lieto per tempo
ove io senza parlar sia sempre inteso.

Giudizio sopra Dante, Tasso e Petrarca

TASSO, i leggiadri e graziosi detti
de' duoi maggior della tosca favella
dilettan ben, perchè la vesta è bella,
onora l'esquisiti alti concetti;
ma via più giova il fuoco de' lor petti,
onde nell'alma a virtù non rubella
nasce il soave ardor e la fiammella
ch'è propria dei ben nati spirti eletti.

Doubtful warfare makes virtues known. Short is every other time before eternity, and nothing is lighter than a pleasing load. I bear the image of my love upon my forehead, sure of arriving happily, in good time, where without speaking I shall be ever understood.

His Estimate of Dante, Tasso, and Petrarch

TASSO, the graceful and easy expressions of the two greatest of the Tuscan tongue give much delight, because the garment is fair and does honour to the high, exquisite thoughts; but far more profitable is the fire in their bosoms, from which springs, in the soul not hostile to virtue, that spark and sweet burning which is proper to well-born, chosen spirits.

Voi gli aggiungete e trapassate in dire,
ma il cor per l'ale vostre ancor non sente
ergersi al Ciel, e punger da giuste ire.
Deh! quando fuor della smarrita gente
ci sentirem dal vostro stil rapire
al degno oggetto dell'umana gente?

*Dalla « Lamentevole orazione profetale dal profondo della
fossa dove stava incarcerato»*

A TE tocca, o Signore,
se invan non m'hai creato,
d'esser mio salvatore.
Per questo notte e giorno
a te lagrimo e grido.
Quando ti parrà ben ch'io sia ascoltato?
Più parlar non mi fido,
chè i ferri c'ho d'intorno,
ridonsi e fanmi scorno
del mio invano pregare,
degli occhi secchi e del rauco esclamare.

You equal and surpass them in expression, but the heart does not
yet feel itself lifted to heaven on your wings, nor pricked with
righteous anger. Oh! when will we feel ourselves snatched by your
art from the erring throng to humankind's worthy end?

*From 'Prophetic Prayer of Lament from the Depth of the Pit in
Which He Was Imprisoned'*

IT is for you, o Lord, if you have not created me in vain, to prove
my saviour. For this I weep and cry to you night and day. When
will it seem good to you that I should be heard? I do not trust myself to say more, for the irons I have about me laugh and mock me
for praying in vain, for my dried-up eyes and hoarse exclaiming.

*Dalle «Oraẓioni tre in salmodia metafisicale
congiunte insieme»*

OMNIPOTENTE Dio, benchè del fato
invittissima legge e lunga pruova
d'esser non sol mie' prieghi invano sparsi,
ma al contrario esauditi, mi rimuova
dal tuo cospetto, io pur torno ostinato,
tutti gli altri rimedi avendo scarsi.
Che s'altro Dio potesse pur trovarsi,
io certo per aiuto a quel n'andrei.
Nè mi si potria dir mai ch'io fosse empio,
se da te, che mi scacci in tanto scempio,
a chi m'invita mi rivolgerei.
Deh, Signor, io vaneggio; aita, aita!
pria che del Senno il tempio
divenga di stoltizia una meschita.

*

BEN so che non si trovano parole
che muover possan te a benivolenza
di chi *ab aeterno* amar non destinasti;
chè 'l tuo consiglio non ha penitenza,

*From 'Three Prayers in Metaphysical Psalm-form
Joined Together'*

ALMIGHTY God, although the unconquerable law of fate, and long
experience not simply of my prayers' being poured forth in vain,
but of their being taken in contrary sense, banish me from your
sight, I still return obstinately, since all other remedies are not
enough for me. For if there were, say, another God, certainly I
would go to him for help. Nor could anyone ever say I was wicked,
if I turned from you who thrust me into such destruction to one
who welcomes me. O, Lord, I wander; help! help! before the
temple of Wisdom becomes a mosque of foolishness.

WELL do I know that no words are to be found that will move
you to benevolence towards one whom you did not destine for
your love from all eternity; for your counsel is without remorse,

nè può eloquenza di mondane scuole
piegarti a compassion, se decretasti
che 'l mio composto si disfaccia e guasti
fra miserie cotante ch'io patisco.
E se sa tutto il mondo il mio martoro,
il ciel, la terra, e tutti i figli loro;
perchè a te, che lo fai, l'istoria ordisco?
E s'ogni mutamento è qualche morte,
Tu, Dio immortal ch'io adoro,
come ti muterai a cangiar mia sorte?

*

Io pur ritorno a dimandar mercede,
dove 'l bisogno e 'l gran dolor mi caccia.
Ma non ho tal retorica nè voce,
ch'a tanto tribunal poi si confaccia.
Nè poca carità, nè poca fede,
nè la poca speranza è che mi nuoce.
E se, com'altri insegna, pena atroce

nor can the eloquence of worldly assemblies bend you to pitying,
if you decreed that my mixed being is to be unmade and to waste
among the many miseries I suffer. And if the whole world knows
of my martyrdom, heaven, earth, and all their children; why do I
rehearse the tale to you who have caused this? And if every change
is something of a death, You, immortal God whom I adore, how
will you change so as to alter my fate?

STILL I come back to ask for mercy, where need and great grief
hunts me. But I have not the eloquence or voice that would be
fitting then for such a jury. Nor is it little charity, nor little faith,
nor little hope that obstructs me. And if, as some teach, there is

che l'anima pulisca e renda degna
della tua grazia, si ritrova al mondo,
non han l'alpe cristallo così mondo,
ch'alla mia puritade si convegna.
Cinquanta prigioni, sette tormenti
passai, e pur son nel fondo;
e dodici anni d'ingiurie e di stenti.

*

Io, con gli amici pur sempre ti scuso
ch'altro secolo in premio a tuo' riserbi,
e che i malvagi in sè sieno infelici,
sempre affliggendo gli animi superbi
sdegno, ignoranza e sospetto rinchiuso;
e che di lor fortune traditrici
traboccan sempre al fine. Ma gli amici,
se, quelli dentro, e noi di fuor, siamo
tutti meschini, chieggon la cagione,
che fa nel nostro mal tue voglie buone;

unspeakable pain in the world which cleanses the soul and makes it
worthy of your grace, the alps have not crystal so clean as would
be needed for my purifying. Fifty prisons, seven torturings, have I
passed through and still am I in the depths; after twelve years of
humiliations and sufferings.

I STILL excuse you constantly with friends, saying that you keep
another world for your own, and that the wicked are unhappy in
themselves, as disdain, ignorance, and close-kept suspicion continually afflict proud minds; and they are always overwhelmed in
the end by their own treacherous fortune. But my friends ask why,
if we are all miserable, those others inwardly, we in an outward
way, your good designs should be effected through our wicked-

che se gli altri enti, e noi, figli d'Adamo,
doveamo trasmutarci a ben del tutto
di magione in magione,
perchè non fai tal muta senza lutto?

*

SE mi sciogli, io far scuola ti prometto
di tutte nazioni
a Dio liberator, verace e vivo,
s'a cotanto pensier non è disdetto
il fine cui mi sproni;
gl'idoli abbatter, far di culto privo
ogni dio putativo
e chi di Dio si serve, e a Dio non serve;
por di ragione il seggio e lo stendardo
contra il vizio codardo;
a libertà chiamar l'anime serve,
umiliar le proterve.
Nè a tetti, ch'avvilisce
fulmine o belva, dir canzon novelle,
per cui Sion languisce.
Ma tempio farò il cielo, altar le stelle.

ness; for if other creatures and we, children of Adam, must be transformed from stage to stage for the good of all, why do you not bring about such change without our lamenting?

IF you free me, I promise to make all nations into a school for true and living God the liberator, if so daring a thought is not to be denied the fulfilment to which you spur me; to throw down the idols, deprive every imaginary god of worship and him who makes God serve his own purposes, and is of no service to God; raise the seat and banner of reason against cowardly vice; call enslaved souls to freedom, humble the froward. Nor sing new psalms, for which Sion is faint, under roofs that lightning or beast may spoil. But I shall make the heavens your temple, your altar the stars.

Dispregio della Morte

QUANTE prende dolcezze e meraviglie
l'anima, uscendo dal gravante e cieco
nostro terreno speco!
Snella per tutto il mondo e lieta vola,
riconosce l'essenze, e vede seco
gli ordini santi e l'eroica famiglia,
che la guida e consiglia,
e come il primo Amor tutti consola,
e quanti mila n'ha una stella sola.

*

MIRANDO 'l mondo e le delizie sacre
e quanti onor a Dio fan gli almi spirti,
comincerai stupirti
come Egli miri pur la nostra terra
picciola, nera, brutta e, più vo' dirti,
dove ha tante biastemme orrende ed acre,
che par che si dissacre;
dove sta l'odio, la morte e la guerra,
e l'ignoranza troppo più l'afferra.

Scorn at Death

HOW much sweetness and wonder seizes on the soul, when it
comes out from this heavy, blinded cave of ours! Clean and glad
it flies through all the universe, recognizes the essences of things,
and sees by its side the orders of saints and the heroic family,
which guide and counsel it, and how first Love comforts all, and
how many spirits a single star holds.

LOOKING on the universe and its holy joys and how many
tributes the benign spirits pay to God, you will begin to be amazed
that He can look on our little, black, ugly earth, and – I shall say
more to you – in which there are so many terrifying and bitter
evils, that it seems to lose all sacredness; where hate, death, and
war are found, and ignorance, infinitely greater, grips it.

*Canzone a Berillo di pentimento desideroso di confessione
ecc. fatta nel Caucaso*

SIGNORE, troppo peccai, troppo, il conosco;
Signor, più non m'ammiro
del mio atroce martìro.
Nè le mie abbominevoli preghiere
di medicina, ma di mortal tosco
fur degne. Ahi, stolto e losco!
Dissi: – Giudica, Dio, – non – Miserere. –
Ma l'alta tua benigna sofferenza,
per cui più volte non mi fulminasti,
mi dà qualche credenza
che perdonanza alfin mi riserbasti.

*

Io mi credevo Dio tener in mano,
non seguitando Dio,
ma l'argute ragion del senno mio,
che a me ed a tanti ministrâr la morte.
Benchè sagace e pio, l'ingegno umano
divien cieco e profano,
se pensa migliorar la comun sorte,

*Song of Repentance for Beryl (Don Brigo of Pavia) with the Desire
to be Confessed, etc., Composed in the 'Caucasus'*

LORD, too much I sinned, too much, I know; Lord, I no longer
wonder at my appalling torment. Nor were my loathsome prayers
worthy of balm, but of deadly poison. Ah! foolish and darkened! I
said: Judge, God, – not – Have mercy. But your high kindly
patience, thanks to which, many times, you have not blasted me,
gives me some assurance that you have reserved pardon for me at
the last.

I BELIEVED I held God in my hand, though not following God,
but the subtle reasonings of my intellect, that to me and so many
have dealt death. Although wise and pious, human wit becomes
blind and profane, if it thinks to better the common fate before you,

pria che mostrarti a' sensi suoi, Dio vero,
e mandarlo ed amarlo non ti degni,
come tuo messaggiero,
di miracoli e prove e contrassegni.

*

TARDI, Padre, ritorno al tuo consiglio,
tardi il medico invoco;
tanto aggravato, il morbo non dà loco.
Quanto più alzar vo' gli occhi al tuo splendore,
più mi sento abbagliar, gravarmi il ciglio.
Poi con fiero periglio
dal lago inferior tento uscir fuore
con quelle forze che non ho, meschino.
Meschino me, per me stesso perduto,
chè l'aiuto divino,
che sol salvarmi può, bramo e rifiuto!

*

MERTI non ho per quelli gran peccata,
che contra te ho commesso,
Madre di Cristo, e voi che state appresso,

true God, see fit to reveal yourself to its faculties, and love it and
send it as your messenger, with miracles and proofs and signs.

LATE, father, I come back for your counsel, late I summon the
doctor; so worsened the disease that it does not yield. The more
I wish to raise my eyes to your brightness, the more I feel dazzled,
my eyelids weighing. Then, to my fierce danger, I try to get out of
the bottommost lake with those powers that, wretch, I do not possess. Wretch that I am, lost thanks to myself, since I desire and
refuse the divine aid which alone can save me!

I HAVE no merit, thanks to those great sins which I have committed against you, Mother of Christ, and you who are near her,

spirti beati, abitator del lume,
che 'l mondo adempie, e sol la terra ingrata
ancor non ha purgata,
prego contra ragion, contra il costume,
ch'al vostro capital fiero inimico
impetrate da lui qualche perdono,
ch' a' peccator fu amico;
poichè tra gli empi il maggior empio io sono.

GIOVAN BATTISTA MARINO

Donna che si lava le gambe

Sovra basi d'argento in conca d'oro
io vidi due colonne alabastrine
dentro linfe odorate e cristalline
franger di perle un candido tesoro.
O (dissi) del mio mal posa e ristoro,
di Natura e d'Amor metà divine,
stabilite per ultimo confine
ne l'Oceano de le dolcezze loro.

blessed spirits, inhabitants of the light which fills the world, and has not cleansed the ungrateful earth alone; I pray unreasonably, against use, for you to beg some pardon for your fierce major enemy from him who was the friend of sinners; because among the wicked, the greatest one am I.

Woman Washing Her Legs

In a shell of gold upon silver base I saw two columns of alabaster amid perfumed and crystal currents breaking a white treasure of pearls. O (I said) resting-place and balm of my suffering, divine ends of Nature and Love, set as the utmost bounds in the Ocean of their own delights.

Fossi Alcide novel, chè i miei trofei
dove mai non giungesse uman desio
traspiantandovi in braccio erger vorrei.
O stringer, qual Sanson, vi potess'io,
chè col vostro cader dolce darei
tomba a la morte e morte al dolor mio.

Dafne in Lauro

D EH, perchè fuggi, o Dafne,
da chi ti segue ed ama,
e fuor che i tuoi begli occhi altro non brama?
Se' molle ninfa? o duro tronco forse
di questo alpestro monte,
rigida e sorda a chi ti prega e chiama?
Ma se tu tronco sei,
come al fuggir le piante hai così pronte?
Come non sai fermarti ai preghi miei?
Così dicea, ma scorse
in vero tronco allor cangiata Apollo
la bella fuggitiva
fermarsi immobilmente in su la riva.

Might I be a new Alcides, for, taking you up in my arms, I
would raise my trophies where human desire had never reached. Or
might I crush you together, like Samson, for I would give death a
tomb with your sweet fall and death to my grief.

Daphne into Laurel

O WHY do you flee, o Daphne, from him who follows and loves
you, and desires nothing other than your lovely eyes? Are you a
soft nymph? or perhaps a hard tree-trunk of this flinty mountain-
side, unbending and deaf to him who begs and calls you? But if you
are a trunk, why are your feet so ready to flee? How can you not
stay for my entreaties? So Apollo was speaking, but he saw then
the lovely fugitive, changed into a real trunk, stay unmovingly
upon the bank.

Fede rotta

Sovra l'umida arena
de le latine sponde
di propria man Tirrena
queste parole un dì scriver vid'io:
Mirzio è sol l'amor mio.
Ahi fu ben degna di sì fral parola,
crudel, l'arena sola; onde poi l'onde
e del Tebro in un punto e de l'oblio
Mirzio, ch'era il tu'amore,
radessero dal lido e dal tuo core.

Bella schiava

Nera sì, ma se' bella, o di Natura
fra le belle d'Amor leggiadro mostro.
Fosca è l'alba appo te; perde e s'oscura
presso l'ebeno tuo l'avorio e l'ostro.
Or quando, or dove il mondo antico o il nostro
vide sì viva mai, senti sì pura
o luce uscir di tenebroso inchiostro,
o di spento carbon nascere arsura?

Broken Vows

On the damp sands of the Italian shore, I saw Tirrena with her own hand writing these words one day: Mirtius is my only love. Ah, cruel fair, the sand alone was fit for words so frail; since the waves of the Tiber and forgetfulness at the one instant erased Mirtius, who was your love, from the beach and from your heart.

Beautiful Slave

Black, yes, but you are beautiful, or a graceful monster of Nature's among Love's beauties. The dawn is gloomy where you are; ivory and the pearl fade and are darkened beside your ebony. When or where did the ancient world, or ours, see so living, feel so pure a light come from shady ink, or burning spring from burnt-out coal?

Servo di chi m'è serva, ecco ch'avvolto
porto di bruno laccio il core intorno,
che per candida man non fia mai sciolto.
Là 've più ardi, o Sol, sol per tuo scorno
un sole è nato; un Sol, che nel bel volto
porta la notte ed ha negli occhi il giorno.

Dipartita

Già fuor de l'onde il Sol sferza i destrieri,
ecco del mio partir l'ora che giunge;
Lilla, intanto, s'Amor ne scalda e punge,
sieno i fidi sospir nostri corrieri.
E come per incogniti sentieri
con Aretusa Alfeo si ricongiunge,
così mentre vivranno i corpi lunge,
a visitarsi tornino i pensieri.

Slave of her who is slave to me, look, I bear a dusky noose round my heart that will never be loosed by white hand. Where you most burn, o Sun, a sun has been born for your sole shaming; a sun that wears night upon her face, and in her eyes has day.

Leave-taking

ALREADY the sun whips his coursers from the waves, and now the hour of my leave-taking arrives; Lilla, the while, if Love warms and pricks us on, let our faithful sighs be our messengers. And as by unknown ways Alpheus joins himself with Arethusa again, so while our bodies live far apart, let our thoughts come back to visit one another.

Spesso due stelle in ciel destre e felici,
se ben per vario sito il corso fanno,
scontrarsi almen con lieti aspetti amici.
E due piante talor divise stanno,
ma sotterra però con le radici
se non co' rami, a ritrovar si vanno.

L'amore incostante

(al Signor Marcello Sacchetti)

CHI vuol veder, Marcello,
Proteo d'amor novello,
novel camaleonte,
a me giri la fronte,
ch'ognor pensier volgendo,
forme diverse e color vari apprendo.

Già defender non oso
il mio fallo amoroso;
anzi l'error confesso,
la colpa accuso io stesso:

Often two stars, nimble and happy in heaven, even though they take their way through different parts, have met at least with glad and loving look. And two plants often stand separate, but move to find one another again, if not with their branches, still with their roots underground.

Inconstant Love

(to Signor Marcello Sacchetti)

WHOEVER cares to see a Proteus of new love, Marcello, a new chameleon, let him turn his eyes on me, for, as my thoughts come back to this subject at all times, so do I embrace different forms and various colours.

I do not in the least dare defend my amorous failing; rather I confess my being wrong, and charge myself with the fault: but

ma chi fia che raccoglia
sul corso fren de la sfrenata voglia?

Chi d'un cupido amante
il desir vaneggiante
o circoscrive o lega,
che si move e si piega
lieve più ch'alga o fronda
che tremi in ramo a l'aura, in lido a l'onda?

Non ha sol un oggetto
il mio bramoso affetto:
cento principi e cento
trov' io del mio tormento;
sempre che vada o miri,
sempre ho nove cagioni ond'io sospiri.

Ogni beltà, ch'io veggia,
il cor mi tiranneggia;
d' ogni cortese sguardo
subito avampo ed ardo.
Lasso! ch'a poco a poco
son fatto esca continua ad ogni foco.

who is there who can catch the bridle of the unbridled will as it
careers?

Who can circumscribe or bind the wandering desire of a covet-
ous lover which moves and bends lightly as seaweed or leaf trembles
on the branch in the breeze, by the seashore in the wave?

My burning affection has not just a single object: I find a hundred
causes for torment and a hundred more; as long as I go or look
about, I always have new reasons for sighing.

Every beauty I see dominates my heart; I flame and burn in-
stantly at each kind look. Alas! I gradually grow to be unfailing
fuel for every fire.

Quante forme repente
offre l'occhio a la mente,
tante son lacci ed ami
perch'io vie più sempr'ami:
or per una languisco,
or per altra mi struggo e 'ncenerisco.

Me la fresca beltate,
me la più tarda etate
infiamma e punge e prende:
quella però m'incende
con le grazie e co' lumi,
questa con gli atti gravi e co' costumi.

L'una per la sua pura
semplicetta natura,
l'altra per l'altra parte
de l'ingegno e de l'arte,
egualmente mi piace
e la rozza bellezza e la sagace.

Usi fregiarsi: i fregi
chi fia che non appregi?
Vada inculta e sprezzata,
sol di se stessa ornata:

The sudden forms the eye offers to the mind are so many traps
and hooks to make me love much more and more: now I languish
for one woman, now for another am destroyed and turned to ashes.

Fresh beauty or maturer age inflame and spur and take me: the
former sets me on fire with her graces and her eyes, the latter with
her stately gestures and her ways.

The first for her pure simple nature, the other for the other en-
dowment of wit and art, – the uncultivated beauty and the wise one
please me equally.

Let a woman be in the habit of tricking herself out: who will
not appreciate her ornaments? Let her be unsophisticated and

quella schiettezza adoro,
quella sua povertate è mio tesoro.

O vezzosa e lasciva,
o ritrosetta e schiva,
quella mi fa sperare
che sia tal qual appare,
questa il pensier lusinga
ch'ami d'esser amata e che s'infinga.

Colei, perchè si vede
che di statura eccede:
costei, perchè mi sembra
più sciolta ne le membra:
preso di doppio nodo,
ambedue fra me stesso ammiro e lodo.

Gota bianca e vermiglia
m'alletta a maraviglia;
pallido e smorto volto
sovente il cor m'ha tolto:
ma s'ama ancor talora
bruno ciglio, occhio oscuro e guancia mora.

negligent, adorned only with herself: I adore that directness, that poverty is my treasure.

Let her be winning and lascivious, or shy and backward, the first makes me hope she will be as she seems, the second gives me the flattering idea that she loves to be loved and pretends.

This one, because she is seen to be of uncommon height; that one because she seems more supple of limb: taken in a double knot, I admire and praise each to myself.

A white and crimson cheek weans me to admiration; a pale, white face has often claimed my heart: but dusky brow, dark eye and swarthy cheek are also to be loved at times.

O crin d'or biondo e terso
tra vivi fior cosperso,
che si confonda e spieghi,
leggiadra man disleghi,
scorger parmi in quell'atto
de l'Aurora purpurea il bel ritratto;

o chiome altra mi mostri
del color degl'inchiostri,
raccolte o pur cadenti
sovra due stelle ardenti,
l'assomiglio non meno
della Notte tranquilla al bel sereno.

Se ride un'angeletta,
quel suo viso è saetta;
se piange, a la mia vita
quel suo pianto è ferita;
se non piange nè ride,
senza stral, senza piaga ancor m'uccide.

Ninfa ch'or alta, or grave,
snoda voce soave
soavemente, e cria

Let a carefree hand unbind a head of gleaming fair hair, cluster-ing, smooth, loosed about living flowers, I seem to see in that action the fair portrait of the purple Dawn;
    or let another show me hair as black as ink, gathered up or fall-ing above two burning stars, I compare her no less to the lovely calm of quiet Night.
    If an angelic little creature laughs, that face of hers is an arrow; if she weeps, her weeping is a wound in my life; if she neither weeps nor laughs, without arrow, or wound, she still kills me.
    A nymph who looses her soft voice softly, now high, now deep,

angelica armonia,
chi fia che non invoglie
a baciar quella bocca, onde la scioglie?

Ove fra lieta schiera
fanciulla lusinghiera
batta con dite argute
dolci fila minute,
qual alma non fia vaga
d'aver da man sì dotta e laccio e piaga?

Veder per piagge o valli
giovinetta che balli,
in vago abito adorno
portar con arte intorno
il piede e la persona;
e qual rustico cor non imprigiona?

Se m'incontro in bellezza
a star tra l' coro avvezza
de le nove sirene
di Pindo e d'Ippocrene,
con gli sguardi e co' carmi
può ferirmi in un punto e può sanarmi.

and utters angelic harmonies, who is there who does not have the desire to kiss that mouth whence she frees her voice?

Where an alluring girl in a gay company strikes the sweet, fine cords with subtle fingers, what soul would not desire to be caught and wounded by so expert a hand?

See a young girl dancing by bank or valley, made prettier by a charming dress, who skilfully whirls body and foot; and what rustic heart does she not imprison?

If I meet a beauty that can take her place beside the nine sirens of Pindus and Hippocrene, with her looks and songs she can wound me and, at the same time, heal me.

Havvi donna gentile
ch'al ciel alza il mio stile.
Costei, ch'ama il mio canto,
amo e bramo altrettanto,
e stato cangerei
sol per esserle in sen co' versi miei.

Altra, qualor mi legge,
mi riprende e corregge.
Allor convien ch'io dica:
– O pur l'avessi amica,
o soggiacer felice
a sì bella maestra e correttrice!

Insomma, e queste e quelle
per me tutte son belle,
di tutte arde il desio.
Marcello, or, s'avess'io
mill'alme e mille cori,
sarei nido capace a tanti amori?

There is a courteous lady who extols my style to heaven. Her who loves my song I love and desire as much, and I would change my nature to be in her bosom with my poems.

Another, when she reads me, reproves and corrects me. Then must I needs say: 'O might I yet have her as lover, – o happy submission to so lovely a teacher and corrector!'

In short, these ones and those, they are all beautiful to me, my desire burns for them all. Now, Marcello, if I had a thousand souls and a thousand hearts, would I be a nest large enough for so many loves?

PIETRO METASTASIO

La Libertà

GRAZIE agl' inganni tuoi,
alfin respiro, o Nice;
alfin d'un infelice
ebber gli Dei pietà:
    sento da' lacci suoi,
sento che l'alma è sciolta;
non sogno questa volta,
non sogno libertà.

Mancò l'antico ardore,
e son tranquillo a segno,
che in me non trova sdegno
per mascherarsi amor.
    Non cangio più colore
quando il tuo nome ascolto;
quando ti miro in volto
più non mi batte il cor.

Liberty

THANKS to your deceits, at last I can breathe, o Nice; at last the Gods have had pity upon an unfortunate man: I feel that my soul is freed from its snares; I am not dreaming this time, I am not dreaming of liberty.

The old ardour has failed, and I am so calm that love does not find any scorn in me to mask itself with. I no longer change colour when I hear your name; when I look you in the face, my heart no longer quickens.

Sogno, ma te non miro
sempre ne' sogni miei;
mi desto, e tu non sei
il primo mio pensier.

    Lungi da te m'aggiro,
senza bramarti mai;
son teco, e non mi fai
nè pena, nè piacer.

Di tua beltà ragiono,
nè intenerir mi sento;
i torti miei rammento,
e non mi so sdegnar.

    Confuso più non sono
quando mi vieni appresso;
col mio rivale istesso
posso di te parlar.

Volgimi il guardo altero,
parlami in volto umano;
il tuo disprezzo è vano,
è vano il tuo favor.

    Chè più l'usato impero
quei labbri in me non hanno;
quegli occhi più non sanno
la via di questo cor.

I dream but I do not see you constantly in my dreams; I wake, and you are not my first thought. I go about in places far removed from you without ever wishing for you; I am with you, and it gives me neither pain nor joy.

I speak of your beauty, nor feel myself melting; I recall my misfortunes, and cannot be offended. I am no longer confused when you approach me; I can talk of you to my rival himself.

Turn your haughty look on me, speak to me with kind face; your contempt is vain, and vain, your favour. For those lips no longer have their accustomed sway over me; those eyes no longer know the way to this heart.

Quel che or m'alletta o spiace,
se lieto o mesto or sono,
già non è più tuo dono,
già colpa tua non è:
    che senza te mi piace
la selva il colle il prato;
ogni soggiorno ingrato
m'annoia ancor con te.

Odi, s'io son sincero:
ancor mi sembri bella,
ma non mi sembri quella
che paragon non ha:
    e (non t'offenda il vero)
nel tuo leggiadro aspetto
or vedo alcun difetto,
che mi parea beltà.

Quando lo stral spezzai,
(confesso il mio rossore)
spezzar m'intesi il core,
mi parve di morir.
    Ma, per uscir di guai,
per non vedersi oppresso,
per riacquistar se stesso
tutto si può soffrir.

What delights or displeases me, if I am merry or sad, is no longer
your gift, nor your fault: for without you I take pleasure in wood
and hill and meadow; even with you every joyless place is tedious.

Listen, to judge if I am sincere: you still strike me as beautiful,
but you do not seem the woman who has no equal: and (do not be
offended by the truth) I now see in your glad face some blemishes
which I once took for beauties.

When I broke off the arrow, I felt my heart breaking, (I confess
my blushes), I seemed to be dying. But we can suffer anything to
free ourselves from woes, to see ourselves no longer tyrannized, to
repossess ourselves.

Nel visco, in cui s'avvenne
quell' augellin talora,
lascia le penne ancora,
ma torna in libertà:
    poi le perdute penne
in pochi dì rinnova;
cauto divien per prova,
nè più tradir si fa.

So che non credi estinto
in me l'incendio antico,
perchè sì spesso il dico,
perchè tacer non so.
    Quel naturale istinto,
Nice, a parlar mi sprona,
per cui ciascun ragiona
de' rischi che passò.

Dopo il crudele cimento
narra i passati sdegni,
di sue ferite i segni
mostra il guerrier così.
    Mostra così contento
schiavo, che uscì di pena,
la barbara catena
che strascinava un dì.

In the lime where it has chanced to come, the little bird sometimes leaves even feathers, but returns to liberty: then grows its
lost feathers again in a few days; becomes wary from experience,
and does not let itself be betrayed another time.

I know you do not think the old flame dead in me, because I say
it so often, because I do not know how to keep silent. The natural
instinct which makes every one dwell on risks they have escaped –
that, Nice, spurs me to talk.

After the cruel danger we tell of threats that are past, the warrior
in this way shows the marks of his wounds. In this way the slave,
who has escaped from pain, happily shows the barbarous chain
which he once dragged.

Parlo, ma sol parlando
me soddisfar procuro:
parlo, ma nulla io curo
che tu mi presti fe';

    parlo, ma non dimando
se approvi i detti miei,
nè se tranquilla sei
nel ragionar di me.

Io lascio un'incostante,
tu perdi un cor sincero:
non so di noi primiero
chi s'abbia a consolar.

    So che un sì fido amante
non troverà più Nice;
che un'altra ingannatrice
è facile a trovar.

Nel comporre l' Olimpiade

Sogni e favole io fingo; e pure in carte
mentre favole e sogni orno e disegno,
in lor, folle ch'io son, prendo tal parte,
che del mal che inventai piango e mi sdegno.

I speak, but in speaking have satisfaction myself alone: I speak, but do not in the least care that you should credit what I say; I speak, but do not ask if you approve my words, nor if you are calm in talking of me.

I leave an inconstant heart, you lose a sincere one: I do not know which of us will be first to be consoled. I know that Nice will never again find so faithful a lover; that it is easy to find another deceiving woman.

While Writing the Olympiad

Dreams and fables I fashion; and even while I sketch and elaborate fables and dreams upon paper, fond as I am, I so enter into them that I weep and am offended at ills I invent. But am I wiser

Ma forse, allor che non m'inganna l'arte,
più saggio sono? È l'agitato ingegno
forse allor più tranquillo? O forse parte
da più salda cagion l'amor, lo sdegno?

Ah! che non sol quelle ch'io canto o scrivo
favole son; ma quanto temo e spero,
tutto è menzogna, e delirando io vivo.
Sogno della mia vita è il corso intero.
Deh tu, Signor, quando a destarmi arrivo,
fa' ch'io trovi riposo in sen del vero.

UGO FOSCOLO

Di sè stesso

PERCHÈ taccia il rumor d'una catena,
di lagrime, di speme, e d'amor vivo,
e di silenzi; chè pietà mi affrena
se con lei parlo, o di lei penso o scrivo.
Tu sol mi ascolti, o solitario rivo,
ove ogni notte Amor seco mi mena,
qui affido il pianto e i miei danni descrivo,
qui tutta verso del dolor la piena.

when art does not deceive me? Is my disturbed mind perhaps
calmer then? Or does love and scorn perhaps spring from firmer
cause?

Ah, not only what I sing and write are fables; but what I fear
and hope for, all is falsehood, and I live in a feverishness. The
whole course of my life has been dream. O Lord, let me find rest
in the bosom of truth, when finally I come to wake.

On Himself

So that the stirring of a chain may be silent, I live on tears, on
hope, on love, and silences; for tenderness restrains me, if I speak
with her, or think or write of her. You alone listen to me, o lonely
stream, where every night Love leads me in his company, here I
confide my tears and declare my sufferings, and here pour out the
fullness of my grief.

E narro come i grandi occhi ridenti
arsero d'immortal raggio il mio core,
come la rosea bocca, e i rilucenti
odorati capelli, ed il candore
delle divine membra, e i cari accenti
m'insegnarono alfin pianger d'amore.

Alla sua donna lontana

MERITAMENTE, però ch'io potei
abbandonarti, or grido alle frementi
onde che batton l'alpi, e i pianti miei
sperdon sordi del Tirreno i venti.
Sperai, poichè mi han tratto uomini e Dei
in lungo esilio fra spergiure genti
dal bel paese ove or meni sì rei,
me sospirando, i tuoi giorni fiorenti,
sperai che il tempo, e i duri casi, e queste
rupi ch' io varco anelando, e le eterne,
ov'io qual fiera dormo, atre foreste,
sarien ristoro al mio cor sanguinente;
Ahi, vota speme! Amor fra l'ombre inferne
seguirammi immortale, onnipotente.

And tell how those great laughing eyes burnt my heart with an immortal ray, how the rose-like mouth, and the shining fragrant locks, and the whiteness of the divine limbs, and the dear cadence taught me at last to weep for love.

To His Distant Love

RIGHTLY, since I could leave you, do I now cry to the trembling waves that beat upon the Alps, and the Tyrrhenian winds deafly scatter my lament. I hoped, after men and Gods dragged me into long exile among peoples self-betrayed from the fair region where you so poorly pass your Florentine days, sighing for me, I hoped that time, and hardships, and these rocks which I cross panting, and the eternal black forests where I sleep like a wild beast, that these might mean comfort to my bleeding heart. Ah, empty hope! Love will follow me amid the infernal shades immortal, all-powerful.

Il proprio ritratto

SOLCATA ho fronte, occhi incavati intenti;
crin fulvo, emunte guance, ardito aspetto;
labbri tumidi, arguti, al riso lenti,
capo chino, bel collo, irsuto petto;
membra esatte; vestir semplice eletto;
ratti i passi, il pensier, gli atti, gli accenti:
prodigo, sobrio; umano, ispido, schietto;
avverso al mondo, avversi a me gli eventi.

Mesto i più giorni e solo; ognor pensoso,
alle speranze incredulo e al timore;
il pudor mi fa vile; e prode l'ira;
cauta in me parla la ragion; ma il core,
ricco di vizi e di virtù, delira –
Morte, tu mi darai fama e riposo.

Alla sera

FORSE perchè della fatal quiete
tu sei l'immago a me sì cara vieni,
o sera! E quando ti corteggian liete
le nubi estive e i zeffiri sereni,

Self-portrait

MY brow is furrowed, my eyes, sunk and intense; hair, tawny,
cheeks, colourless, look, bold; thick, well-drawn lips, slow to
laughter, bent head, fine neck, my chest, hairy; compact limbs;
choice and simple style of dress; quick in step, in thought, in
speech: prodigal and sober; kindly and bristling, open; hostile to
the world, events are hostile to me.

Melancholy most days, and alone; constantly thoughtful; doubting before hopes and fears; fine modesty makes me craven; and
anger, brave; reason speaks cautioning me, but my heart, rich in
vices and virtues, raves – Death, you will give me fame and rest.

To Evening

PERHAPS because you are the image of that fatal quiet your coming is so dear to me, o evening! When the summer clouds and calm

e quando dal nevoso aere inquiete
tenebre e lunghe all'universo meni
sempre scendi invocata, e le secrete
vie del mio cor soavemente tieni.

Vagar mi fai co' miei pensier su l'orme
che vanno al nulla eterno; e intanto fugge
questo reo tempo, e van col lui le torme
delle cure onde meco egli si strugge;
e mentre io guardo la tua pace, dorme
quello spirto guerrier ch'entro mi rugge.

A Zacinto

Nè più mai toccherò le sacre sponde
ove il mio corpo fanciulletto giacque,
Zacinto mia, che te specchi nell'onde
del greco mar da cui vergine nacque
Venere, e fea quelle isole feconde
col suo primo sorriso, onde non tacque
le tue limpide nubi, e le tue fronde
l'inclito verso di colui che l'acque

breezes woo you, and again when from the snowy air you bring
long and troubled shades to the world, you always come down as
one prayed for, and gently follow out the secret ways of my heart.

You make me linger in thought, upon the paths that go towards
eternal nothingness; and, meanwhile, this evil time flies, and with it
go the swarms of cares in which it wastes itself and me; and as I
look upon your peace, that warrior spirit which roars in me is
sleeping.

To Zante

NEVER more shall I touch the sacred shores where my infant body
lay, my Zante, who look at yourself in the mirror of the Greek
waves from which the virgin Venus rose to life, and made these
islands fertile with her first smile; so that the rough verse does not
pass over in silence your serene clouds and leafiness, the verse of

cantò fatali ed il diverso esiglio
per cui bello di fama e di sventura
baciò la sua petrosa Itaca Ulisse.
Tu non altro che il canto avrai del figlio,
o materna mia terra; a noi prescrisse
il fato illacrimata sepoltura.

In morte del fratello Giovanni

Un dì, s'io non andrò sempre fuggendo
di gente in gente, mi vedrai seduto
su la tua pietra, o fratel mio, gemendo
il fior dei tuoi gentili anni caduto.
La madre or sol, suo dì tardo traendo,
parla di me col tuo cenere muto:
ma io deluse a voi le palme tendo;
e se da lunge i miei tetti saluto,
sento gli avversi Numi, e le secrete
cure che al viver tuo furon tempesta,
e prego anch'io nel tuo porto quiete.
Questo di tanta speme oggi mi resta!
Straniere genti, l'ossa mie rendete
allora al petto della madre mesta.

him who sang the fatal waters and the various exile through which, lovely with fame and misfortune, Ulysses came to kiss his rocky Ithaca. You will not have more than the song of your child, o my mother earth; for us fate has ordained an unwept sepulchre.

Upon the Death of His Brother John

One day, if I am not to keep fleeing from people to people, you will see me seated upon your stone, o my brother, weeping for the fallen flower of your generous years. Our mother alone now, drawing out her late day, speaks to your dumb ashes of me: but I stretch out vain hands to you both; and if from afar I hail the roofs of home, I am aware of the hostile Gods, and the secret cares which were a tempest to your life, and I too pray for quietness in your haven. This is what is left to me today of so much hope! Foreign peoples, give back my bones then to the bosom of my sad mother.

A Luigia Pallavicini caduta da cavallo

I BALSAMI beati
per te le Grazie apprestino,
per te i lini odorati
che a Citerea porgeano
quando profano spino
le punse il piè divino,

quel dì che insana empiea
il sacro Ida di gemiti,
e col crine tergea,
e bagnava di lagrime
il sanguinoso petto
al ciprio giovinetto.

Or te piangon gli Amori,
te fra le Dive liguri
Regina e Diva! e fiori
votivi all'ara portano
d'onde il grand'arco suona
del figlio di Latona.

To Luigia Pallavicini Who Fell from Her Horse

LET the Graces make ready the blessed oils for you, for you the
scented garments that they held out for Venus when a profane
thorn pricked her foot divine,
   that day when distractedly she filled sacred Ida with her moaning, and wiped with her hair, and bathed with her tears the bloody
breast of the Cypriot youth.
   Now the Cupids weep for you, you Queen and Goddess among
the Ligurian Goddesses! and bear offerings of flowers to the altar
from whence the great bow of Latona's son rings out.

E te chiama la danza
ove l'aure portavano
insolita fragranza,
allor che a' nodi indocile
la chioma al roseo braccio
ti fu gentile impaccio.

Tal nel lavacro immersa,
che fior, dall'inachio
clivo cadendo, versa,
Palla i dall'elmo liberi
crin sulla man che gronda
contien fuori dell'onda.

Armoniosi accenti
dal tuo labbro volavano,
e dagli occhi ridenti
traluceano di Venere
i disdegni e le paci,
la speme, il pianto, e i baci.

And the dance calls for you, to which the breezes came with rare
fragrance when, untamed by its knots, your hair formed a gentle
impediment to your rosy arm.

Just as when Pallas, immersed in the bath that fills with the pouring stream from the Inachian cliff, holds her hair, free of the helmet,
out of the water with dripping hand.

Loving accents flew from your lips, and in your laughing eyes
shone the scorn and the peace of Venus, the hope, the weeping, and
the kisses.

Deh! perchè hai le gentili
forme e l'ingegno docile
volto a studi virili?
Perchè non dell'Aonie
seguivi, incauta, l'arte,
ma i ludi aspri di Marte?

Invan presaghi i venti
il polveroso agghiacciano
petto e le reni ardenti
dell'inquieto alipede,
ed irritante il morso
accresce impeto al corso.

Ardon gli sguardi, fuma
la bocca, agita l'ardua
testa, vola la spuma,
ed i manti volubili
lorda, e l'incerto freno,
ed il candido seno;

O why have you turned your gentle form and mild understanding to manly pursuits? Why did you follow, rash one, not the
Aonian arts but the rough games of Mars?

Vainly prophetic the winds froze the dusty chest and the burning
haunches of the restless wingèd steed, and the bit, chafing, gave
greater impulse to its career.

Its glances burn, its mouth steams, the high head shakes, the
foam flies, and streaks the flowing skirts, and the uncertain bridle,
and the white bosom;

e il sudor piove, e i crini
sul collo irti svolazzano,
suonan gli antri marini
allo incalzato scalpito
della zampa che caccia
polve e sassi in sua traccia.

Già dal lito si slancia
sordo ai clamori e al fremito;
già già fino alla pancia
nuota . .". e ingorde si gonfiano
non più memori l'acque
che una Dea da lor nacque.

Se non che il re dell'onde
dolente ancor d'Ippolito
surse per le profonde
vie del tirreno talamo,
e respinse il furente
col cenno onnipotente.

and sweat rains down, and the mane flutters on the bristling neck, the ocean caves resound to the hurried beating of the hoof that spurns dust and stones from its track.

Already it throws itself from the shore deaf to the cries and the shuddering; now, now up to the belly it swims ... and the waters swell, as if they gorged their fill, no longer mindful that a Goddess was born from them.

But, no, the king of the waves, still grieving for Hippolytus, rose from the deep paths of the Tyrrhenian bed, and threw back the furious beast with an all-powerful sign.

Quei dal flutto arretrosse
ricalcitrando e, orribile!
sovra l'anche rizzosse;
scuote l'arcion, te misera
su la petrosa riva
strascinando mal viva.

Pèra chi osò primiero
discortese commettere
a infedele corsiero
l'agil fianco femineo,
e aprì con rio consiglio
nuovo a beltà periglio!

Chè or non vedrei le rose
del tuo volto sì languide,
non le luci amorose
spiar ne' guardi medici
speranza lusinghiera
della beltà primiera.

It drew back from the surge, trampling backwards and, horror!
reared up; it shakes the saddle and drags you, unfortunate one,
scarce alive, over the stony beach.

May he perish who first was unmannerly enough to dare to en-
trust the soft female side to faithless steed, and, with evil counsel,
uncover a new danger to beauty.

For now I would not see the roses of your face so lifeless, nor
your loving eyes search the doctor's looks for a flattering hope of
your first beauty.

Di Cintia il cocchio aurato
le cerve un dì traevano,
ma al ferino ululato
per terrore insanirono,
e dalla rupe etnea
precipitâr la Dea.

Gioian d'invido riso
le abitatrici olimpie,
perchè l'eterno viso,
silenzioso e pallido,
cinto apparia d'un velo
ai conviti del cielo:

ma ben piansero il giorno
che dalle danze efesie
lieta facea ritorno
fra le devote vergini,
e al ciel salia più bella
di Febo la sorella.

One day the hinds were drawing the golden coach of Diana, but they went mad with terror at the wild beasts' howling, and hurled the Goddess from the Etnean cliff.

The female dwellers on Olympus rejoiced with envious smile, because the immortal face, silent and pale, was veiled when she appeared before the guests of heaven:

but they sorely wept the day she returned happy to the Ephesian dances among the dedicated virgins, and the sister of Phoebus rose more lovely in heaven.

De' Sepolcri

(A Ippolito Pindemonte)

DEORUM MANIUM IURA SANCTA
SUNTO (XII TAB.)

ALL'OMBRA de' cipressi e dentro l'urne
confortate di pianto è forse il sonno
della morte men duro? Ove più il Sole
per me alla terra non fecondi questa
bella d'erbe famiglia e d'animali,
e quando vaghe di lusinghe innanzi
a me non danzeran l'ore future,
nè da te, dolce amico, udrò più il verso
e la mesta armonia che lo governa,
nè più nel cor mi parlerà lo spirto
delle vergini Muse e dell'Amore,
unico spirto a mia vita raminga,
qual fia ristoro a' dì perduti un sasso
che distingua le mie dalle infinite
ossa che in terra e in mar semina morte?

On Tombs

(To Ippolito Pindemonte)

LET THE LAWS BY THE GODS' HANDS
BE SACRED (XII TAB)

IN the shade of cypresses and within urns comforted by weeping is
the sleep of death perhaps less hard? When for me the sun no
longer makes this fair family of plants and animals fertile, and when
future hours will not dance before me, lovely with vain promise,
and when I shall not hear your verse, sweet friend, nor the sad
harmony that sways it, nor in my heart will the spirit any longer
speak of the virgin Muses and of love, only spirit of my wandering
life, what recompense for days lost will a stone be that may mark
out my bones from the infinite number that death sows on land and

Vero è ben, Pindemonte! Anche la Speme,
ultima Dea, fugge i sepolcri; e involve
tutte cose l'obblio nella sua notte;
e una forza operosa le affatica
di moto in moto; e l'uomo e le sue tombe
e l'estreme sembianze e le reliquie
della terra e del ciel traveste il tempo.

Ma perchè pria del tempo a sè il mortale
invidierà l'illusion che spento
pur lo sofferma al limitar di Dite?
Non vive ei forse anche sotterra, quando
gli sarà muta l'armonia del giorno,
se può destarla con soavi cure
nella mente de' suoi? Celeste è questa
corrispondenza d'amorosi sensi,
celeste dote è negli umani; e spesso
per lei si vive con l'amico estinto
e l'estinto con noi, se pia la terra
che lo raccolse infante e lo nutriva,
nel suo grembo materno ultimo asilo

in the sea? True it is indeed, Pindemonte! Even Hope, the last of
goddesses, flies from tombs; and oblivion wraps all things in its
night; and a busy force wears them from one movement to the next;
and time disguises man and his tombs and last appearances and the
relics of earth and sky.

But why, before time, will mortal man deny himself the illusion
which, lost, still arrests him on the threshold of the underworld?
Does he perhaps not live even below ground, when day's harmony
is silent to him, if he can awaken it with sweet cares in the minds of
his own? Heavenly is this meeting of tender feelings, a heavenly
gift to humans; and often through it we live with the departed
friend and the departed with us, if reverently the earth which re-
ceived him as a child and fed him, keeps his relics sacred from the

porgendo, sacre le reliquie rendà
dall'insultar de' nembi e dal profano
piede del vulgo, e serbi un sasso il nome,
e di fiori odorata arbore amica
le ceneri di molli ombre consoli.

Sol chi non lascia eredità d'affetti
poca gioia ha dell'urna; e se pur mira
dopo l'esequie, errar vede il suo spirto
fra 'l compianto de' templi acherontei,
o ricovrarsi sotto le grandi ale
del perdono d'Iddio: ma la sua polve
lascia alle ortiche di deserta gleba
ove nè donna innamorata preghi,
nè passeggier solingo oda il sospiro
che dal tumulo a noi manda Natura.

Pur nuova legge impone oggi i sepolcri
fuor de' guardi pietosi, e il nome a' morti
contende. E senza tomba giace il tuo
sacerdote, o Talìa, che a te cantando
nel suo povero tetto educò un lauro
con lungo amore, e t'appendea corone;

assault of lightning and the profane feet of the crowd, offering a last
refuge in its motherly lap, and if a stone retains his name, and a
fragrant tree, kind with flowers, consoles his ashes with soft shade.

Only he who leaves no inheritance of affection has little joy in
urns; and if he should look beyond funeral rites, he sees his spirit
wandering amid the general weeping of Acherontian temples, or
stealing under the great wings of the pardon of God: but his dust
he leaves to the nettles of the desert where no loving woman prays,
nor lonely traveller hears the sigh that Nature sends to us from the
tomb.

Yet a new law today sets graves beyond pitying glances, and to
the dead denies their name. And your priest, o Thalia, lies without
sepulchre, he, who singing to you in his poor dwelling, raised up a
laurel with enduring love, and hung crowns to you there; and you,

e tu gli ornavi del tuo riso i canti
che il lombardo pungean Sardanapàlo,
cui solo è dolce il muggito de' buoi
che dagli antri abdùani e dal Ticino
lo fan d'ozi beato e di vivande.
O bella Musa, ove sei tu? Non sento
spirar l'ambrosia, indizio del tuo Nume,
fra queste piante ov'io siedo e sospiro
il mio tetto materno. E tu venivi
e sorridevi a lui sotto quel tiglio
ch'or con dimesse frondi va fremendo
perchè non copre, o Dea, l'urna del vecchio
cui già di calma era cortese e d'ombre.
Forse tu fra plebei tumuli guardi
vagolando, ove dorma il sacro capo
del tuo Parini? A lui non ombre pose
tra le sue mura la città, lasciva
d'evirati cantori allettatrice,
non pietra, non parola; e forse l'ossa
col mozzo capo gl'insanguina il ladro
che lasciò sul patibolo i delitti.

with your laughter, enriched the songs in which he struck the
Lombard Sardanapalus, who only hearkens to the lowing, that
comes from the Abduan hollows and the Ticino, of cattle that
make him blissful with ease and feasting. O fair Muse, where are
you? I do not scent the ambrosia exhaled, which is sign of your
presence, here where I sit among these plants and sigh for my
mother's house. And you would come and smile upon him under
that lime-tree which now with downcast, leafy boughs keeps shiver-
ing, because it does not cover, o Goddess, the urn of that old man
to whom it was once generous in giving calm and shade. Perhaps,
wandering among humble graves, you look for the spot where
sleeps the sacred head of your Parini? This city, the whorish nurse
of unmanned singers, gave him no shade within its walls, no stone,
no word; and perhaps the thief who parted from his crimes upon
the scaffold, now stains, with the blood of his severed head, those

Senti raspar fra le macerie e i bronchi
la derelitta cagna ramingando
su le fosse e famelica ululando;
e uscir del teschio, ove fuggìa la Luna,
l'upupa e svolazzar su per le croci
sparse per la funerea campagna,
e l'immonda accusar col luttuoso
singulto i rai di che son pie le stelle
alle obbliate sepolture. Indarno
sul tuo poeta, o Dea, preghi rugiade
dalla squallida notte. Ahi! su gli estinti
non sorge fiore, ove non sia d'umane
lodi onorato e d'amoroso pianto.

Dal dì che nozze e tribunali ed are
dier alle umane belve essere pietose
di sè stesse e d'altrui, toglieano i vivi
all'etere maligno ed alle fere
i miserandi avanzi che Natura
con veci eterne a sensi altri destina.

bones. You hear the stray bitch, that roams over the burial pits
and howls from hunger, scraping among the rubble and undergrowth; and hear the owl, that flies out from the skull where it
shunned the moon, and glides among the crosses scattered over
the funereal scene, defiled bird, with mournful sob, cry out against
the rays which the stars in pity shed on forgotten graves. Vainly,
o Goddess, do you pray for dews to descend upon your poet from
the dismal night. Ah! no flower rises over the deceased, unless it is
honoured by human praise and tears of love.

From the day that marriage and law courts and altars bade
human animals be tender of themselves and of one another, the
living took those remains, which Nature with constant varying
destines for other purposes, from the corrupting atmosphere and
from wild beasts. Tombs were the testimony of deeds, and the altar

Testimonianza a' fasti eran le tombe,
ed are a' figli e uscian quindi i responsi
de' domestici Lari, e fu temuto
su la polve degli avi il giuramento:
religion che con diversi riti
le virtù patrie e la pietà congiunta
tradussero per lungo ordine d'anni.
Non sempre i sassi sepolcrali a' templi
fean pavimento; nè agli incensi avvolto
de' cadaveri il lezzo i supplicanti
contaminò; nè le città fur meste
d'effigiati scheletri: le madri
balzan ne' sonni esterrefatte, e tendono
nude le braccia su l'amato capo
del lor caro lattante onde nol desti
il gemer lungo di persona morta
chiedente la venal prece agli eredi
dal santuario. Ma cipressi e cedri
di puri effluvi i zefiri impregnando
perenne verde protendean su l'urne
per memoria perenne, e preziosi
vasi accoglean le lacrime votive.

for a man's sons, and from them came the answers of the household gods, and an oath sworn upon the dust of ancestors was awful; a religion which fatherly virtues and wedded devotion transmitted for a long succession of years. Sepulchral stones did not always serve as the floors of temples; nor did the stench of corpses surrounded with incense infect those who came to pray; nor were cities sad with figured skeletons: mothers start terrified in sleep, and stretch their arms, bare, over the beloved head of their dear suckling so that the continuous moaning of one dead begging his heirs to grant him the sanctuary's hireling prayer does not wake her child. But cypresses and cedars loading the breeze with their freshness stretched out perennial green over urns in perennial remembrance, and precious vases held the suppliant tears. Friends

Rapian gli amici una favilla al Sole
a illuminar la sotterranea notte,
perchè gli occhi dell'uom cercan morendo
il Sole; e tutti l'ultimo sospiro
mandano i petti alla fuggente luce.
Le fontane versando acque lustrali
amaranti educavano e viole
su la funebre zolla; e chi sedea
a libar latte e a raccontar sue pene
ai cari estinti, una fragranza intorno
sentia qual d'aura de' beati Elisi.
Pietosa insania che fa cari gli orti
de' suburbani avelli alle britanne
vergini dove le conduce amore
della perduta madre, ove clementi
pregaro i Geni del ritorno al prode
che tronca fe' la trionfata nave
del maggior pino, e si scavò la bara.
Ma ove dorme il furor d'inclite geste
e sien ministri al vivere civile
l'opulenza e il tremore, inutil pompa
e inaugurate immagini dell'Orco
sorgon cippi e marmorei monumenti.

stole a spark from the Sun to light the subterranean night, because the eyes of man in dying search out the Sun; and all breasts send their last sigh to the light that flies. The fountains pouring waters of purification raised up amaranths and violets on the turf of the grave; and whoever sat there to pour out offerings of milk and to tell over his sorrows to the dear departed, sensed a fragrance around him as of the air of blessed Elysium. A tender madness, that makes the gardens of suburban cemeteries dear to British girls, where they are led by love for a mother lost, where they implore the Fates to be favourable to the return of the brave man who had the tallest mast cut from the ship he overcame, and hewed his coffin from it.* But where the fever for bold deeds sleeps and wealth and fear are the ministers of civil life, half columns and marble monuments rise as useless pomp and unpropitious images of Mammon. Already the

---

* Nelson.

Già il dotto e il ricco ed il patrizio vulgo,
decoro e mente al bello italo regno,
nelle adulate reggie ha sepoltura
già vivo, e i stemmi unica laude. A noi
Morte apparecchi riposato albergo,
ove una volta la fortuna cessi
dalle vendette, e l'amistà raccolga
non di tesori eredità, ma caldi
sensi di liberal carme l'esempio.

A egregie cose il forte animo accendono
l'urne de' forti, o Pindemonte; e bella
e santa fanno al peregrin la terra
che le ricetta. Io quando il monumento
vidi ove posa il corpo di quel grande
che temprando lo scettro a' regnatori
gli allòr ne sfronda, ed alle genti svela
di che lagrime grondi e di che sangue;
e l'arca di colui che nuovo Olimpo
alzò in Roma a' Celesti; e di chi vide

learned and rich and noble mob, the ornament and mind of the fair
Italian kingdom, have their grave still living, in the flattered courts,
and their family crest as their only fame. For us let death prepare a
restful abode, when fortune has once ceased from vengeance, and let
friendship gather no treasure of possessions but the warm feelings
and the example of liberal song.

The urns of the strong fire the strong soul to excelling deeds, o
Pindemonte; and make the earth that is their receptacle lovely and
holy to the pilgrim. When I myself saw the monument where lies
the body of that great man who, even as he strengthened the sceptre
of rulers, took leaves from their laurel, and revealed to peoples with
what tears and with what blood it runs; * and the ark of him who
in Rome raised a new Olympus to the Deities; † and of him who

---

* Machiavelli.   † Michelangelo.

sotto l'etereo padiglion rotarsi
più mondi, e il Sole irradiarli immoto,
onde all'Anglo che tanta ala vi stese
sgombrò primo le vie del firmamento;
te beata, gridai, per le felici
aure pregne di vita, e pe' lavacri
che da' suoi gioghi a te versa Apennino!
Lieta dell' aer tuo veste la Luna
di luce limpidissima i tuoi colli
per vendemmia festanti, e le convalli
popolate di case e d'oliveti
mille di fiori al ciel mandano incensi:
e tu prima, Firenze, udivi il carme
che allegrò l'ira al Ghibellin fuggiasco,
e tu i cari parenti e l'idioma
desti a quel dolce di Calliope labbro
che Amore in Grecia nudo e nudo in Roma
d'un velo candidissimo adornando,
rendea nel grembo a Venere Celeste:

saw more worlds turning under the ethereal canopy, and the Sun, motionless, lighting them,* whence he first cleared the ways of the firmament for the Englishman who there stretched so great a wing;† I cried out, you blessed one, for your happy breezes stirring with life, and for the streams that Apennine pours down to you from her crests! The moon, glad with your air, clothes your hills, that are rejoicing for the wine-harvest, with clearest light, and the clustering valleys peopled with houses and olive groves send up a thousand flowering incenses: and you first, Florence, heard the song that lightened the anger of the fugitive Ghibelline,‡ and you gave parents and speech to that soft lip of Calliope § who, adorning Love, naked in Greece and naked in Rome, with a veil of the whitest, restored her to the lap of Heavenly Venus: but more

---

* Galileo. † Newton. ‡ Dante. § Petrarch.

ma più beata chè in un tempio accolte
serbi l'itale glorie, uniche forse
da che le mal vietate Alpi e l'alterna
onnipotenza delle umane sorti
armi e sostanze t'invadeano ed are
e patria e, tranne la memoria, tutto.
Che ove speme di gloria agli animosi
intelletti rifulga ed all'Italia,
quindi trarrem gli auspici. E a questi marmi
venne spesso Vittorio ad ispirarsi.
Irato a' patri Numi, errava muto
ove Arno è più deserto, i campi e il cielo
desioso mirando; e poi che nullo
vivente aspetto gli molcea la cura,
qui posava l'austero; e avea sul volto
il pallor della morte e la speranza.
Con questi grandi abita eterno: e l'ossa
fremono amor di patria. Ah sì! da quella
religiosa pace un Nume parla:
e nutria contro a' Persi in Maratona
ove Atene sacrò tombe a' suoi prodi,

blessed because you keep, gathered in one temple, Italian glories,
that are unique perhaps, since the ill-contested Alps and the changing omnipotence of human fate have spoiled you of arms and possessions and altars and native land and everything, except memory.
So when hope of glory comes to shine upon daring minds and
upon Italy, from these shall we draw auguries. And to these marble
tombs Vittorio * came often for inspiration. Angry with his country's gods, he would wander silently where the Arno is most barren, and look longingly at the fields and the sky; and when no living sight softened his cares, here the austere man rested; and on his
face there was the pallor of death and hope. He lives eternally with
these great: and his bones tremble with love for his country. Ah,
even so! a deity speaks from that religious peace: and fed the Greek
valour and anger against the Persians at Marathon where Athens

* Alfieri.

la virtù greca e l'ira. Il navigante
che veleggiò quel mar sotto l'Eubea,
vedea per l'ampia oscurità scintille
balenar d'elmi e di cozzanti brandi,
fumar le pire igneo vapor, corrusche
d'armi ferree vedea larve guerriere
cercar la pugna; e all'orror de' notturni
silenzi si spandea lungo ne' campi
di falangi un tumulto, e un suon di tube,
e un incalzar di cavalli accorrenti
scalpitanti su gli elmi a' moribondi,
e pianto, ed inni, e delle Parche il canto.

Felice te che il regno ampio de' venti,
Ippolito, a' tuoi verdi anni correvi!
E se il piloto ti drizzò l'antenna
oltre l'isole egee, d'antichi fatti
certo udisti suonar dell'Ellesponto
i liti, e la marea mugghiar portando
alle prode retee l'armi d'Achille
sovra l'ossa d'Ajace: a' generosi
giusta di glorie dispensiera è morte;

consecrated tombs to her brave. The sailor who coasted Euboea
saw through the broad dusk sparks flashing off from helmets and
crashing swords, and pyres reeking with fiery smoke, saw phantom
warriors glaring with steely arms seek out combat; and in the awfulness of the silences of night a tumult of formations spread far into
the plains, and a sound of trumpets, and an urging of horses as they
rushed forward, trampling on the helmets of the dying, and
lamentation, and hymns, and the song of the Fates.

Happy you who travelled the broad reign of the winds, Ippolito,
in your green years! And if the helmsman set the tiller beyond the
Aegean Isles, certainly you heard the shores of the Hellespont resound with ancient deeds, and the surge bellowing as it brought the
arms of Achilles to the Retean beaches, over the tomb of Ajax:
death is the fair bestower of glories to the great-hearted; nor did

nè senno astuto nè favor di regi
all'Itaco le spoglie ardue serbava
chè alla poppa raminga le ritolse
l'onda incitata dagl'inferni Dei.

E me che i tempi ed il desio d'onore
fan per diversa gente ir fuggitivo,
me ad evocar gli eroi chiamin le Muse
del mortale pensiero animatrici.
Siedon custodi de' sepolcri, e quando
il tempo con sue fredde ale vi spazza
fin le rovine, le Pimplee fan lieti
di lor canto i deserti, e l'armonia
vince di mille secoli il silenzio.
Ed oggi nella Tròade inseminata
eterno splende a' peregrini un loco
eterno per la Ninfa a cui fu sposo
Giove, ed a Giove diè Dardano figlio
onde fur Troja e Assàraco e i cinquanta
talami e il regno della giulia gente.

searching wisdom, nor the favour of kings, keep the hard won trophies for the man of Ithaca, for the waves stirred up by the infernal gods took them back from the wandering bark.

And me whom the times and the wish for honour cause to seek refuge among different peoples, let the Muses, the inspirers of mortal thought, summon me to invoke heroes. They sit, the Pimplean sisters,* guardians of sepulchres, and when time, with his cold wings, has shattered even the ruins there, they make deserts glad with their song, and harmony overcomes the silence of a thousand centuries. And today in the unsown Troad, a place shines eternally to pilgrims, eternal because of the Nymph to whom Jove was lord, and she gave to Jove a son, Dardanus, from whom came Troy, Assaracus, and the fifty bridal beds, and the reign of the Giulian

* The Muses.

Però che quando Elettra udì la Parca
che lei dalle vitali aure del giorno
chiamava a' cori dell'Eliso, a Giove
mandò il voto supremo: E se, diceva,
a te fur care le mie chiome e il viso
e le dolci vigilie, e non mi assente
premio miglior la volontà de' fati,
la morta amica almen guarda dal cielo
onde d'Elettra tua resti la fama.
Così orando moriva. E ne gemea
l'Olimpio; e l'immortal capo accennando
piovea dai crini ambrosia su la Ninfa
e fe' sacro quel corpo e la sua tomba.
Ivi posò Erittonio, e dorme il giusto
cenere d'Ilo; ivi l'iliache donne
sciogliean le chiome, indarno ahi! deprecando
da' lor mariti l'imminente fato;
ivi Cassandra, allor che il Nume in petto
le fea parlar di Troia il dì mortale,
venne; e all'ombre cantò carme amoroso,
e guidava i nepoti, e l'amoroso
apprendeva lamento a' giovinetti.

people. For when Electra heard one of the Fates calling her from the living breezes of the day to the courts of Elysium, she sent up this last prayer to Jove: And if, she said, my tresses and my face were dear to you and those sweet sleepless nights, and if the will of the Fates does not grant me a better prize, at least look upon your dead beloved from heaven so that the fame of your Electra may survive. So praying, she died. And Olympus wept at it; and the immortal head bowing rained ambrosia from its locks upon the Nymph; and made that body sacred and her tomb. There Erichtonius rested, and there slept the just ashes of Ilus; there the Iliachan women would loose their hair, alas, in vain! and cry out against the impending fate of their husbands: there Cassandra came when the God in her breast made her speak of Troy's fatal day; and sang a song of love to the shades, and brought their grandsons, and taught the loving dirge to these youths. And said, sighing: If ever

E dicea sospirando: Oh se mai d'Argo,
ove al Tidide e di Laerte al figlio
pascerete i cavalli, a voi permetta
ritorno il cielo, invan la patria vostra
cercherete! Le mura opra di Febo
sotto le lor reliquie fumeranno.
Ma i Penati di Troia avranno stanza
in queste tombe; chè de' Numi è dono
servar nelle miserie altero nome.
E voi, palme e cipressi, che le nuore
piantan di Priamo, e crescerete, ahi presto!
di vedovili lagrime innaffiati,
proteggete i miei padri: e chi la scure
asterrà pio dalle devote frondi
men si dorrà di consanguinei lutti
e santamente toccherà l'altare.
Proteggete i miei padri. Un dì vedrete
mendico un cieco errar sotto le vostre
antichissime ombre, e brancolando
penetrar negli avelli, e abbracciar l'urne,
e interrogarle. Gemeranno gli antri
secreti, e tutta narrerà la tomba

heaven allows you to return from Argos where you will graze the horses of Tydides and of the son of Laertes, you will search for your native country in vain! The walls that are the work of Phoebus will smoke under their remains. But the Gods of Troy will be lodged in these tombs; since it is the gift of deities to keep their proud name amid misfortunes. And you, palms and cypresses whom the women of Priam's family plant, and who will grow, soon alas! quickened by widow's tears, protect my ancestors: and whoever shall keep his axe from these dedicated leaves will be less grief-stricken for internecine woes, and he will touch the altar holily. Protect my ancestors. One day you will see a blind beggar wandering under your most ancient shades, and, mumbling, penetrate them to the burial place, and embrace the urns, and question them. The secret caves will moan, and the tomb relate all, Ilium razed

Ilio raso due volte e due risorto
splendidamente su le mute vie
per far più bello l'ultimo trofeo
ai fatali Pelidi. Il sacro vate,
placando quelle afflitte alme col canto,
i prenci argivi eternerà per quante
abbraccia terre il gran padre Oceano.
E tu onore di pianti, Ettore, avrai
ove fia santo e lagrimato il sangue
per la patria versato, e finchè il Sole
risplenderà su le sciagure umane.

Dai «Frammenti del Carme le Grazie»

ERA più lieta
Urania un dì, quando le Grazie a lei
il gran peplo fregiavano. Con esse
qui Galileo sedeva a spiar l'astro
della loro regina; e il disviava
col notturno rumor l'acqua remota,
che sotto a' pioppi delle rive d'Arno
furtiva e argentea gli volava al guardo.

twice and twice arisen splendidly above the silent ways so as to
make finer the last trophy of the fateful sons of Peleus. The sacred
bard, soothing those tormented souls with song, will immortalize
the Argive princes through as many lands as great father Ocean embraces. And you, Hector, will be honoured in tears wherever they
deem holy and lament blood shed for one's country, and as long as
the Sun shines upon human sorrows.

From 'Fragments of a Hymn to the Graces'

URANIA was happier one day, when the Graces fringed her great
blue robe. With them Galileo sat here to spy out the star of their
queen; and the far water that flew from his gaze, furtive and silver,
under the poplars on the banks of Arno, would draw him away
with its nocturnal sound. Here the dawn, the moon, and the sun

Qui a lui l'alba, la luna e il sol mostrava,
gareggiando di tinte, or le severe
nubi su la cerulea alpe sedenti,
or il piano che fugge alle tirrene
Nereidi, immensa di città e di selve
scena e di templi e d'arator beati,
or cento colli, onde Appennin corona
d'ulivi e d'antri e di marmoree ville
l'elegante città, dove con Flora
le Grazie han serti e amabile idioma.

*

Già del piè, delle dita, e dell'errante
estro, e degli occhi vigili alle corde
ispirata sollecita le note
che pingon come l'armonia diè moto
agli astri, all'onda eterea e alla natante
terra per l'oceano, e come franse
l'uniforme creato in mille volti
co' raggi e l'ombre e il ricongiunse in uno,

displayed for him, vying in their hues, now the stern clouds sitting on the sky-blue mountain, now the plain that flies towards the Tyrrhenian Nereids, vast scene of cities and woods and temples and blessed ploughmen, now a hundred hills, with which the Apennine crowns, with olives and caves and marble villas, the shapely city, where with Flora the Graces have garlands and a delightful speech.

ALREADY with her foot, her fingers, and wandering fire, and with her eyes watchful of the strings, inspired she summons the notes that depict how harmony gave motion to the stars, to the ethereal wave and to the earth coming forth from the ocean, and how it broke the created whole into a thousand aspects with light and shade, and reassembled them into one, and gave sounds to the air

e i suoni all'aere, e diè i colori al sole,
e l'alterno continuo tenore
alla fortuna agitatrice e al tempo;
sì che le cose dissonanti insieme
rendan concento d'armonia divina
e innalzino le menti oltre la terra.
Come quando più gaio Euro provòca
sull'alba il queto Lario, e a quel sussurro
canta il nocchiero e allegransi i propinqui
liuti, e molle il flauto si duole
d'innamorati giovani e di ninfe
su le gondole erranti; e dalle sponde
risponde il pastorel con la sua piva:
per entro i colli rintronano i corni
terror del cavriol, mentre in cadenza
di Lecco il malleo domator del bronzo
tuona dagli antri ardenti; stupefatto
perde le reti il pescatore, ed ode.
Tal dell'arpa diffuso erra il concento
per la nostra convalle; e mentre posa
la sonatrice, ancora odono i colli.

*

and colours to the sun, and varying, continuous course to time and unsettling chance; so that dissonant things together should give out chords of divine harmony and raise minds beyond the earth. As when the wind Eurus merrily stirs the quiet Lake of Como at dawn, and the helmsman sings to that rustling and nearby lutes rejoice, and the flute, soft, laments for love-sick youths and nymphs in the wandering gondolas; and from the banks the shepherd answers with his pipe: from the hills' depth blare the horns that are the doe's terror, while, rhythmically from Lecco, the hammer, master of bronze, thunders from the burning caverns; the fisherman, amazed, lets slip the net, and listens. So does the harp's symphony wander through our hollow vale; and while the player rests, the hills still listen.

Io dal mio poggio
quando tacciono i venti fra le torri
della vaga Firenze, odo un Silvano
ospite ignoto a' taciti eremiti
del vicino Oliveto: ei sul meriggio
fa sua casa un frascato, e a suon d'avena
le pecorelle sue chiama alla fonte.
Chiama due brune giovani la sera,
nè piegar erba mi parean ballando.
Esso mena la danza.

*

Spesso per l'altre età, se l'idioma
d'Italia correrà puro a' nepoti,
(e vostro, e voi, deh! lo serbate, o Grazie!)
tento ritrar ne' versi miei la sacra
danzatrice, men bella allor che siede,
men di te bella, o gentile sonatrice,
men amabil di te quando favelli,
o nutrice dell'api. Ma se danza,
vedila! tutta l'armonia del suono
scorre dal suo bel corpo, e dal sorriso

From my hilltop I, when the winds hush among the towers of
fairest Florence, hear a Sylvan guest who is unknown to the silent
hermits of the nearby Olivet: about noon he makes his house of a
green bower, and with the reed's sound, calls the sheep to the fountain. He calls two dark girls in the evening, and they do not seem to
bend the grass as they dance. He leads the dance.

Often for other ages, if the speech of Italy is to run pure to our
grandchildren (it is yours, and o! do you preserve it, you Graces!),
I attempt to trace in my lines the sacred dancer, less lovely when
she sits, less lovely than you, o gentle harpist, less loveable than
you when you give voice, o nurse of the bees. But if she dances, see
her! all the harmony of sound flows from her fair body, and from

della sua bocca; e un moto, un atto, un vezzo,
manda agli sguardi venustà improvvisa.
E chi pinger la può? Mentre a ritrarla
pongo industre lo sguardo, ecco m'elude,
e le carole che lente disegna
affretta rapidissima, e s'invola
sorvolando su' fiori; appena veggio
il vel fuggente biancheggiar fra' mirti.

*

E IL velo delle Dee manda improvviso
un suon, qual di lontana arpa, che scorre
sopra i vanni de' Zeffiri soave;
qual venìa dall'Egeo per l'isolette
un'ignota armonia, poi che al reciso
capo e al bel crin d'Orfeo la vaga lira
annodaro scagliandola nell'onde
le delire Baccanti; e sospirando
con l'Ionio propinquo il sacro Egeo
quell'armonia serbava, e l'isolette
stupefatte l'udiro e i continenti.

*

her mouth's smile, and a movement, a gesture, a grace, flashes sudden beauty at the onlookers. And who can paint her? While I fix my gaze intently to draw her, there she slips me, and speeds the circling dance she was slowly weaving, and flies off skimming over the flowers; I scarcely see the fleeting veil whiten among the myrtles.

AND the veil of the Goddesses suddenly gives forth a sound, like that of a distant harp, that softly runs on the wings of Zephyr; as unknown harmony came among the islands from the Aegean, when the raving Bacchantes tied the wondrous lyre to the severed head and fair locks of Orpheus, hurling it into the waves; and the sacred Aegean, sighing with nearby Ionia, kept up that harmony, and the islets, astonished, heard it, and the continents.

DATE candidi giorni a lei che sola,
da che più lieti mi fioriano gli anni,
m'arse divina d'immortale amore.
Sola vive al cor mio cura soave,
sola e secreta spargerà le chiome
sovra il sepolcro mio, quando lontano
non prescrivano i fati anche il sepolcro.
Vaga e felice i balli e le fanciulle
di nera treccia insigni e di sen colmo,
sul molle clivo di Brianza un giorno
guidar la vidi: oggi le vesti allegre
obliò lenta e il suo vedovo coro.
E se alla Luna e all'etere stellato
più azzurro il scintillante Èupili ondeggia,
il guarda avvolta in lungo velo, e plora
col rosignuol, finchè l'Aurora il chiami
a men soave tacito lamento.
A lei da presso il piè volgete, o Grazie,
e nel mirarvi, o Dee, tornino i grandi
occhi fatali al lor natìo sorriso.

GIVE fair days to her who alone, since my years flowered more happily, divine, has burnt my heart with immortal love. She alone lives as a sweet care in my heart, alone and in secret will she shake out her hair upon my tomb, if the fates do not decree that even my tomb should be a distant one. Delighting and happy I saw her lead the dance and maidens who are favoured with black locks and full bosom, on the soft slope of Brianza one day: today she slowly turns from the happy dress and her widowed train. And if the Lake of Pusiano ripples more blue to the moon and the starry ether, she looks on it, wrapped in a long veil, and mourns with the nightingale, until Dawn calls him to less charmed and silent lament. Turn your step near to her, o you Graces, and in seeing you, o Goddesses, let her great fatal eyes light once more with their true-born smile.

GIOVANNI BERCHET

Il trovatore

Va per la selva bruna
solingo il trovator
domato dal rigor
  della fortuna.

La faccia sua sì bella
la disfiorò il dolor;
la voce del cantor
  non è più quella.

Ardea nel suo segreto;
e i voti, i lai, l'ardor
alla canzon d'amor
  fidò indiscreto.

Dal talamo inaccesso
udillo il suo signor:
l'improvido cantor
  tradì se stesso.

The Minstrel

Solitary, the minstrel goes through the dusky wood, cast down by the hardness of fate.

Sorrow has wasted the face that was so handsome; the singer's voice is no longer what it was.

He burned with secret passion; and carelessly, he confided his wishes, his pangs, his heat, in a love-song.

His lord heard him from the secluded wedding-couch: the unwary singer betrayed himself.

Pei dì del giovinetto
tremò alla donna il cor,
ignara fino allor
     di tanto affetto.

E supplice al geloso,
ne contenea il furor:
bella del proprio onor
     piacque allo sposo.

Rise l'ingenua. Blando
l'accarezzò il signor:
ma il giovin trovator
     cacciato è in bando.

De' cari occhi fatali
piu non vedrà il fulgor;
non berrà piu da lor
     l'obblìo de' mali.

Varcò quegli atri muto
ch'ei rallegrava ognor
con gl'inni del valor
     col suo liuto.

The woman's heart trembled for the youth's days; she had not known so much feeling until then.

And pleading with the jealous man, she restrained his fury: fair with her own honour, she delighted her husband.

The simple woman laughed. Softly her lord caressed her: but the young minstrel is banished.

He will no longer look on the lustre of those dear fatal eyes; he will no more drink forgetfulness of wrongs from them.

He passed through those halls that he would always cheer, playing hymns of bravery on his lute.

Scese, varcò le porte;
stette, guardolle ancor:
e gli scoppiava il cor
      come per morte.

Venne alla selva bruna;
quivi erra il trovator,
fuggendo ogni chiaror
      fuor che la luna.

La guancia sua sì bella
più non somiglia un fior;
la voce del cantor
      non è più quella.

ALESSANDRO MANZONI

Morte di Ermengarda

SPARSA le trecce morbide
sull'affannoso petto,
lenta le palme, e rorida
di morte il bianco aspetto,
giace la pia, col tremolo
sguardo cercando il ciel.

He went down and out through the gates; he stood still, he
looked at them again: his heart burst in his bosom as if at the
moment of death.

He came to the dusky wood; there the minstrel wanders, flying
from every brightness except the moon.

His cheek, once so fair, no longer is like the flower; the singer's
voice is no longer what it was.

The Death of Ermengarda

THE soft locks scattered upon the heaving bosom, the hands slow,
and the white features dewed with death, the pious girl lies, searching heaven with trembling gaze.

Cessa il compianto: unanime
s'innalza una preghiera:
calata in su la gelida
fronte, una man leggiera
sulla pupilla cerula
stende l'estremo vel.

Sgombra, o gentil, dall'ansia
mente i terrestri ardori;
leva all'Eterno un candido
pensier d'offerta, e muori:
fuor della vita è il termine
del lungo tuo martir.

Tal della mesta, immobile
era quaggiuso il fato:
sempre un obblio di chiedere
che le saria negato;
e al Dio de' santi ascendere,
santa del suo patir.

Ahi! nelle insonni tenebre,
pei claustri solitari,
tra il canto delle vergini,
ai supplicati altari,
sempre al pensier tornavano
gl'irrevocati dì;

The weeping hushes: a general prayer rises: a hand fallen lightly
upon the cold forehead, stretches the last veil over her vivid blue
eyes.

Clear worldly passions from your troubled mind, o gentle
one; raise a pure thought in offering to the Eternal, and die: the end
of your long suffering lies beyond life.

Such was the unchanging fate of this sad creature: always to ask
for forgetfulness that was denied her; and to ascend to the God of
saints, saintly through her forbearance.

Ah! in the unsleeping shadows, through the deserted cloisters,
amid the song of the virgins, at the altars implored, those irre-
vocable days always came back to her;

quando ancor cara, improvvida
d'un avvenir mal fido,
ebbra spirò le vivide
aure del Franco lido,
e tra le nuore Saliche
invidiata uscì:

quando da un poggio aereo,
il biondo crin gemmata,
vedea nel pian discorrere
la caccia affaccendata,
e sulle sciolte redini
chino il chiomato sir;

e dietro a lui la furia
de' corridor fumanti;
e lo sbandarsi, e il rapido
redir dei veltri ansanti;
e dai tentati triboli
l'irto cinghiale uscir;

e la battuta polvere
rigar di sangue, còlto
dal regio stral: la tenera
alle donzelle il volto
volgea repente, pallida
d'amabile terror.

when still beloved, unprepared for a treacherous future, she eagerly breathed the quickening air of French ground, and went out, envied, among the Salic brides:

when, bejewelled her fair hair, from an airy height she watched the flurried chase breaking over the plain, and her long-haired sire bent over the loose reins;

and behind him the fury of the steaming chargers; and the ranging and quick grouping of the panting hounds; and the prickly boar come out from the disturbed undergrowth;

and, struck by the royal shaft, streak the trampled dust with blood: the tender girl suddenly turned her face to her companions, pale with a lovable terror.

Oh Mosa errante! oh tepidi
lavacri d'Aquisgrano!
ove, deposta l'orrida
maglia, il guerrier sovrano
scendea del campo a tergere
il nobile sudor!

Come rugiada al cespite
dell'erba inaridita,
fresca negli arsi calami
fa rifluir la vita,
che verdi ancor risorgono
nel temperato albor;

tale al pensier, cui l'empia
virtù d'amor fatica,
discende il refrigerio
d'una parola amica,
e il cor diverte ai placidi
gaudii d'un altro amor.

Ma come il sol che reduce
l'erta infocata ascende,
e con la vampa assidua
l'immobil aura incende,
risorti appena i gracili
steli riarde al suol;

O winding Meuse! o warm springs of Aix-la-Chapelle! where, putting by his fearful coat of mail, the warrior king would come away from the field to cleanse himself of valour's sweat!

As dew makes life flow fresh again in the burnt stalks of a clump of dry grass which rise green again in the mild dawn;

so the refreshment of a friendly word falls upon the thoughts with which love, in its wicked power, tires us, and turns the heart to the calm enjoyment of a different love.

But as the sun that, returning, goes up its fiery slope and kindles the unmoving breeze with its steady flame, burns the newly risen stems back to the ground;

ratto così dal tenue
obblio torna immortale
l'amor sopito, e l'anima
impaurita assale,
e le sviate immagini
richiama al noto duol.

Sgombra, o gentil, dall'ansia
mente i terrestri ardori;
leva all'Eterno un candido
pensier d'offerta, e muori:
nel suol che dee la tenera
tua spoglia ricoprir,

altre infelici dormono,
che il duol consunse; orbate
spose dal brando, e vergini
indarno fidanzate;
madri che i nati videro
traffitti impallidir.

Te dalla rea progenie
degli oppressor discesa,
cui fu prodezza il numero,
cui fu ragion l'offesa,
e dritto il sangue, e gloria
il non aver pietà,

as quickly does slumbering love come back immortal from slight forgetfulness, and assails the frightened mind, and brings back the deluding images of the old grief.

Clear worldly passions from your troubled mind, o gentle one; raise a pure thought in offering to the Eternal, and die; in the ground which must cover your tender frame,

sleep other unhappy women whom grief consumed; wives bereaved by the sword, and virgins vainly betrothed; mothers who saw their children paling as they were stabbed.

You, the descendant of the evil race of oppressors, for whom number was bravery; injury, argument; blood, right; and glory, not to have pity;

te collocò la provida
sventura in fra gli oppressi:
muori compianta e placida;
scendi a dormir con essi:
alle incolpate ceneri
nessuno insulterà.

Muori, e la faccia esanime
si ricomponga in pace;
com'era allor che improvida
d'un avvenir fallace,
lievi pensier virginei
solo pingea. Così

dalle squarciate nuvole
si svolge il sol cadente,
e, dietro il monte, imporpora
il trepido occidente:
al pio colono augurio
di più sereno dì.

you were placed among the oppressed by provident misfortune:
die mourned and calm; go down to sleep with them: no one will
desecrate your blameless ashes.

Die, and let your face, lifeless, be composed again to peace; as it
was when, unprepared for a deceptive future, you simply painted
glad, virgin fancies on the air. So

from the rent clouds the descending sun issues, and reddens the
alarmed east, behind the mountain: sign to the pious crofter of a
calmer day.

GIACOMO LEOPARDI

L'infinito

SEMPRE caro mi fu quest'ermo colle,
e questa siepe, che da tanta parte
dell'ultimo orizzonte il guardo esclude.
Ma sedendo e mirando, interminati
spazi di là da quella, e sovrumani
silenzi, e profondissima quiete
io nel pensier mi fingo; ove per poco
il cor non si spaura. E come il vento
odo stormir tra queste piante, io quello
infinito silenzio a questa voce
vo comparando: e mi sovvien l'eterno,
e le morte stagioni, e la presente
e viva, e il suon di lei. Così tra questa
immensità s'annega il pensier mio:
e il naufragar m'è dolce in questo mare.

The Infinite

IT was always dear to me, this solitary hill, and this hedge which
shuts off the gaze from so large a part of the uttermost horizon.
But sitting and looking out, in thought I fashion for myself endless
spaces beyond, more-than-human silences, and deepest quiet;
where for a while the heart is not alarmed. And as I hear the wind
rustling among these plants, I go on and compare this voice to that
infinite silence: and I recall the eternal, and the dead seasons, and
the present, living one and her sound. So in this immensity my
thoughts drown: and shipwreck is sweet to me in this sea.

La sera del dì di festa

Dolce e chiara è la notte e senza vento,
e queta sovra i tetti e in mezzo agli orti
posa la luna, e di lontan rivela
serena ogni montagna. O donna mia,
già tace ogni sentiero, e pei balconi
rara traluce la notturna lampa:
tu dormi, che t'accolse agevol sonno
nelle tue chete stanze; e non ti morde
cura nessuna; e già non sai nè pensi
quanta piaga m'apristi in mezzo al petto.
Tu dormi: io questo ciel, che sì benigno
appare in vista, a salutar m'affaccio,
e l'antica natura onnipossente,
che mi fece all'affanno. A te la speme
nego, mi disse, anche la speme; e d'altro
non brillin gli occhi tuoi se non di pianto.
Questo dì fu solenne: or da' trastulli
prendi riposo; e forse ti rimembra
in sogno a quanti oggi piacesti, e quanti
piacquero a te: non io, non già ch'io speri,

The Evening of the Holiday

Mild and clear is the night and without wind, and quietly above
the roofs and among the orchards the moon rests and reveals clear
in the distance every mountain. O my love, every street is already
silent, and only here and there does a night lamp glimmer from the
balconies. You sleep, for easy slumber welcomes you in your quiet
rooms; and no care gnaws you; and certainly you do not know or
guess what a wound you have opened in my breast. You sleep: I
turn to greet this heaven, which in appearance seems so kindly, and
ancient all-powerful nature which made me for pain. To you I deny
hope, nature said to me -- even hope; and your eyes shall not shine
from other than tears. This day was a holiday: now you take rest
from games; and perhaps you remember in dream how many liked
you today, how many you liked: but I do not, not that I can hope

al pensier ti ricorro. Intanto io chieggo
quanto a viver mi resti, e qui per terra
mi getto, e grido, e fremo. O giorni orrendi
in così verde etate! Ahi, per la via
odo non lunge il solitario canto
dell'artigian, che riede a tarda notte,
dopo i sollazzi, al suo povero ostello;
e fieramente mi si stringe il core,
a pensar come tutto al mondo passa,
e quasi orma non lascia. Ecco è fuggito
il dì festivo, ed al festivo il giorno
volgar succede, e se ne porta il tempo
ogni umano accidente. Or dov'è il suono
di que' popoli antichi? or dov'è il grido
de' nostri avi famosi, e il grande impero
di quella Roma, e l'armi e il fragorio
che n'andò per la terra e l'oceano?
Tutto è pace e silenzio, e tutto posa
il mondo, e più di lor non si ragiona.
Nella mia prima età, quando s'aspetta
bramosamente il dì festivo, or poscia
ch'egli era spento, io doloroso, in veglia,

it, recur to your mind. Meanwhile I ask how much is left for me to
live, and here upon the ground I throw myself, and cry aloud, and
tremble. O horrible days in so green an age! Ah, I hear on the road,
not far away, the lonely song of the tradesman who returns late at
night, after his amusements, to his poor lodging; and my heart is
fiercely oppressed to think how everything in the world passes, and
leaves almost no trace. Here is the holiday flown, and the normal
day succeeds the festive, and time bears away every human circum-
stance. Where now is the sound of those ancient peoples? Where
now is the fame of our illustrious ancestors, and the great empire of
that Rome, and the arms and the martial noise that went over land
and ocean? All is peace and silence, and the world rests entirely,
and we do not talk of them now. In my earliest years when a holiday is fervently awaited, when once it was passed, I lay, sorrow-

premea le piume; ed alla tarda notte
un canto che s'udia per li sentieri
lontanando morire a poco a poco,
già similmente mi stringeva il core.

Alla luna

O GRAZIOSA luna, io mi rammento
che, or volge l'anno, sovra questo colle
io venia pien d'angoscia a rimirarti:
e tu pendevi allor su quella selva
siccome or fai, che tutta la rischiari.
Ma nebuloso e tremulo dal pianto
che mi sorgea sul ciglio, alle mie luci
il tuo volto apparia, che travagliosa
era mia vita: ed è, nè cangia stile,
o mia diletta luna. E pur mi giova
la ricordanza, e il noverar l'etate
del mio dolore. Oh come grato occorre
nel tempo giovanil, quando ancor lungo
la speme e breve ha la memoria il corso,
il rimembrar delle passate cose,
ancor che triste, e che l'affanno duri!

ful and awake, sunk in my pillow; and in the late night, a song that
was heard in the streets going off, dying little by little, would
oppress my heart in the same way.

To the Moon

FAIR moon, I am reminded that (a year has almost run since then)
I came upon this hill full of anguish to look upon you once more:
and you hung there over that wood as you do now so as to brighten
it all. But your face appeared misty and trembling to my eyes from
the tears which rose at their brim, for troubled was my life: and is,
nor does it change tenour, o my beloved moon. And yet the recall-
ing and telling over the years of my grief helps me. O how pleasantly in youth when hope has still a long course and memory a
short one, does recollection of past things come to us, though they
be sad, and the pain still last!

A Silvia

SILVIA, rimembri ancora
quel tempo della tua vita mortale,
quando beltà splendea
negli occhi tuoi ridenti e fuggitivi,
e tu, lieta e pensosa, il limitare
di gioventù salivi?

Sonavan le quiete
stanze, e le vie dintorno,
al tuo perpetuo canto,
allor che all'opre femminili intenta
sedevi, assai contenta
di quel vago avvenir che in mente avevi.
Era il maggio odoroso: e tu solevi
così menare il giorno.

Io gli studi leggiadri
talor lasciando e le sudate carte,
ove il tempo mio primo
e di me si spendea la miglior parte,
d'in su i veroni del paterno ostello
porgea gli orecchi al suon della tua voce,

To Silvia

SILVIA, do you still remember that time in your mortal life when beauty shone in your laughing, sidelong eyes, and you, gay and thoughtful, mounted the threshold of youth?

The quiet rooms and the streets around hummed to your continual song, when you sat intent upon your womanly work, content with that lovely future you had in mind. It was the scented Maytime: and you used, like this, to pass the day.

Sometimes leaving my pleasant studies and the soiled pages where my first years and the best part of myself were spent, from the balconies of my father's house I would strain my ear to catch

ed alla man veloce
che percorrea la faticosa tela.
Mirava il ciel sereno,
le vie dorate e gli orti,
e quinci il mar da lungi, e quindi il monte.
Lingua mortal non dice
quel ch'io sentiva in seno.

Che pensieri soavi,
che speranze, che cori, o Silvia mia!
Quale allor ci apparia
la vita umana e il fato!
Quando sovviemmi di contanta speme,
un affetto mi preme
acerbo e sconsolato,
e tornami a doler di mia sventura.
O natura, o natura,
perchè non rendi poi
quel che prometti allor? perchè di tanto
inganni i figli tuoi?

Tu pria che l'erbe inaridisse il verno,
da chiuso morbo combattuta e vinta,
perivi, o tenerella. E non vedevi
il fior degli anni tuoi;

the sound of your voice, and of your hand which ran across the toiling loom. I would look at the clear sky, the gilded streets, and the gardens, and on this side the sea at a distance, and on that the mountains. Mortal tongue cannot tell what I felt in my bosom.

What sweet thoughts, what hopes, what hearts, o my Silvia! How did human life and fate appear to us then! When I am reminded of so much promise, a harsh, disconsolate feeling oppresses me, and I come again to grieve at my misfortune. O nature, o nature, why do you not yield afterwards what you promised then? Why do you deceive your children so much?

You, before winter withered the grass, beset and overcome by secret disease, you perished, o my tender one. And you did not see

non ti molceva il core
la dolce lode or delle negre chiome,
or degli sguardi innamorati e schivi;
nè teco le compagne ai dì festivi
ragionavan d'amore.

Anche peria fra poco
la speranza mia dolce: agli anni miei
anche negaro i fati
la giovanezza. Ahi come,
come passata sei,
cara compagna dell'età mia nova,
mia lacrimata speme!
Questo è quel mondo? questi
i diletti, l'amor, l'opre, gli eventi
onde cotanto ragionammo insieme?
Questa la sorte delle umane genti?
All'apparir del vero
tu, misera, cadesti: e con la mano
la fredda morte ed una tomba ignuda
mostravi di lontano.

the flower of your years; your heart was not touched by the sweet
praise, now of your black hair, now of your loving, shy looks, nor
did your friends speak with you of love upon holidays.

My sweet hope also perished in a little while; to my years, too,
fate denied youth. Ah, how, how you have passed, dear companion
of my early years, my lamented hope? Is this the same world? these
the delights, the love, the works, the happenings of which we
spoke so much together? This the fate of humankind? At the coming of truth, unfortunate one, you fell: and with your hand pointed
in the distance cold death and a naked tomb.

Canto notturno di un pastore errante dell' Asia

CHE fai tu, luna in ciel? dimmi, che fai,
silenziosa luna?
Sorgi la sera, e vai,
contemplando i deserti: indi ti posi.
Ancor non sei tu paga
di riandare i sempiterni calli?
Ancor non prendi a schivo, ancor sei vaga
di mirar queste valli?
Somiglia alla tua vita
la vita del pastore.
Sorge in sul primo albore,
move la greggia oltre pel campo, e vede
greggi, fontane ed erbe;
poi stanco si riposa in su la sera:
altro mai non ispera.
Dimmi, o luna: a che vale
al pastor la sua vita,
la vostra vita a voi? dimmi: ove tende
questo vagar mio breve,
il tuo corso immortale?

Night Song of a Wandering Shepherd of Asia

WHAT are you doing, moon, there in the sky? tell me, what are
you doing, silent moon? You rise in the evening, and go, con-
templating deserts: then you rest. Are you not sated with going
over the everlasting paths? Do you not feel a loathing, are you still
eager to look upon these valleys? The shepherd's life is like yours.
He rises at the first dawning, moves his flocks onwards over the
fields, and sees flocks, fountains, and grass; then, tired, towards
evening rests: he never hopes for anything else. Tell me, o moon:
what worth has his life for the shepherd, your life for you? tell me:
where does my brief wandering lead, where, your undying course?

Vecchierel bianco, infermo,
mezzo vestito e scalzo,
con gravissimo fascio in su le spalle,
per montagna e per valle,
per sassi acuti, ed alta rena, e fratte,
al vento, alla tempesta, e quando avvampa
l'ora, e quando poi gela,
corre via, corre, anela,
varca torrenti e stagni,
cade, risorge, e più e più s'affretta,
senza posa o ristoro,
lacero, sanguinoso; infin ch'arriva
colà dove la via
e dove il tanto affaticar fu volto:
abisso orrido, immenso,
ov'ei precipitando, il tutto obblia.
Vergine luna, tale
è la vita mortale.

Nasce l'uomo a fatica,
ed è rischio di morte il nascimento.
Prova pena e tormento
per prima cosa; e in sul principio stesso
la madre e il genitore
il prende a consolar dell'esser nato.

Shrunken old man, white-haired, failing, half-naked, and barefoot, with a most heavy burden upon his shoulders, who runs
through valleys and over mountains, over sharp stones, deep sand,
and brakes, in wind, in storm, when the hour is burning, and when
it freezes – runs on, panting, crosses torrents and marshes, falls
rises again, and hurries more and more, without rest or refreshment, torn and bleeding; until he arrives where the road and all
his travail have led: a horrible, vast abyss into which he falls head-
long, and forgets everything. Virgin moon, such is mortal life.

Man is born to labour, and birth is a risk of death. He experiences
pain and anguish as the first of things; and at the very beginning his
mother and father take to consoling him for being born. Then

Poi che crescendo viene,
l'uno e l'atro il sostiene, e via pur sempre
con atti e con parole
studiasi fargli core,
e consolarlo dell'umano stato:
altro ufficio più grato
non si fa da parenti alla lor prole.
Ma perchè dare al sole,
perchè reggere in vita
chi poi di quella consolar convenga?
Se la vita è sventura,
perchè da noi si dura?
Intatta luna, tale
è lo stato mortale.
Ma tu mortal non sei,
e forse del mio dir poco ti cale.

Pur tu, solinga, eterna peregrina,
che sì pensosa sei, tu forse intendi,
questo viver terreno,
il patir nostro, il sospirar, che sia;
che sia questo morir, questo supremo
scolorar del sembiante,

when he comes to grow, the one and the other support him, and, on and on, ceaselessly, try with words and actions to give him heart, and console him for the human state: no more gratifying service is to be rendered by parents to their children. But why give to the sun, why keep in life one who must then be consoled for it? If life is misfortune, why do we last it out? Inviolate moon, such is the mortal state. But you are not mortal, and perhaps care little for my words.

Yet, lonely, eternal wanderer, who are so thoughtful, perhaps you understand what this earthly life is, our suffering and sighing, and what this dying is, this ultimate fading of the features, and

e perir dalla terra, e venir meno
ad ogni usata, amante compagnia.
E tu certo comprendi
il perchè delle cose, e vedi il frutto
del mattin, della sera,
del tacito, infinito andar del tempo.
Tu sai, tu certo, a qual suo dolce amore
ride la primavera,
à chi giovi l'ardore, e che procacci
il verno co' suoi ghiacci.
Mille cose sai tu, mille discopri,
che son celate al semplice pastore.
Spesso quand'io ti miro
star così muta in sul deserto piano,
che, in suo giro lontano, al ciel confina;
ovver con la mia greggia
seguirmi viaggiando a mano a mano;
e quando miro in cielo arder le stelle;
dico fra me pensando:
a che tante facelle?
Che fa l'aria infinita, e quel profondo
infinito seren? che vuol dir questa
solitudine immensa? ed io che sono?

perishing from the earth, and falling away from every familiar,
loving company. And certainly you understand the why of things,
and see the fruit of morning, of evening, of the silent, endless going
of time. You know, you certainly, to what sweet love of hers
the springtime laughs, whom the heat serves, and what winter with
its ice effects. A thousand things you know, a thousand discover
that are hidden to the simple shepherd. Often when I see you stay
so silently above the empty plain which, in its far sweep, borders on
the sky; or see you follow me with my flock, travelling slow and
steady; and when I look on the stars burning in heaven; in thought
I say to myself: wherefore, so many torches? What does the infinite
air serve, and what the deep infinite sky? What does this boundless
solitude mean? And what am I? So I discuss with myself: both of

Così meco ragiono: e della stanza
smisurata e superba,
e dell'innumerabile famiglia;
poi di tanto adoprar, di tanti moti
d'ogni celeste, ogni terrena cosa,
girando senza posa,
per tornar sempre là donde son mosse;
uso alcuno, alcun frutto
indovinar non so. Ma tu per certo,
giovinetta immortal, conosci il tutto.
Questo io conosco e sento,
che degli eterni giri,
che dell'esser mio frale,
qualche bene o contento
avrà fors'altri; a me la vita è male.

O greggia mia che posi, oh te beata,
che la miseria tua, credo, non sai!
Quanta invidia ti porto!
Non sol perchè d'affanno
quasi libera vai;
ch'ogni stento, ogni danno,
ogni estremo timor subito scordi;
ma più perchè giammai tedio non provi.

the sumptuous and unbounded mansion, and the numberless
family; then, in so much activity, in the so many movements of
every heavenly, every earthly thing, going on without rest, always
coming back to the point from which they were moved, in these I
cannot see any use, any fruit. But you for sure, immortal maiden,
know the sum of all. I know and feel this, that others may have
some profit or contentment from the eternal revolvings, from my
frail being; to me life is evil.

O my flock that rest, o happy you, who, I imagine, do not know
your misery! How much envy I bear you! Not only because you go
nearly free of worry; for you immediately forget every effort,
every blow, every extreme fear; but rather because you never know

Quando tu siedi all'ombra, sovra l'erbe,
tu se' queta e contenta;
e gran parte dell'anno
senza noia consumi in quello stato.
Ed io pur seggo sovra l'erbe, all'ombra,
e un fastidio m'ingombra
la mente, ed uno spron quasi mi punge
sì che, sedendo, più che mai son lunge
da trovar pace o loco.
E pur nulla non bramo,
e non ho fino a qui cagion di pianto.
Quel che tu goda o quanto,
non so già dir; ma fortunata sei.
Ed io godo ancor poco,
o greggia mia, nè di ciò sol mi lagno.
Se tu parlar sapessi, io chiederei:
dimmi: perchè giacendo
a bell'agio, ozioso,
s'appaga ogni animale;
me, s'io giaccio in riposo, il tedio assale?

boredom. When you sit in the shade upon the grass, you are quiet and contented; and you spend untroubled a great part of the year in that state. And yet I sit upon the grass in the shade, and a weariness clouds my mind, and it is as if a spur pricks me so that, sitting as I am, I am farther than ever from finding peace and haven. And yet I desire nothing, and till now have no cause for tears. I cannot even say what it is you enjoy, or how much; but you are lucky. And I continue to enjoy little, o my flock, nor do I sorrow only for this. If you could speak, I would ask you: tell me: why is every animal satisfied lying at dear ease, idle; why if I lie at rest, does tedium assail me?

Forse s'avess'io l'ale
da volar su le nubi,
e noverar le stelle ad una ad una,
o come il tuono errar di giogo in giogo,
più felice sarei, dolce mia greggia,
più felice sarei, candida luna.
O forse erra dal vero,
mirando all'altrui sorte, il mio pensiero:
forse in qual forma, in quale
stato che sia, dentro covile o cuna,
è funesto a chi nasce il dì natale.

Il sabato del villaggio

La donzelletta vien dalla campagna,
in sul calar del sole,
col suo fascio dell'erba; e reca in mano
un mazzolin di rose e di viole,
onde, siccome suole,
ornare ella si appresta
dimani al dì di festa, il petto e il crine.

Perhaps if I had wings to fly above the clouds, and number the stars one by one, or like the thunder roam from crest to crest, I would be happier, my sweet flock, I would be happier, white moon. Or perhaps my thoughts wander from the truth when I look at the fate of others: perhaps in whatever form, in whatever state he may have his being, in den or in cot, the day of birth is gloomy to him who is born.

Saturday in the Village

The girl comes from the country, at the sinking of the sun, with her bundle of grass, and carries in her hand a little bunch of roses and violets with which she is ready to deck her bosom and her hair tomorrow, on the holiday, as is her custom. With neighbours,

Siede con le vicine
su la scala a filar la vecchierella,
incontro là dove si perde il giorno;
e novellando vien del suo buon tempo,
quando al dì della festa ella si ornava,
ed ancor sana e snella
solea danzar la sera intra di quei
ch'ebbe compagni dell'età più bella.
Già tutta l'aria imbruna,
torna azzurro il sereno, e tornan l'ombre
giù da' colli e da' tetti,
al biancheggiar della recente luna.
Or la squilla dà segno
della festa che viene;
ed a quel suon diresti
che il cor si riconforta.
I fanciulli gridando
su la piazzuola in frotta,
e qua e là saltando,
fanno un lieto romore:
e intanto riede alla sua parca mensa,
fischiando, il zappatore,
e seco pensa al dì del suo riposo.

upon the steps, the old woman sits spinning, facing towards where
the light is fading; and goes on talking of her own good season,
when she on holidays, still fresh and supple, would dance the evening away with those youths who were the friends of her fairer age.
Now all the air has darkened, the heavens take on a blue again, and
again the shadows fall from hills and roofs, in the whitening of the
young moon. Now the peal of bells announces the holiday that is
coming, and you would say that at the sound the heart is comforted. The children shouting in the little square in swarms, and
leaping here and there, make a happy din: meanwhile the hoer goes
back whistling to his meagre spread, and thinks in himself of his
day of rest.

Poi quando intorno è spenta ogni altra face,
e tutto l'altro tace,
odi il martel picchiare, odi la sega
del legnaiuol, che veglia
nella chiusa bottega alla lucerna,
e s'affretta, e s'adopra
di fornir l'opra anzi il chiarir dell'alba.

Questo di sette è il più gradito giorno,
pien di speme e di gioia:
diman tristezza e noia
recheran l'ore, ed al travaglio usato
ciascun in suo pensier farà ritorno.

Garzoncello scherzoso,
cotesta età fiorita
è come un giorno d'allegrezza pieno,
giorno chiaro, sereno,
che precorre alla festa di tua vita.
Godi, fanciullo mio; stato soave,
stagion lieta è cotesta.
Altro dirti non vo'; ma la tua festa
ch'anco tardi a venir non ti sia grave.

Then when every other light has gone out, and everything else is silent, you hear the hammer rapping, hear the saw of the carpenter who works all night in his closed shop by a lantern, and hurries, and exerts himself to have the job ready before the lightening of dawn.

This is the most welcome of seven days, full of hope and joy. Tomorrow the hours will bring sadness and boredom, and each will go back in thought to his usual labour.

Mischievous boy, this flowering age of yours is like a day full of joy, a clear cloudless day which precedes the holiday of your life. Have enjoyment of it, my son; a sweet state, a happy season, it is. I do not want to say anything more to you; but may your holiday which still hesitates to come, not be heavy.

A sè stesso

OR poserai per sempre,
stanco mio cor. Perì l'inganno estremo,
ch'eterno io mi credei. Perì. Ben sento,
in noi di cari inganni,
non che la speme, il desiderio è spento.
Posa per sempre. Assai
palpitasti. Non val cosa nessuna
i moti tuoi, nè di sospiri è degna
la terra. Amaro e noia
la vita, altro mai nulla; e fango è il mondo.
T'acqueta omai. Dispera
l'ultima volta. Al gener nostro il fato
non donò che il morire. Omai disprezza
te, la natura, il brutto
poter, che, ascoso, a comun danno impera,
e l'infinita vanità del tutto.

To Himself

NOW you will rest for ever, tired heart of mine. The last deception
has perished which I believed eternal. It has perished. Well do I feel
it, in us has been extinguished not only the hope of dear illusions,
but the desire for them as well. Rest for ever. You have laboured
much. Nothing can repay your stirring, nor is the earth worthy of
sighs. Life is bitterness and tedium, never anything else; and the
world is mud. Be quietened now. Despair for the last time. To
human kind fate has only appointed dying. Scorn nature now, the
brutal power which governs to the universal hurt, and the infinite
vanity of everything.

Coro di morti

SOLA nel mondo eterna, a cui si volve
ogni creata cosa,
in te morte, si posa
nostra ignuda natura;
lieta no, ma sicura
dell'antico dolor. Profonda notte
nella confusa mente
il pensier grave oscura;
alla speme, al desio, l'arido spirto
lena mancar si sente:
così d'affanno e di temenza è sciolto,
e l'età vote e lente
senza tedio consuma.
Vivemmo: e qual di paurosa larva,
e di sudato sogno,
a lattante fanciullo erra nell'alma
confusa ricordanza:
tal memoria n'avanza
del viver nostro: ma da tema è lunge
il rimembrar. Che fummo?
Che fu quel punto acerbo
che di vita ebbe nome?

Chorus of the Dead

DEATH who alone are eternal in this world, to whom every
created thing comes, our naked being rests in you; not happy, but
safe from the ancient grief. Deep night darkens the heavy thought
in the mind confused; the arid spirit feels its will to hope, to desire,
failing: freed thus from anxiety and fear, it spends the empty, slow
ages without weariness. We lived: and as the troubled memory of
frightening spectre and sweated dream haunts the soul of the child
still suckling: so does memory of our life keep with us: but our
remembering is far from fear. What were we? What was that bitter
point that had the name of life? Life is today a dark and awful thing

Cosa arcana e stupenda
oggi è la vita al pensier nostro, e tale
qual de' vivi al pensiero
l'ignota morte appar. Come da morte
vivendo rifuggìa, così rifugge
dalla fiamma vitale
nostra ignuda natura
lieta no ma sicura,
però ch'esser beato
nega ai mortali e nega a' morti il fato.

La ginestra
o *il Fiore del deserto*

E gli uomini vollero piuttosto le tenebre
che la luce – Giovanni iii, 19

QUI su l'arida schiena
del formidabil monte
sterminator Vesevo,
la qual null'altro allegra arbor nè fiore,
tuoi cespi solitari intorno spargi,

to our minds, just as unknown death appears to the minds of the
living. As our naked nature fled from death while we lived, so it
flies from the vital flame now, not happy but safe, because fate
denies happiness to the mortal and the dead.

The Broom
or
The Flower of the Desert

And men loved darkness rather
than light – John iii, 19

HERE upon the arid back of the redoubtable mountain, destroyer
Vesuvius, which no other tree or flower cheers, you scatter your

odorata ginestra,
contenta dei deserti. Anco ti vidi
de' tuoi steli abbellir l'erme contrade
che cingon la cittade
la qual fu donna de' mortali un tempo,
e del perduto impero
par che col grave e taciturno aspetto
faccian fede e ricordo al passeggero.
Or ti riveggo in questo suol, di tristi
lochi e dal mondo abbandonati amante,
e d'afflitte fortune ognor compagna.
Questi campi cosparsi
di ceneri infeconde, e ricoperti
dell'impietrata lava,
che sotto i passi al peregrin risona;
dove s'annida e si contorce al sole
la serpe, e dove al noto
cavernoso covil torna il coniglio;
fur liete ville e colti.
E biondeggiar di spiche, e risonaro
di muggito d'armenti;
fur giardini e palagi,

lonely bushes around, fragrant broom, content with deserts. A while ago I saw you beautify with your stems the bare country places that girdle the city which was once the mistress of mortals, and it seems that with their grave and silent look they serve as a testimony and a reminder of that lost empire to the traveller. Now I see you again on this ground, the lover of sad places that are abandoned by the world, and the unfailing companion of adverse fates. These fields that are scattered over with infertile ash and covered with solid lava that resounds to the pilgrim's tread, where nests and twists in the sun the snake, and where the rabbit comes home to his familiar, cave-like burrow, were once happy country houses and cultivated places. And they grew gold with corn, and echoed to the lowing of herds; there were gardens and mansions,

agli ozi de' potenti
gradito ospizio, e fur città famose,
che coi torrenti suoi l'altero monte
dall'ignea bocca fulminando oppresse
con gli abitanti insieme. Or tutto intorno
una ruina involve,
ove tu siedi, o fior gentile, e quasi
i danni altrui commiserando, al cielo
di dolcissimo odor mandi un profumo,
che il deserto consola. A queste piagge
venga colui che d'esaltar con lode
il nostro stato ha in uso, e vegga quanto
è il gener nostro in cura
all'amante natura. E la possanza
qui con giusta misura
anco estimar potrà dell'uman seme,
cui la dura nutrice, ov'ei men teme,
con lieve moto in un momento annulla
in parte, e può con moti
poco men lievi ancor subitamente
annichilare in tutto.
Dipinte in queste rive
son dell'umana gente
«le magnifiche sorti e progressive».

the welcome retreat for the leisure of the great, and famous cities
which the proud mountain, thundering with the torrents of its
flaming mouth, crushed along with their inhabitants. Now one
ruin claims everything around the place where you sit, o kindly
flower, and, almost sympathizing for the losses of others, send up
to heaven a perfume of sweetest smell that consoles the desert. Let
him who is accustomed to extol our state come to these slopes and
see how greatly mankind enjoys the care of loving Nature. And
here, too, he will be able to guess rightly the power of humankind which that hard nurse, when we least fear, in a moment, with a
light motion, nullifies in part, and can, with motions scarcely less
light, in no time, annihilate altogether. Displayed upon these banks
are 'the magnificent and progressive destinies of the human race'.

Qui mira e qui ti specchia,
secol superbo e sciocco,
che il calle insino allora
dal risorto pensier segnato innanti
abbandonasti, e volti addietro i passi,
del ritornar ti vanti,
e procedere il chiami.
Al tuo pargoleggiar gl'ingegni tutti
di cui lor sorte rea padre ti fece
vanno adulando, ancora
ch'a ludibrio talora
t'abbian fra sè. Non io
con tal vergogna scenderò sotterra;
ma il disprezzo piuttosto che si serra
di te nel petto mio,
mostrato avrò quanto si possa aperto:
bench'io sappia che obblio
preme chi troppo all'età propria increbbe.
Di questo mal, che teco
mi fia comune, assai finor mi rido.
Libertà vai sognando, e servo a un tempo
vuoi di novo il pensiero,

Here look and here see yourself mirrored, proud, foolish century,
that have abandoned the path, leading forward till now, of new-
risen thought, and turned your steps backwards, and boast of the
regression, and call it advancing. To your babbling all gifted souls,
whose evil fate has given them you for an father, pay tribute even
although sometimes they hold you in scorn among themselves. I
shall not go underground with such shame; but I shall rather have
shown, as much as can be shown openly, the scorn of you which is
locked in my breast, although I know that oblivion presses upon
those who are too hateful to their own age. Much already have I
laughed at this evil which I shall share with you. You keep dreaming of Liberty and you want thought to be once more the slave of

sol per cui risorgemmo
dalla barbarie in parte, e per cui solo
si cresce in civiltà, che sola in meglio
guida i pubblici fati.
Così ti spiacque il vero
dell'aspra sorte e del depresso loco
che natura ci diè. Per questo il tergo
vigliaccamente rivolgesti al lume
che il fe palese: e, fuggitivo, appelli
vil chi lui segue, e solo
magnanimo colui
che sè schernendo o gli altri, astuto o folle,
fin sopra gli astri il mortal grado estolle.

Uom di povero stato e membra inferme,
che sia dell'alma generoso ed alto,
non chiama sè nè stima
ricco d'or nè gagliardo,
e di splendida vita o di valente
persona infra la gente
non fa risibil mostra;

a single age, thought by which alone we have risen a little above barbarism, and by which alone one grows in civilization, and which alone guides public destinies for the best. So unpleasant have proved the truths of the hard fate and the low place that nature gave you. Because of this you have turned your backs cravenly on the light which made them clear, and fleeing you call coward him who follows it, and great-hearted only him who, mocking himself or others, in cunning or foolishness, extols the human state above the stars.

Always a creature of scant power and weak limbs, a man who is also generous and exalted of soul does not boast or value himself for being lusty or rich in gold, and does not make a laughable show of splendid life or strength among people; but lets himself appear

ma sè di forza e di tesor mendico
lascia parer senza vergogna, e noma
parlando, apertamente, e di sue cose
fa stima al vero uguale.
Magnanimo animale
non credo io già, ma stolto,
quel che nato a perir, nutrito in pene,
dice, a goder son fatto,
e di fetido orgoglio
empie le carte, eccelsi fati e nove
felicità, quali il ciel tutto ignora,
non pur quest'orbe, promettendo in terra
a' popoli che un'onda
di mar commosso, un fiato
d'aura maligna, un sotterraneo crollo
distrugge sì, ch'avanza
a gran pena di lor la rimembranza.
Nobil natura è quella
ch'a sollevar s'ardisce
gli occhi mortali incontra
al comun fato, e che con franca lingua,
nulla al ver detraendo,
confessa il mal che ci fu dato in sorte,
e il basso stato e frale;

beggared of strength and treasure, and talks of this openly, and
gives a value that is the true one to his possessions. I do not at all
believe him a great-hearted creature who, born to perish, nourished
in pains, says, I was made to have enjoyment, and fills pages with
noisome pride, promising exalted fortunes and new happinesses,
unknown to heaven, far less this world, to peoples whom a wave
of the sea aroused, a breath of pestilent wind, a subterranean col-
lapse so destroys that the memory of them hardly remains. His is a
noble nature who dares to raise mortal eyes against the common
fate, and who, with free tongue, not detracting anything from the
truth, attests the evil and the low weak state that has been given to
us as destiny; that nature which shows itself great and strong in

quella che grande e forte
mostra sè nel soffrir, nè gli odii e l'ire
fraterne, ancor più gravi
d'ogni altro danno, accresce
alle miserie sue, l'uomo incolpando
del suo dolor, ma dà la colpa a quella
che veramente è rea, che de' mortali
è madre in parto ed in voler matrigna.
Costei chiama inimica; e incontro a questa
congiunta esser pensando,
siccom'è il vero, ed ordinata in pria
l'umana compagnia,
tutti fra sè confederati estima
gli uomini, e tutti abbraccia
con vero amor, porgendo
valida e pronta ed aspettando aita
negli alterni perigli e nelle angosce
della guerra comune. Ed alle offese
dell'uomo armar la destra, e laccio porre
al vicino ed inciampo,
stolto crede così qual fora in campo
cinto d'oste contraria, in sul più vivo
incalzar degli assalti,

suffering, and does not add to its miseries with hates and anger against brother men (things clearly graver than every other ill), blaming man for its grief, but gives the blame to her who is truly evil, who is the mother of humankind in bearing them, and their stepmother in feelings. He calls her enemy; and considering the human brotherhood to be, first of all, ordered and united against her, as is true, he deems all men to be allies, and embraces all with true love, offering genuine and ready help, and expecting as much, in the successive perils and anguishes of the common war. And to take up arms to the hurt of man, and to set snares and obstacles for his neighbour, he thinks as foolish an action as it would be on the battlefield, surrounded by a hostile army, in the most desperate moment of attack, to begin fierce struggles with friends, while

gl'inimici obbliando, acerbe gare
imprender con gli amici,
e sparger fuga e fulminar col brando
infra i proprii guerrieri.
Così fatti pensieri
quando fien, come fur, palesi al volgo,
e quell'orror che primo
contra l'empia natura
strinse i mortali in social catena,
fia ricondotto in parte
da verace saper, l'onesto e il retto
conversar cittadino,
e giustizia e pietade, altra radice
avranno allor che non superbe fole,
ove fondata probità del volgo
così star suole in piede
qual star può quel ch'ha in error la sede.

Sovente in queste rive,
che, desolate, a bruno
veste il flutto indurato, e par che ondeggi,
seggo la notte; e su la mesta landa
in purissimo azzurro
veggo dall'alto fiammeggiar le stelle,

enemies are forgotten, and to spread flight and descend with the
sword among one's own warriors. When thoughts of this kind are, as
they were, revealed to the crowd, together with the horror that first
drew mortals together in a social chain against unholy Nature, then
shall the honest and upright intercourse of the city be brought back,
in part, by right knowledge, and justice and piety will then have
another root than that of proud follies, upon which the established
morality of the vulgar is used to stand, as well as that may stand
which is founded upon error.

  Often upon these slopes which, abandoned as they are, the solid
flow clothes in brown, and, it seems, still undulates, I sit at night
and, upon the sad waste, see the stars that flame from purest blue,

cui di lontan fa specchio
il mare, e tutto di scintille in giro
per lo voto seren brillare il mondo.
E poi che gli occhi a quelle luci appunto,
ch'a lor sembrano un punto,
e son immense in guisa
che un punto a petto a lor son terra e mare
veracemente; a cui
l'uomo non pur, ma questo
globo ove l'uomo è nulla,
sconosciuto è del tutto; e quando miro
quegli ancor più senz'alcun fin remoti
nodi quasi di stelle,
ch'a noi paion qual nebbia, a cui non l'uomo
e non la terra sol, ma tutte in uno,
del numero infinite e della mole,
con l'aureo sole insiem, le nostre stelle
o son ignote, o così paion come
essi alla terra, un punto
di luce nebulosa; al pensier mio
che sembri allora, o prole
dell'uomo? E rimembrando
il tuo stato quaggiù, di cui fa segno
il suol ch'io premo; e poi dall'altra parte,

mirrored from afar by the sea, and see the world all shining with
sparks that turn through empty heaven. And then I focus my eyes
on those lights that seem a point to them, and are so huge that the
sea and the earth compared to them are, in reality, a point; to which
not only man, but this globe where man is nothing, is completely
unknown; and when I gaze at those knots, almost, of stars which
are even more, are infinitely remote, which to us seem like a mist,
and to which, not only man or the earth, but all the sum of our
stars, infinite in number and size, together with the golden sun are
either unknown, or appear a point of misty light as those knots
themselves do to the earth, what do you seem in my judgement
then, o children of men? And when I remember your condition
here below, which the ground I press on testifies; and then, on the

che te signora e fine
credi tu data al Tutto, e quante volte
favoleggiar ti piacque, in questo oscuro
granel di sabbia, il qual di terra ha nome,
per tua cagion, dell'universe cose
scender gli autori, e conversar sovente
co' tuoi piacevolmente, e che i derisi
sogni rinnovellando, ai saggi insulta
fin la presente età, che in conoscenza
ed in civil costume
sembra tutte avanzar; qual moto allora,
mortal prole infelice, o qual pensiero
verso te finalmente il cor m'assale?
No so se il riso o la pietà prevale.

Come d'arbor cadendo un picciol pomo,
cui là nel tardo autunno
maturità senz'altra forza atterra,
d'un popol di formiche i dolci alberghi
cavati in molle gleba
con gran lavoro, e l'opre,
e le ricchezze ch'adunate a prova

other hand, that you believe you have been appointed master and
end of All, and how often you like to tell tales of the authors of
universal things, how they come down upon this unknown grain
of sand called the earth on your account, and often speak with you
pleasantly; and when I remember too, that, renewing these laughable dreams, you insult the wise right to the present age, which
seems to surpass all others in knowledge and social usage; what
feeling, then, or what thought for you, assails my heart, o unhappy
humankind? I do not know if laughter or pity predominates.

As a little apple which ripeness, with no other aid, brings to
earth in the late autumn, falls, crushes, lays waste, and covers at one
and the same moment the sweet mansions of a people of ants which
had been hollowed out of the soft loam with great labour, and their
works and their riches which the industrious tribe, vying with one

con lunga affaticar l' assidua gente
avea provvidamente al tempo estivo,
schiaccia, diserta e copre
in un punto; così d'alto piombando,
dall'utero tonante
scagliata al ciel profondo,
di ceneri e di pomici e di sassi
notte e ruina, infusa
di bollenti ruscelli,
o pel montano fianco
furïosa tra l'erba
di liquefatti massi
e di metalli e d'infocata arena
scendendo immensa piena,
le cittadi che il mar là su l'estremo
lido aspergea, confuse
e infranse e ricoperse
in pochi istanti: onde su quelle or pasce
la capra, e città nove
sorgon dall'altra banda, a cui sgabello
son le sepolte, e le prostrate mura
l'arduo monte al suo piè quasi calpesta.
Non ha natura al seme
dell'uom più stima o cura

another, with long fatigue, had gathered in the summertime, so
were the cities which the sea washed, on its very edge, shattered
and covered over in a few minutes by a night and ruin of ashes,
pumice, stones, in molten streams, which, shot up to far heaven
from the thundering womb, rained down from on high, or by the
huge overflowing of liquified masses, of metals and burning sand,
which came down the mountain side furiously through the grass: so
that over those cities now browses the goat, and new cities rise
opposite which have for their seat the buried and prostrate walls
that the mountain almost tramples at its foot. Nature has no more
regard or care for the seed of man than for the ant: and if the mas-

ch'alla formica: e se più rara in quello
che nell'altra è la strage,
non avvien ciò d'altronde
fuor che l'uom sue prosapie ha men feconde.

Ben mille ed ottocento
anni varcàr poi che spariro, oppressi
dall'ignea forza, i popolati seggi,
e il villanello intento
ai vigneti che a stento in questi campi
nutre la morta zolla e incenerita,
ancor leva lo sguardo
sospettoso alla vetta
fatal, che nulla mai fatta più mite
ancor siede tremenda, ancor minaccia
a lui strage ed ai figli ed agli averi
lor poverelli. E spesso
il meschino in sul tetto
dell'ostel villereccio, alla vagante
aura giacendo tutta notte insonne,
e balzando più volte, esplora il corso
del temuto bollor, che si riversa
dall'inesausto grembo
su l'arenoso dorso, a cui riluce

sacre of the one is less frequent than that of the other, this happens for no other reason than that man is less fertile in offspring.

Full a thousand and eight hundred years have passed away since the peopled places disappeared, crushed by fiery might, and the peasant busy at his vine which the dead and ashy soil of these fields barely nourishes, still lifts his eyes suspiciously to the fatal peak that, not for a moment milder, still sits awesome, still threatens destruction to him and his children and their poor little possessions. And often the wretch lying sleepless in the wandering breeze upon the roof of his rustic dwelling, jumps up repeatedly and scans the course of the fearful molten lava which pours from the unexhausted womb on to the sandy sides, and its light is reflected in the bay of

di Capri la marina
e di Napoli il porto e Mergellina.
E se appressar lo vede, o se nel cupo
del domestico pozzo ode mai l'acqua
fervendo gorgogliar, desta i figliuoli,
desta la moglie in fretta, e via, con quanto
di lor cose rapir posson, fuggendo,
vede lontan, l'usato
suo nido, e il picciol campo,
che gli fu dalla fame unico schermo,
preda al flutto rovente,
che crepitando giunge, e inesorato
durabilmente sopra quei si spiega.

Torna al celeste raggio
dopo l'antica obblivion l'estinta
Pompei, come sepolto
scheletro, cui di terra
avarizia o pietà rende all'aperto;
e dal deserto foro
diritto infra le file
de' mozzi colonnati il peregrino
lunge contempla il bipartito giogo

Capri, and the port of Naples, and Mergellina. And if he sees it
approaching, or if he ever hears the water gurgling feverishly in
the gloom of the household well, he wakes his children, he hur-
riedly wakes his wife, and, fleeing with as much of their belongings
as they can snatch up, he sees from safe distance his accustomed nest
and the little field which was his only shield against hunger, fall
prey to the white-hot tide that arrives crackling and, relentless,
spreads over these things durably.

After ancient obliteration lifeless Pompeii returns to daylight
like a buried skeleton that the earth's greed or pity gives back to
the air; and from the deserted forum the pilgrim gazes for long
where, rising between the lines of truncated columns, he sees the

e la cresta fumante,
ch'alla sparsa ruina ancor minaccia.
E nell'orror della secreta notte
per li vacui teatri,
per li templi deformi e per le rotte
case, ove i parti il pipistrello asconde,
come sinistra face
che per voti palagi atra s'aggiri,
corre il baglior della funerea lava,
che di lontan per l'ombre
rosseggia e i lochi intorno intorno tinge.
Così, dell'uomo ignara e dell'etadi
ch'ei chiama antiche, e del seguir che fanno
dopo gli avi i nepoti,
sta natura ognor verde, anzi procede
per sì lungo cammino
che sembra star. Caggiono i regni intanto,
passan genti e linguaggi: ella nol vede:
e l'uom d'eternità s'arroga il vanto.

divided peak and the smoking summit which still threaten the scattered ruin. And in the horror of the secret night, through the empty theatres, and the deformed temples and broken houses where the bat conceals its young, the glow of the deathly lava hastens like an evil torch circling blackly through vacant palaces, and from afar reddens through the shades, and stains all the places about. So, heedless of man and the ages which he calls ancient, and of the way in which the youngest generation follow their ancestors, Nature keeps green at all times, rather goes forward by so long a road that it seems to stand still. Meanwhile kingdoms fall, races and languages pass away: she does not see this: and man usurps the boast of eternity.

E tu, lenta ginestra,
che di selve odorate
queste campagne dispogliate adorni,
anche tu presto alla crudel possanza
soccomberai del sotterraneo foco,
che ritornando al loco
già noto, stenderà l'avaro lembo
su tue molli foreste. E piegherai
sotto il fascio mortal non renitente
il tuo capo innocente:
ma non piegato insino allora indarno
codardamente supplicando innanzi
al futuro oppressor; ma non eretto
con forsennato orgoglio inver le stelle,
nè sul deserto, dove
e la sede e i natali
non per voler ma per fortuna avesti;
ma più saggia, ma tanto
meno inferma dell'uom, quanto le frali
tue stirpi non credesti
o dal fato o da te fatte immortali.

And you, slow bush of broom, that deck these bare country places with fragrant copses, you too will soon fall to the cruel power of the subterranean fire, which, coming again to its known limit, will stretch its rapacious hem over your soft forests. And you will bend your innocent head beneath the mortal burden without struggling; but a head that has not been bent in cowardly supplication, vainly, before the coming oppressor; nor raised with vainglorious pride towards the stars, nor upon the desert where you sprang and grew not by choosing to, but by chance. But you will have been wiser and so much the less infirm than man, as you did not believe your frail kind made immortal by fate or by yourself.

GIUSEPPE GIUSTI

La guigliottina a vapore

Hanno fatto nella China
una macchina a vapore
per mandar la guigliottina:
questa macchina in tre ore
fa la testa a cento mila
         messi in fila.

L'instrumento ha fatto chiasso,
e quei preti han presagito
che il paese passo passo
sarà presto incivilito;
rimarrà come un babbeo
         l'Europeo.

L'imperante è un uomo onesto;
un po' duro, un po' tirato,
un po' ciuco, ma del resto
ama i sudditi e lo Stato,
e protegge i bell'ingegni
         de' suoi regni.

The Steam-driven Guillotine

They have made a steam engine in China to oust the guillotine: this machine in three hours looks after the heads of a hundred thousand, queueing in a line.

The instrument has caused a stir, and the local priests have predicted that the country will soon, step by step, be civilized; the European will meantime seem a dunce.

The Emperor is an honest man, a little hard, a little stingy, a little stupid, but, for the rest, he loves his subjects and the State, and he patronizes the brilliant minds of his dominions.

V' era un popolo ribelle
che pagava a malincuore
i catasti e le gabelle:
il benigno imperatore
ha provato in quel paese
           quest'arnese.

La virtù dell'istrumento
ha fruttato una pensione
a quel boia di talento,
col brevetto d'invenzione,
e l'ha fatto Mandarino
           di Pekino.

Grida un frate: oh! bella cosa!
gli va dato anco il battesimo.
ah perchè, (dice al Canosa
un Tiberio in diciottesimo),
questo genio non m'è nato
           nel Ducato!

There was a rebellious people who payed taxes and import duty with an ill-will: the kindly emperor has tried this apparatus in that country.

The worth of the instrument has produced a pension for that talented executioner, with patent rights for his invention, and has made him a Mandarin of Peking.

A friar shouts: Oh! What a fine thing! It is also to be baptized. Ah why, (says a thumbnail Tiberius * to Canosa †), wasn't this genius born in my Duchy!

---

* The Duke of Modena.   † His minister.

La chiocciola

Viva la chiocciola,
viva una bestia
che unisce il merito
alla modestia.
Essa all'astronomo
e all'architetto
forse nell'animo
destò il concetto
del cannocchiale,
e delle scale:
    viva la chiocciola,
    caro animale.

Contenta ai comodi
che Dio la fece,
può dirsi il Diogene
della sua spece.
Per prender aria
non passa l'uscio;
nelle abitudini
del proprio guscio
sta persuasa
e non intasa:
    viva la chiocciola
    bestia da casa.

The Snail

Long live the snail, long live a beast that unites merit with modesty. It perhaps suggested to the astronomer and the architect the telescope and the spiral staircase. Long live the snail, dear animal.

Content with the comforts which God provided, it could be called the Diogenes of its species. To take the air it doesn't step across its threshold; it is confirmed in the habits of its own shell and does not catch colds: long live the snail, household beast.

Di cibi estranei
acre prurito
svegli uno stomaco
senza appetito:
essa, sentendosi
bene in arnese,
ha gusto a rodere
del suo paese
tranquillamente
l'erba nascente:
  viva la chiocciola,
  bestia astinente.

Nessun procedere
sa colle buone,
e più d'un asino
fa da leone.
Essa al contrario,
bestia com'è,
tira a proposito
le corna a sè;
non fa l'audace,
ma frigge e tace:
  viva la chiocciola,
  bestia di pace.

 Let the piquancy of exotic foods stimulate a stomach without appetite: the snail feels itself in good shape and likes to nibble the springing grass of its home country: long live the snail, abstemious beast.

 No one knows how to get on with kindness and so every one acts like a lion rather than an ass. The snail, on the contrary, draws its horns in just at the right moment; it does not go in for daring, but splutters and is silent: long live the snail, peaceful beast.

Natura, varia
ne' suoi portenti,
la privilegia
sopra i viventi
perchè (carnefici,
sentite questa)
le fa rinascere
perfin la testa;
cosa mirabile,
ma indubitabile;
     viva la chiocciola,
     bestia invidiabile.

Gufi dottissimi,
che predicate
e al vostro simile
nulla insegnate;
e, voi, girovaghi,
ghiotti, scapati,
padroni idrofobi,
servi arrembati,
prego a cantare
l'intercalare:
     viva la chiocciola,
     bestia esemplare.

Nature, that varies in its prodigies, has favoured the snail more than ordinary living beings, because (listen to this, you executioners) she makes even its head grow again; a wonderful thing, but not to be doubted: long live the snail, enviable beast.

Most learned owls who preach and teach your neighbour nothing; and you, scavengers, gluttons, numbskulls, rabid masters, brokendown servants, I beg you to sing the refrain: long live the snail, exemplary beast.

Sant' Ambrogio

VOSTRA Eccellenza, che mi sta in cagnesco
per que' pochi scherzucci di dozzina,
e mi gabella per anti-tedesco
perche metto le birbe alla berlina,
o senta il caso avvenuto di fresco
a me, che girellando, una mattina
càpito in Sant'Ambrogio di Milano,
in quello vecchio, là, fuori di mano.

M'era compagno il figlio giovinetto
d'un di que' capi un po' pericolosi
di quel tal Sandro, autor d'un romanzetto,
ove si tratta di Promessi Sposi. ...
Che fa il nesci, Eccellenza? o non l'ha letto?
Ah, intendo: il suo cervel, Dio lo riposi,
in tutt'altre faccende affaccendato,
a questa roba è morto e sotterrato.

Entro, e ti trovo un pieno di soldati,
di que' soldati settentrionali,
come sarebbero Boemi e Croati,
messi qui nella vigna a far da pali:

The Church of Sant' Ambrogio

YOUR Excellency, who is cross with me for those few trifling little
jokes of mine, and labels me for anti-German because I pillory
rogues, oh listen to this experience which recently came my way
when, wandering around one morning, I happened to enter
Sant'Ambrogio, the old one, there, out of the way.

I was accompanied by the young son of one of those slightly
dangerous brains, of that certain Sandro, author of a little novel
which deals with The Betrothed. ... Why look as if you know
nothing about it, Excellency? or haven't you read it? Oh, I understand: your brain, God rest it, is busied with quite different busi-
ness, and is dead and buried to stuff of this kind.

I go in, and I find a full house of soldiers, those northern soldiers, likely to be Bohemians and Croats, stuck here in the vineyard

difatto se ne stavano impalati,
come sogliono in faccia a' generali,
co' baffi di capecchio e con que' musi,
davanti a Dio, diritti come fusi.

Mi tenni indietro; chè, piovuto in mezzo
di quella maramaglia, io non lo nego
d' aver provato un senso di ribrezzo,
che lei non prova in grazia dell'impiego.
Sentiva un'afa, un alito di lezzo;
scusi, Eccellenza, mi parean di sego,
in quella bella casa del Signore,
fin le candele dell'altar maggiore.

Ma, in quella che s'appresta il sacerdote
a consacrar la mistica vivanda,
di subita dolcezza mi percuote
su, di verso l'altare, un suon di banda.
Dalle trombe di guerra uscian le note
come di voce che si raccomanda,
d'una gente che gema in duri stenti
e de' perduti beni si rammenti.

to serve as poles: in fact they stood planted there as they do normally before a general, with their tow moustaches and those faces
of theirs, before God, straight as spindles.

I kept back; for, when I landed in among that mob, I don't deny
it, I experienced a sense of revulsion, which you don't experience
thanks to your job. My nostrils were assailed by a mugginess, a
faint stink; 'beg your pardon, Excellency, but even the candles on
the great altar seemed of suet in that fine house of God.

But at the moment when the priest makes ready to consecrate the
mystic food, the music of a band, from up near the altar, struck me
with instant sweetness. Notes came from the war-trumpets that
were like the pleading voice of a people who groan in hardship and
remember lost possessions.

Era un coro del Verdi; il coro a Dio
là de' Lombardi miseri, assetati;
quello: *O Signore, dal tetto natìo,*
che tanti petti ha scossi e inebriati.
Qui cominciai a non esser più io;
e, come se que' così diventati
fossero gente della nostra gente,
entrai nel branco involontariamente.

Che vuol ella, Eccellenza, il pezzo è bello,
poi nostro, e poi sonato come va:
e coll'arte di mezzo, e col cervello
dato all' arte, l'ubbie si buttan là.
Ma, cessato che fu, dentro, bel bello,
io ritornava a star come la sa;
quand'eccoti per farmi un altro tiro,
da quelle bocche che parean di ghiro,

un cantico tedesco, lento lento,
per l'aer sacro a Dio mosse le penne:
era preghiera, e mi parea lamento,
d'un suono grave, flebile, solenne,

It was a chorus by Verdi; that chorus to God sung by the Lom-
bards, thirsting and sorrowful; that: *O Lord, from the houses where
we were born*, which has shaken and filled so many bosoms. At this
point I began to be myself no longer; and, as if those others had at
this become people of our people, I entered involuntarily into the
crowd.

What's surprising, Excellency, the piece is a fine one, then ours,
and then played as it should be: and when art comes between, and
when the mind is given to art, prejudices are thrown aside. But
when it had finished, gradually in myself I came again to feel you
know how; when, there, to play me another trick, from those
mouths like those of dormice,

a German song slowly, slowly moved its wings through that air
sacred to God: it was a prayer and it seemed a lament to me, one
of earnest, plaintive, solemn tone, such that I keep hearing it in

tal, che sempre nell'anima lo sento;
e mi stupisco che in quelle cotenne,
in quei fantocci esotici di legno,
potesse l'armonia fino a quel segno.

Sentia, nell'inno, la dolcezza amara
de' canti uditi da fanciullo: il core,
che da voce domestica gl'impara,
ce li ripete i giorni del dolore:
un pensier mesto della madre cara,
un desiderio di pace e d'amore,
uno sgomento di lontano esilio,
che mi faceva andare in visibilio.

E, quando tacque, mi lasciò pensoso
di pensieri più forti e più soavi.
– Costor, dicea tra me, re pauroso
degl'italici moti e degli slavi,
strappa a' lor tetti, e qua, senza riposo,
schiavi gli spinge, per tenerci schiavi;
gli spinge di Croazia e di Boemme,
come mandre a svernar nelle Maremme.

my soul; and I marvel that in those squareheads, in those out-
landish, wooden puppets, harmony could achieve so much.

I heard, in the hymn, the bitter sweetness of songs listened to in
childhood: the heart, which learns them from a familiar voice, sings
them over in days of sorrow: a sad thought of our dear mother, a
desire for peace and love, dismay at distant exile, which melted me.

And when it hushed, it left me thinking stronger, sweeter
thoughts. These men, I said to myself, are snatched from their
homes by a king afraid of Italian and Slav stirrings, and are forced
here, without pause, as slaves to keep us slaves; he drives them
from Croatia and Bohemia as flocks are driven to winter in the
Maremma.

A dura vita, a dura disciplina,
muti, derisi, solitari stanno,
strumenti ciechi d'occhiuta rapina,
che lor non tocca e che forse non sanno:
e quest'odio, che mai non avvicina
il popolo lombardo all'alemanno,
giova a chi regna dividendo, e teme
popoli avversi affratellati insieme.

Povera gente! lontana da' suoi,
in un paese, qui, che le vuol male,
chi sa che, in fondo all'anima, po' poi,
non mandi a quel paese il principale!
Gioco che l'hanno in tasca come noi. –
Qui, se non fuggo, abbraccio un caporale,
colla su' brava mazza di nocciolo,
duro e piantato lì come un piolo.

Living a hard life, subject to hard discipline, they remain silent,
mocked at, and alone, blind instruments of keen-eyed rapine, which
does not fall to them and which they perhaps do not know of. And
this hate which never lets the Lombard people approach the German, serves the purposes of a king who reigns by dividing, and
who fears hostile peoples banded in brotherliness.

Poor souls! far from their own, in a country, here, that wishes
them harm, who knows but that they, deep down, would have the
emperor at the devil! I bet they loathe him as we do. – At this
point, if I do not fly, I shall embrace a corporal with his brave hazel
staff, standing there stiff and rooted as a stake.

GIOSUÈ CARDUCCI

Pianto antico

L'ALBERO a cui tendevi
la pargoletta mano,
il verde melograno
da' bei vermigli fior,

nel muto orto solingo
rinverdì tutto or ora
e giugno lo ristora
di luce e di calor.

Tu fior de la mia pianta
percossa e inaridita,
tu de l'inutil vita
estremo unico fior,

sei ne la terra fredda,
sei ne la terra negra;
nè il sol più ti rallegra
nè ti risveglia amor.

Ancient Lament

THE tree to which you stretched your baby hand, the green
pomegranate-tree with its fine scarlet flowers,
has just grown green again in the deserted, silent courtyard and
June is reviving it with light and heat.
You, flower of my stricken, dried-up plant, you the last only
flower of my useless life,
you are in the cold earth, you are in the black earth, nor does the
sun any longer delight, nor can love wake you.

Il comune rustico

O CHE tra faggi e abeti erma su i campi
smeraldini la fredda orma si stampi
al sole del mattin puro e leggero,
o che foscheggi immobile nel giorno
morente su le sparse ville intorno
a la chiesa che prega o al cimitero

che tace, o noci de la Carnia, addio!
Erra tra i vostri rami il pensier mio
sognando l'ombre d'un tempo che fu.
Non paure di morti ed in congreghe
diavoli goffi con bizzarre streghe,
ma del comun la rustica virtù

accampata a l'opaca ampia frescura
veggo ne la stagion de la pastura
dopo la messa il giorno de la festa.
Il consol dice, e poste ha pria le mani
sopra i santi segnacoli cristiani:
– Ecco, io parto fra voi quella foresta

The Country Community

WHETHER between beech-trees and firs your cold imprint be left,
lone upon the emerald fields in the sun of pure and lightsome morning, or it gloom motionless in the day that dies upon the scattered
dwellings around the praying church or the cemetery that

is silent, farewell, o chestnut-trees of Carnia! My thoughts roam
among your branches, dreaming of the shades of a time that is gone.
Not fears of the dead or gross devils leagued with fantastic witches
do I see, but the rustic virtue of the community

displayed in the dim and spreading chill in the season of pasturage, after mass on a holiday. The Consul says, and first he has laid
his hands upon the sacred Christian symbols: 'There, I divide
among you that forest

d'abeti e pini ove al confin nereggia.
E voi trarrete la mugghiante greggia
e la belante a quelle cime là.
E voi, se l'unno o se lo slavo invade,
eccovi, o figli, l'aste, ecco le spade,
morete per la nostra libertà. –

Un fremito d'orgoglio empieva i petti,
ergea le bionde teste; e de gli eletti
in su le fronti il sol grande feriva.
Ma le donne piangenti sotto i veli
invocavan la Madre alma de' cieli.
Con la man tesa il console seguiva:

– Questo, al nome di Cristo e di Maria,
ordino e voglio che nel popol sia. –
A man levata il popol dicea Sì.
E le rosse giovenche di su 'l prato
vedean passare il piccolo senato,
brillando su gli abeti il mezzodí.

of firs and pines where it blackens at the edge. And you will take
the lowing herd and the bleating one to those peaks there. And if
the Hun or the Slav invades, here, my sons, is the spear, here are
swords for you, you will die for your liberty.'

A shiver of pride possessed their breasts, it raised the fair heads,
and the sun struck upon the foreheads of the chosen. But the women
weeping beneath their veils, called upon the kindly mother of the
heavens. With outstretched hand the Consul continued:

'This, in the name of Christ and Mary, I order and desire should
have effect among the people.' With raised hands the people said,
So let it be. And the young red heifers on the meadow saw the little
senate pass, as noon shone upon the firs.

Alla stazione in una mattina d'autunno

O H quei fanali come s'inseguono
accidiosi là dietro gli alberi,
tra i rami stillanti di pioggia
sbadigliando la luce su 'l fango!

Flebile, acuta, stridula fischia
la vaporiera da presso. Plumbeo
il cielo e il mattino d'autunno
come un grande fantasma n'è intorno.

Dove e a che move questa, che affrettasi
a' carri foschi, ravvolta e tacita
gente? a che ignoti dolori
o tormenti di speme lontana?

Tu pur pensosa, Lidia, la tessera
al secco taglio dài de la guardia,
e al tempo incalzante i begli anni
dài, gl'istanti gioiti e i ricordi.

At the Station, One Morning in Autumn

O H THOSE lamps how drearily they succeed one another behind the trees, amid branches dripping with rain, their light yawning upon the ground!

Near at hand the train whistles desolate, sharp, shrilling. Leaden, the sky, and the autumn morning is like a great phantom around us.

Where and to what end does this thing move that people, muffled and silent, hurry to dark coaches? to what unknown griefs? to what torment of distant hopes?

You Lydia, thoughtful also, give your ticket to the dry clipping of the collector, and give your lovely years, moments enjoyed, memories, to hastening time.

Van lungo il nero convoglio e vengono
incappucciati di nero i vigili,
come ombre; una fioca lanterna
hanno, e mazze di ferro: ed i ferrei

freni tentati rendono un lugubre
rintocco lungo: di fondo a l'anima
un'eco di tedio risponde
doloroso, che spasimo pare.

E gli sportelli sbattuti al chiudere
paion oltraggi: scherno par l'ultimo
appello che rapido suona:
grossa scroscia su' vetri la pioggia.

Già il mostro, conscio di sua metallica
anima, sbuffa, crolla, ansa, i fiammei
occhi sbarra; immane pe 'l buio
gitta il fischio che sfida lo spazio.

Va l'empio mostro; con traino orribile
sbattendo l'ale gli amor miei portasi.
Ahi, la bianca faccia e 'l bel velo
salutando scompar ne la tènebra.

The guards come and go along the black train, hooded in black,
like shades; they have a dim lantern and iron hammers, and the
iron brakes, tested, respond with a long funeral ring: from the
soul's depth an echo of tedium, lamenting answers, that seems a
start of agony.

And the carriage-doors slammed shut seem outrages: the last
call that sounds briefly, mockery: the rain beats large upon the
window.

Already the monster, conscious of its metallic soul, snorts,
shakes, pants, bares its flaming eyes; huge through the gloom, it
hurls its whistle, challenging space.

The evil monster goes: wings flurrying, it carries away my loves
with its horrible carriages. Ah, the white face and lovely veil disappear, even as they bid farewell, into the shadows.

O viso dolce di pallor roseo,
o stellanti occhi di pace, o candida
tra' floridi ricci inchinata
pura fronte con atto soave!

Fremea la vita nel tepid'aere,
fremea l'estate quando mi arrisero;
e il giovine sole di giugno
si piacea di baciar luminoso

in tra i riflessi del crin castanei
la molle guancia: come un'aureola
più belli del sole i miei sogni
ricingean la persona gentile.

Sotto la pioggia, tra la caligine
torno ora, e ad esse vorrei confondermi;
barcollo com'ebro, e mi tocco,
non anch'io fossi dunque un fantasma.

Oh qual caduta di foglie, gelida,
continua, muta, greve, su l'anima!
io credo che solo, che eterno,
che per tutto nel mondo è novembre.

O soft face of rose-like paleness, o eyes brimming with peace, o
white, pure forehead bent in sweet grace between luxuriant locks!
    Life trembled in the warm air, the summer trembled, when they
smiled on me, and the young sun of June was glad to kiss with light
    the soft cheek amid the auburn lustre of the hair: my dreams,
lovelier than the sun, encircled the gentle form, too, as if with a
halo.
    Under the rain, in the mist, I now go back, and I would be glad
to lose myself in them; I stagger like a drunkard, and touch myself
for fear I too might be a phantom.
    O such a fall of leaves, icy, incessant, silent, grievous, upon the
soul! I believe that only, that eternally, for everything in the world,
it is November.

Meglio a chi 'l senso smarrì de l'essere,
meglio quest'ombra, questa caligine:
io volgio, io voglio adagiarmi
in un tedio che duri infinito.

Mezzogiorno alpino

NEL gran cerchio de l'alpi, su 'l granito
squallido e scialbo, su' ghiacciai candenti,
regna sereno intenso ed infinito
nel suo grande silenzio il mezzodì.

Pini ed abeti senza aura di venti
si drizzano nel sol che gli penètra,
sola garrisce in picciol suon di cetra
l'acqua che tenue tra i sassi fluì.

Congedo

FIOR tricolore,
tramontano le stelle in mezzo al mare
e si spengono i canti entro il mio core.

Luckier he whose senses desert him, better this shadow, this mist; I want, I want to drift in a tedium that stretches to infinity.

Alpine Morning

IN the great circle of the alps, upon the discoloured, pale granite, upon the burning glaciers, noon reigns serene, intense and infinite in its great silence.

Pines and firs untouched by breath of wind rise straight in the sun that penetrates them, only the water that runs thin among the stones protests with the small sound of a lute.

Salute in Farewell

THREE-COLOURED flower,
the stars go down into the midst of the sea
and the songs die within my heart.

GIOVANNI PASCOLI

Allora

ALLORA ... in un tempo assai lunge
felice fui molto; non ora:
ma quanta dolcezza mi giunge
da tanta dolcezza d'allora!

Quell'anno! per anni che poi
fuggirono, che fuggiranno,
non puoi, mio pensiero, non puoi,
portare con te, che quell'anno!

Un giorno fu quello, ch'è senza
compagno, ch'è senza ritorno;
la vita fu van parvenza
sì prima sì dopo quel giorno!

Un punto! ... così passeggero,
che in vero passò non raggiunto,
ma bello così, che molto ero
felice, felice, quel punto!

At that Time

AT that time ... in a most distant time I was very happy; not
now: but how much sweetness comes to me from so much sweetness then!

That year! through all the years that later fled, that will fleet
away, you cannot, my thoughts, you cannot bear with you anything but that year!

It was a day that is without fellow, that is without return; life
was an empty appearance, equally, before and after that day!

A point! ... so passing, that in truth it passed by unattained, but
so lovely that I was happy, very happy, at that point!

Romagna

a Severino

SEMPRE un villaggio, sempre una campagna
mi ride al cuore (o piange), Severino:
il paese ove, andando, ci accompagna
l'azzurra vision di San Marino:

sempre mi torna al cuore il mio paese
cui regnarono Guidi e Malatesta,
cui tenne pure il Passator cortese,
re della strada, re della foresta.

Là nelle stoppie dove singhiozzando
va la tacchina con l'altrui covata,
presso gli stagni lustreggianti, quando
lenta vi guazza l'anatra iridata,

oh! fossi io teco; e perderci nel verde,
e di tra gli olmi, nido alle ghiandaie,
gettarci l'urlo che lungi si perde
dentro il meridiano ozio dell'aie;

The Romagna

to Severino

EVER a village, ever a stretch of countryside laughs at my heart (or
weeps), o Severino: the country where, as we go, we are accompanied by the blue vision of San Marino:

ever my homeland comes back to my heart where Guidi and
Malatesta reigned, which courteous Passator also held, he, king of
the road, and king of the forest.

There among the stubble where the turkey-hen goes wheezing
with a brood not her own, near the shining ponds, where the many-
gleaming duck paddles slow,

oh! might I be with you; and we, lose ourselves in the green,
and from among the elms, the jays' nest, send up the shout which
loses itself in the noon ease of the barn-yards;

mentre il villano pone dalle spalle
gobbe la ronca e afferra la scodella,
e 'l bue rumina nelle opache stalle
la sua laboriosa lupinella.

Da' borghi sparsi le campane in tanto
si rincorron coi lor gridi argentini:
chiamano al rezzo, alla quiete, al santo
desco fiorito d'occhi di bambini.

Già m'accoglieva in quelle ore bruciate
sotto ombrello di trine una mimosa,
che fioria la mia casa ai dì d'estate
co' suoi pennacchi di color di rosa;

e s'abbracciava per lo sgretolato
muro un folto rosaio a un gelsomino;
guardava il tutto un pioppo alto e slanciato,
chiassoso a giorni come un biricchino.

Era il mio nido: dove, immobilmente,
io galoppava con Guidon Selvaggio
e con Astolfo; o mi vedea presente
l'imperatore nell'eremitaggio.

while the farmhand takes the pruning-fork from his humped
shoulders and grasps the bowl, and the ox chews its monotonous
cud in the dim stalls.

From the scattered hamlets, meanwhile, the bells mingle their
silvery shouts: they call to repose, to quiet, to the pious table
decked with the flowers of children's eyes.

Once a mimosa welcomed me under a trailing umbrella in those
burnt hours, a mimosa which decorated my house in summer days
with its pink tassels;

and a thick rose-bush embraced a jasmine through the crumbling wall; a poplar, tall and slender, noisy by day as a cheeky boy,
looked upon the whole scene.

It was my nest: where, without moving, I galloped with Guidon
Selvaggio and with Astolfo; or saw before me the emperor in the
hermitage.

E mentre aereo mi poneva in via
con l'ippogrifo pel sognato alone,
o risonava nella stanza mia
muta il dettare di Napoleone;

udia tra i fieni allor allor falciati
de' grilli il verso che perpetuo trema,
udiva dalle rane dei fossati
un lungo interminabile poema.

E lunghi, e interminati, erano quelli
ch'io meditai, mirabili a sognare:
stormir di frondi, cinguettìo d'uccelli,
risa di donne, strepito di mare.

Ma da quel nido, rondini tardive,
tutti tutti migrammo un giorno nero;
io, la mia patria or è dove si vive;
gli altri son poco lungi; in cimitero.

Così più non verrò per la calura
tra que' tuoi polverosi biancospini,
ch'io non ritrovi nella mia verzura
del cuculo ozioso i piccolini,

And while, aloft, I rode with the hippogriff on the way to the
dreamed-of ring of light, or the sayings of Napoleon echoed in my
noiseless room;

I heard from the hay-fields, cut just then, the cicadas' verse that
endlessly trembles, heard a long, unending poem from the frogs in
the ditches.

And long, and without end, were those which I brooded on,
wonderful things to dream: rustling of leaves, birds' twittering,
women's laughter, roar of the sea.

But from that nest, late swallows, we all, all migrated one black
day; for me, homeland now is where one lives; the others are not
far removed; in the churchyard.

So I shall no longer come in the heat between your dusty haw-
thorns, lest I should find, in my green places, the younglings of the
idle cuckoo,

Romagna solatìa, dolce paese,
cui regnarono Guidi e Malatesta,
cui tenne pure il Passator cortese,
re della strada, re della foresta.

Orfano

LENTA la neve fiocca, fiocca, fiocca.
Senti: una zana dondola pian piano.
Un bimbo piange, il piccol dito in bocca;
canta una vecchia, il mento sulla mano.
La vecchia canta: Intorno al tuo lettino
c'è rose e gigli, tutto un bel giardino.
Nel bel giardino il bimbo s'addormenta.
La neve fiocca lenta, lenta, lenta ...

Novembre

GEMMEA l'aria, il sole così chiaro
che tu ricerchi gli albicocchi in fiore,
e del prunalbo l'odorino amaro
        senti nel cuore ...

lonely Romagna, sweet homeland, where Guidi and Malatesta ruled, which courteous Passator also held, he, king of the road and king of the forest.

Orphan

SLOWLY the snow flakes downward, downward, downward. Listen: a cradle is rocking gently. A child cries, a small finger in its mouth; there is an old woman singing, her chin upon her hand. The old woman is singing: Around your bed there are roses and lilies, a whole lovely garden. In the lovely garden the child is falling asleep. The snow is flaking slowly, slowly, slowly ...

November

GEM-LIKE the air, the sun so clear that you look for the apricots' blossoming, and smell in your heart the bitterish scent of the white-thorn ...

Ma secco è il pruno, e le stecchite piante
di nere trame segnano il sereno,
e vuoto il cielo, e cavo al piè sonante
                sembra il terreno.

Silenzio, intorno: solo, alle ventate,
odi lontano, da giardini ed orti,
di foglie un cader fragile. È l'estate,
                fredda, dei morti.

La voce

C'è una voce nella mia vita,
che avverto nel punto che muore;
   voce stanca, voce smarrita,
col tremito del batticuore:

voce d'una accorsa anelante,
che al povero petto s'afferra
   per dir tante cose e poi tante,
ma piena ha la bocca di terra:

But the thornbush is dry, and the stick-like plants mark the heavens with black designs, and empty is the sky, and the earth seems hollow, echoing to the step.

Silence, around: only, in the wind's quickening, you hear in the distance, from orchard and garden, a brittle falling of leaves. It is the summer, cold, of the dead.

The Voice

THERE is a voice in my life, which I make out just as it dies; a tired voice, a voice lost, with the tremor of my heart-beat:

voice panting from its haste, that clutches the poor breast to say so many things and so many more, but that mouth is full of earth:

tante tante cose che vuole
ch'io sappia, ricordi, sì ... sì ...
ma di tante tante parole
non sento che un soffio ... Zvanì ...

Quando avevo tanto bisogno
di pane e di compassione,
che mangiavo solo nel sogno,
svegliandomi al primo boccone;

una notte, su la spalletta
del Reno, coperta di neve,
dritto e solo (passava in fretta
l'acqua brontolando, Si beve?);

dritto e solo, con un gran pianto
d'aver a finire così,
mi sentii d'un tratto daccanto
quel soffio di voce ... Zvanì ...

Oh! la terra, com'è cattiva!
la terra, che amari bocconi!
ma voleva dirmi, io capiva:
— No ... no ... Di' le devozioni!

so many things that it wants me to know and remember, like
this ... like that ... but of so many, many words I hear only a
breath ... Johnnie ...
When I was in such need of bread and pity, which I ate only in
dream, waking at the first mouthful;
one night, on the snow-covered edge of the Reno, I, upright and
alone (the river passed mumbling, will you drink?);
upright and alone, weeping bitterly to have to end like this, I
suddenly heard at my side that breathing voice ... Johnnie ...
Oh! how wicked the earth is! the earth, what bitter mouthfuls!
but it wanted to say to me, I understood: 'No ... no. ... Say your
prayers!

Le dicevi con me pian piano,
con sempre la voce più bassa:
  la tua mano nella mia mano:
ridille! vedrai che ti passa.

  Non far piangere piangere piangere
(ancora!) chi tanto soffrì!
  il tuo pane, prega il tuo angelo
che te lo porti ... Zvanì ... –

  Una notte dalle lunghe ore
(nel carcere!), che all'improvviso
  dissi – Avresti molto dolore,
tu, se non t'avessero ucciso,

  ora, o babbo! – che il mio pensiero,
dal carcere, con un lamento,
  vide il babbo nel cimitero,
le pie sorelline in convento:

  e che agli uomini, la mia vita,
volevo lasciargiela lì ...
  risentii la voce smarrita
che disse in un soffio ... Zvanì ...

'You used to say them with me quietly with a voice that fell lower and lower: your hand in my hand: say them again! you will see that this will pass from you.

'Do not make her weep, weep, weep (still!) who suffered so much! beg your angel to bring you your bread ... Johnnie ...'

On a night of long hours (in prison!), when suddenly I said, 'You would have grieved much, now, if they had not killed you, o father!' when my thoughts, from prison, saw, with woe, my father in the cemetery, my devout little sisters in the convent:

and when I wished to leave my life to men there ... I heard the lost voice again which said breathingly ... Johnnie ...

Oh! la terra come è cattiva!
non lascia discorrere, poi!
    Ma voleva dirmi, io capiva:
– Piuttosto di' un requie per noi!

    Non possiamo nel camposanto
più prendere sonno un minuto,
    chè sentiamo struggersi in pianto
le bimbe che l'hanno saputo!

    Oh! la vita mia che ti diedi
per loro, lasciarla vuoi qui?
    qui, mio figlio? dove non vedi
chi uccise tuo padre ... Zvanì? –

    Quante volte sei rivenuta
nei cupi abbandoni del cuore,
    voce stanca, voce perduta,
col tremito del batticuore:

    voce d'una accorsa anelante
che ai poveri labbri si tocca
    per dir tante cose e poi tante;
ma piena di terra ha la bocca:

Oh! how wicked the earth is! do not let it be spoken of, then! But you wanted to say to me, I understood: 'Rather say a requiem for us!

'We cannot take our rest in the churchyard a moment, for we hear our daughters who witnessed our end, wasting themselves in weeping.

'Oh! do you want to lay down here that life of mine I gave you for them? Here, my son? Where you do not see who killed your father ... Johnnie?'

How many times have you returned in the dark surrenders of my heart, tired voice, voice lost, with the tremor of my heart-beat:

voice panting from its haste, which touches the poor lips to say so many things and so many more; but that mouth is full of earth:

la tua bocca! con i tuoi baci,
già tanto accorati a quei dì!
 a quei dì beati e fugaci
che aveva i tuoi baci Zvanì!

 che m'addormentavano gravi
campane col placido canto,
 e sul capo biondo che amavi,
sentivo un tepore di pianto!

 che ti lessi negli occhi, ch'erano
pieni di pianto, che sono
 pieni di terra, la preghiera
di vivere e d'essere buono!

 Ed allora, quasi un comando,
no, quasi un compianto, t'uscì
 la parola che a quando a quando
mi dici anche adesso ... Zvanì ...

your mouth! with your kisses, so distressed even in the old days! in those blessed and fleeting days when Johnnie knew your kisses!

for heavy bells would lay me asleep with their peaceful song, and on the fair head which you loved, I would feel the warmth of tears!

for I read in your eyes which were full of tears, which now are full of earth, the prayer to live and be good!

And then, like a command, no, almost a voiced regret, the word escaped from you, which at times you say to me even now ... Johnnie ...

Il gelsomino notturno

E s'aprono i fiori notturni
nell'ora che penso a' miei cari.
Sono apparse in mezzo ai viburni
le farfalle crepuscolari.

Da un pezzo si tacquero i gridi:
là sola una casa bisbiglia.
Sotto l'ali dormono i nidi,
come gli occhi sotto le ciglia.

Dai calici aperti si esala
l'odore di fragole rosse.
Splende un lume là nella sala.
Nasce l'erba sopra le fosse.

Un'ape tardiva sussurra
trovando già prese le celle.
La Chiocetta per l'aia azzurra
va col suo pigolìo di stelle.

Per tutta la notte s'esala
l'odore che passa col vento.

The Jasmine at Night

AND the flowers of night open, in the hour that I think of those dear to me. The twilight butterflies have appeared among the viburnums.

For a while now the cries have ceased: only over there a house whispers. Nests sleep under wings, like eyes under eyelids.

The scent of red strawberries is breathed up from open chalices. A light shines there in the room. Grass springs above ditches.

A late bee murmurs finding the cells already taken. The Hen goes through the blue barnyard followed by her chirping of stars.

All through the night a scent rises that passes with the wind. The

Passa il lume su per la scala;
brilla al primo piano: s'è spento ...

È l'alba: si chiudono i petali
un poco gualciti; si cova,
dentro l'urna molle e segreta,
non so che felicità nuova.

L'ora di Barga

AL mio cantuccio, donde non sento
se non le reste brusir del grano,
il suon dell'ore viene col vento
dal non veduto borgo montano:
suono che uguale, che blando cade,
come una voce che persuade.

Tu dici, È l'ora; tu dici, È tardi,
voce che cadi blanda dal cielo.
Ma un poco ancora lascia che guardi
l'albero, il ragno, l'ape, lo stelo,
cose ch'han molti secoli o un anno
o un'ora, e quelle nubi che vanno.

---

light passes up the stairs: shines out from the first floor: is extinguished ...

It is dawn: the petals close, slightly crumpled; there nests in the soft and secret urn some new happiness, I cannot say what.

Time at Barga

TO my corner, from which I hear nothing but the bearded grain's rustling, the ringing of the hours comes from the unseen mountain hamlet: a sound that falls even, falls mild, like a voice persuading.

You say, It is time; you say, It is late, voice that falls mild from heaven, but let me look a little longer on the tree, the spider, the bee, the stem, things that have many centuries in them, or a year, or an hour, and those clouds that pass.

Lasciami immoto qui rimanere
fra tanto moto d'ale e di fronde;
e udire il gallo che da un podere
chiama, e da un altro l'altro risponde,
e, quando altrove l'anima è fissa,
gli strilli d'una cincia che rissa.

E suona ancora l'ora, e mi manda
prima un suo grido di meraviglia
tinnulo, e quindi con la sua blanda
voce di prima parla e consiglia,
e grave grave grave m'incuora:
mi dice, È tardi; mi dice, È l'ora.

Tu vuoi che pensi dunque al ritorno
voce che cadi blanda dal cielo!
Ma bello è questo poco di giorno
che mi traluce come da un velo!
Lo so ch'è l'ora, lo so ch'è tardi;
ma un poco ancora lascia che guardi.

Let me stay here, unmoving amid so much movement of wing and leaf; and hear the cock that calls from one farm, and from another, the other answers, and, when the soul is elsewhere intent, the shrilling of a tomtit that quarrels.

And the hour rings out again, and addresses me first with its tinkling voice of wonder, and then with its former mild voice speaks and advises and ponderously encourages me: it says to me, It is late; it says to me, It is time.

You want me then to think of my return, voice that falls mild from heaven! But this little part of the day that shines through to me as if from behind a veil is beautiful! I know it is time, I know it is late; but let me stay and watch a little longer.

Lascia che guardi dentro il mio cuore,
lascia ch'io viva del mio passato;
se c'è sul bronco sempre quel fiore,
s'io trovi un bacio che non ho dato!
Nel mio cantuccio d'ombra romita
lascia ch'io pianga su la mia vita!

E suona ancora l'ora, e mi squilla
due volte un grido quasi di cruccio,
e poi, tornata blanda e tranquilla,
mi persuade nel mio cantuccio:
è tardi! è l'ora! Sì, ritorniamo
dove son quelli ch'amano ed amo.

GABRIELE D'ANNUNZIO

Canto del sole

Ecco, e la glauca marina destasi
fresca a' freschissimi favonii; palpita:
ella sente nel grembo
gli amor verdi de l'alighe.

Let me look into my heart. Let me live over my past, to see if there is still that flower upon the tree-stump, if I find a kiss that I have not given! Let me weep over my life from my corner of lonely shade.

And the hour rings again, and a cry almost as of annoyance shakes me with sound twice, and then grown mild and peaceful again, persuades me in my corner: it is late! it is time! Then, let us go back where there are those who love and whom I love.

Song of the Sun

Look, the green sea wakes fresh to freshest breezes; it trembles: it feels in its lap the green loves of the seaweeds.

Sente: la sfiorano a torme i queruli
gabbiani, simili da lunge passano
le fulve e nere vele
pe'l gran sole cullandosi;

e in ampia cerchia ne l'acqua i floridi
poggi specchiantisi paiono imagini
di piramidi vinte
dal trionfo de l'edere.

Thàlatta! thàlatta! Volino, balzino
su su dal giovine core, zampillino
i tuoi brevi pirrichii,
o divino Asclepiade!

O Mare, o gloria, forza d'Italia,
alfin da' liberi tuoi flutti a l'aure
come un acciar temprata
la Giovinezza sfolgori!

Romanza

Dolcemente muor Febbraio
in un biondo suo colore.
Tutta a 'l sol, come un rosaio,
la gran piazza aulisce in fiore.

It feels: the querulous sea-gulls skim it in crowds, similar, in the distance, pass ochre and black sails rocked in the great sun;

and in the broad circle of the water the flowering hills, mirrored, seem images of pyramids overcome in the ivy's triumph.

Thalatta! thalatta! let your short numbers fly, spring from the youthful heart, let them shoot up like sparks, o divine Asclepiades!

O Sea, o glory, strength of Italy, at last from your free surges let Youth flash out like tempered steel to the wind!

Romance

Sweetly dies February in a fairness of its own. All in the sun the great square in flower sends up fragrance like a rose-garden.

Dai novelli fochi accesa,
tutta a l' sol, la Trinità
su la tripla scala ride
ne la pia serenità.

L'obelisco pur fiorito
pare, quale un roseo stelo;
in sue vene di granito
ei gioisce, a mezzo il cielo.

Ode a piè de l'alta scala
la fontana mormorar,
vede a 'l sol l'acque croscianti
ne la barca scintillar.

In sua gloria la Madonna
sorridendo benedice
di su l'agile colonna
lo spettacolo felice.

Cresce il sole per la piazza
dilagando in copia d'or.
È passata la mia bella
e con ella va il mio cuor.

Lit by the new fires, all in the sun, the Trinity laughs above its triple stair-way in the holy clearness.

The obelisque, too, seems to have flowered like a rose-coloured stalk; it glories in its veins of granite amid the heavens.

It hears at the foot of the high stair-way the fountain murmuring, it sees the water pouring in the sun, flashing in the boat.

In her glory the Virgin Mary, smiling from the slender column, bestows a blessing on the happy sight.

The sun grows, flooding the square with abundance of gold. My fair one has passed and with her goes my heart.

A una torpediniera nell' Adriatico

NAVIGLIO d'acciaio, diritto veloce guizzante
bello come un'arme nuda,
vivo palpitante
come se il metallo un cuore terribile chiuda;

tu che solo al freddo coraggio dell'uomo t'affili
come l'arme su la cote,
e non soffri i vili
su la piastra ardente del ponte che il fremito scote;

messaggero primo di morte sul mar guerreggiato,
franco vèlite del mare,
tu passi, – e il tuo fato
io seguo nel flutto guardando la scìa luccicare.

Crollan dal ciel sommo valanghe di nubi difformi
fra colonne alte di raggi;
trapassano a stormi
a stormi gli uccelli radendo con gridi selvaggi;

To a Torpedo-boat in the Adriatic

SHIP of steel, straight, swift, flashing, lovely as a naked weapon,
alive, quivering as if the metal enclosed a terrible heart;
you who are edged only by man's cold courage like the weapon
upon the whetstone, and do not tolerate cowards on the burning
walk of the bridge which the trembling shakes;
first messenger of death on the contested sea, free ranger of the
sea, you pass – and I follow your fate, watching the wake glittering
in the surge.
Phalanxes of misshapen cloud crumble from highest heaven between tall columns of rays; flock after flock of birds skim past with
wild cries;

sotto la bufera cinereo là verso Ancona
l'Adriatico s'oscura:
se di lungi tuona,
il rombo rimbomba giù giù per la cupa calura.

Fa schermo la nube. Ma l'occhio dell'anima scorge
oltremare in lontananza
la città che sorge
alta sul suo golfo splendendo a la nostra speranza,

da tutte le torri splendendo nell'unica fede:
«Sempre a te! Sempre la stessa!»
poi che ancora crede,
la triste sorella domata, a la nostra promessa.

E un'ombra s'allunga, s'aggrava su l'acque (io la scorgo
con un brivido interrotto
crescere, nel gorgo
livido una macchia far come di sangue corrotto);

under the squall the Adriatic darkens to ashen there towards
Ancona: if it thunders in the distance, the rumble re-echoes down,
down through the dark sultriness.

The clouds form a shield. But the soul's eye makes out across the
sea in the distance the city which rises high above its gulf, shining
out to our hope,

from all its towers shining in the one faith: 'Always yours!
Always the same!' since our sad, captive sister still believes in our
promise.

And a shadow stretches, weighs upon the water (I perceive it
growing with an intermittent shudder, making a clot as of bad
blood in the glaring abyss),

s'allunga da Lissa remota a la riva materna.
Ecco, appar Faa di Bruno.
«Sarà dunque eterna
la vergogna?» E ascolta. «Nessun risponde, nessuno?»

Tu, tu, o naviglio d'acciaio, veloce guizzante
bello come un'arme nuda,
vivo palpitante
come se il metallo un cuore terribile chiuda;

tu che solo al freddo coraggio dell'uomo t'affili
come l'arme su la cote,
e non soffri i vili
su la piastra ardente del ponte che il fremito scote;

messaggero primo di morte sul mar guerreggiato,
franco vèlite del mare,
oh rispondi! Il fato
è certo; e a quel Giorno s'accendono i fochi su l'are.

it makes from far Lissa towards the mother shore. And now, Faa di Bruno appears. 'Will the shame last for ever?' And he listens. 'Does no one answer, no one?'

You, you, o ship of steel, straight, swift, flashing, lovely as a naked weapon, alive, quivering as if the metal enclosed a terrible heart;

you who are edged only by man's cold courage like the weapon upon the whetstone, and do not tolerate cowards on the burning walk of the bridge which the trembling shakes;

first messenger of death on the contested sea, free ranger of the sea, oh answer! Fate is certain; and the fires are lit upon the altars for that day.

Assisi

Assisi, nella tua pace profonda
l'anima sempre intesa alle sue mire
non s'allentò; ma sol si finse l'ire
del Tescio quando il greto aspro s'inonda.

Torcesi la riviera sitibonda
che è bianca del furor del suo sitire.
Come fiamme anelanti di salire,
sorgon gli ulivi dalla torta sponda.

A lungo biancheggiar vidi, nel fresco
fiato della preghiera vesperale,
le tortuosità desiderose.

Anche vidi la carne di Francesco,
affocata dal dèmone carnale,
sanguinar su le spine delle rose.

Assisi

Assisi, in your deep peace the soul, ever intent upon its own
ends, did not slacken; but the flowing of the Tescio when the
rough river-bed floods was only imagined.

The thirsty course twists, white with the fury of its thirst. Like
flames panting to ascend, the olives rise on the twisted bank.

In the distance I saw the ardent twistings whitening in the fresh
breath of the evening prayer.

I saw, too, the flesh of Francis, flamed hectic by the fleshly demon,
bleeding on the roses' thorns.

Bocca d'Arno

Bocca di donna mai mi fu di tanta
soavità nell'amorosa via
(se non la tua, se non la tua, presente)
come la bocca pallida e silente
del fiumicel che nasce in Falterona.
Qual donna s'abbandona
(se non tu, se non tu) sì dolcemente
come questa placata correntìa?
Ella non canta,
e pur fluisce quasi melodìa
all'amarezza.

      Qual sia la sua bellezza
      io non so dire,
      come colui che ode
      suoni dormendo e virtudi ignote
      entran nel suo dormire.

Le saltano all'incontro i verdi flutti,
schiumanti di baldanza,
con la grazia dei giovini animali.
In catena di putti
non mise tanta gioia Donatello,

Mouth of the Arno

Woman's mouth to me was never of such soft charm in the ways of love (if not yours, if not yours, which is here) as the pale and silent mouth of the little river that is born in Falterona. What woman gives herself (if not you, if not you) so sweetly as this stilled current? It does not sing and yet flows almost a melody to bitterness.

What its beauty is I cannot say, like one who hears sounds in sleep and unknown powers enter into his slumber.

Towards it leap the green surges, foaming with vigour, with the grace of young animals. Donatello did not put such joy into a chain

fervendo il marmo sotto lo scalpello,
quando ornava le bianche cattedrali.
Sotto ghirlande di fiori e di frutti
svolgeasi intorno ai pergami la danza
infantile, ma non sì fiera danza
come quest'una.

V'è creatura alcuna
che in tanta grazia
viva ed in sì perfetta
gioia, se non quella lodoletta
che in aere si spazia?

Forse l'anima mia, quando profonda
sè nel suo canto e vede la sua gloria
forse l'anima tua, quando profonda
sè nell'amore e perde la memoria
degli inganni fugaci in che s'illuse
ed anela con me l'alta vittoria.
Forse conosceremo noi la piena
felicità dell'onda
libera e delle forti ali dischiuse
e dell'inno selvaggio che si sfrèna.
Adora e attendi!

of little angels, the marble feverish under his chisel, when he
decorated the white cathedrals. The infant dance went round trel-
lises, under garlands of flowers and fruit, but not so proud a dance
as this one.

Is there any creature that lives in such grace, in so perfect a joy,
unless it be that little lark that soars in air?

Perhaps my soul, when, deep in its own song, it sees its glory –
perhaps your soul, when it enters deeply into love and loses remembrance of the fleeting deceptions in which it was caught and
pants with me in high victory. Perhaps we shall know the full
happiness of the free wave and of the strong, opened wings and of
the wild hymn that is loosed. Adore and watch!

Adora, adora, e attendi!
Vedi? I tuoi piedi
nudi lascian vestigi
di luce, ed a' tuoi occhi prodigi
sorgon dall'acque. Vedi?

Grandi calici sorgono dall'acque,
di non so qual leggiere oro intessuti.
Le nubi i monti i boschi i lidi l'acque
trasparire per le corolle immani
vedi, lontani e vani
come in sogni paesi sconosciuti.
Farfalle d'oro come le tue mani
volando a coppia scoprono su l'acque
con meraviglia i fiori grandi e strani,
mentre tu fiuti
l'odor salino.
    Fa un suo gioco divino
    l'Ora solare,
    mutevole e gioconda
    come la gola d'una colomba
    alzata per cantare.

Adore, adore, and watch! Do you see? Your naked feet are leaving tracks of light, and they rise from the water to your miraculous eyes. Do you see?

Great goblets rise up from the water, filigreed with indescribable fine gold. You see the clouds, mountains, woods, the shores, the waters shining through huge petals, far-off and transitory as unknown countries in dream. Golden butterflies like your hands discover with wonder, as they fly over the water in couples, the great strange flowers, while you breathe in the salt smell.

The hour of the sun plays its divine game, changeful and pleased like a dove's throat stretched to sing.

Sono le reti pensili. Talune
pendon come bilance dalle antenne
cui sostengono i ponti alti e protesi
ove l'uom veglia a volgere la fune;
altre pendono a prua dei palischermi
trascorrendo il perenne
specchio che le rifrange; e quando il sole
batte a poppa i navigli, stando fermi
i remi, un gran fulgor le trasfigura:
grandi calici sorgono dall'acque,
gigli di foco.
      Fa un suo divino gioco
      la giovine Ora
      che è breve come il canto
      della colomba. Godi l'incanto,
      anima nostra, e adora!

La pioggia nel pineto

TACI. Su le soglie
del bosco non odo
parole che dici
umane; ma odo

They are the hanging nets. Some hang like scales from the rods fixed to the high platforms stretched out above the stream, where the man watches to pull in the twine; others hang from the prows of fishing-boats, crossing the evergreen mirror that refracts them; and when the sun beats down on the sterns of the boats, the oars at rest, a great radiance transfigures them; great goblets rise from the waters, lilies of fire.

The young Hour plays its divine game which is short as the song of the dove. Enjoy the charm, our soul, and adore!

Rain in the Pine-wood

HUSH. On the edge of the wood I do not hear human words that you are saying; but I hear newer words which far-off drops and

parole più nuove
che parlano gocciole e foglie
lontane.
Ascolta. Piove
dalle nuvole sparse.
Piove su le tamerici
salmastre ed arse,
piove su i pini
scagliosi ed irti,
piove su i mirti
divini,
su le ginestre fulgenti
di fiori accolti,
su i ginepri folti
di coccole aulenti,
piove su i nostri volti
silvani,
piove su le nostre mani
ignude,
su i nostri vestimenti
leggieri,
su i freschi pensieri
che l'anima schiude
novella,
su la favola bella
che ieri
t'illuse, che oggi m'illude,
o Ermione.

---

leaves are speaking. Listen. It is raining from the scattered clouds.
It rains on the salty, burnt tamarinds, on the rough, prickly pines,
on the divine myrtles, on the broom flashing with clustered flowers,
on the junipers thick with odorous berries, it rains upon our woodwild faces, it rains on our naked hands, on our light clothes, on the
fresh thoughts which the soul, renewed, discloses, on the lovely
fable that yesterday beguiled you, that today beguiles me, o
Hermione.

Odi? La pioggia cade
su la solitaria
verdura
con un crepitìo che dura
e varia nell'aria
secondo le fronde
più rade, men rade.
Ascolta. Risponde
al pianto il canto
delle cicale
che il pianto australe
non impaura,
nè il ciel cinerino.
E il pino
ha un suono, e il mirto
altro suono, e il ginepro
altro ancora, stromenti
diversi
sotto innumerevoli dita.
E immersi
noi siam nello spirto
silvestre,
d'arborea vita viventi;
e il tuo volto ebro
è molle di pioggia
come una foglia,

Do you hear? The rain is falling on the lonely greenery with a rustling that keeps on and varies in the air according as the leaves are more spaced or less spaced. Listen. The song of the cicada answers the weeping, the song that the westering lament does not awe, nor the ashen sky. And the pine has one sound, and the myrtle another sound, and the juniper another again, different instruments under numberless fingers. And we are plunged in the forest's spirit, living with a tree-like life; and your exulting face is soft with rain

e le tue chiome
auliscono come
le chiare ginestre,
o creatura terrestre
che hai nome
Ermione.

Ascolta, ascolta. L'accordo
delle aeree cicale
a poco a poco
più sordo
si fa sotto il pianto
che cresce;
ma un canto vi si mesce
più roco
che di laggiù sale,
dall'umida ombra remota.
Più sordo e più fioco
s'allenta, si spegne.
Sola una nota
ancor trema, si spegne,
risorge, trema, si spegne.
Non s'ode voce del mare.
Or s'ode su tutta la fronda
crosciare
l' argentea pioggia
che monda,

like a leaf, and your locks are fragrant like the shining broom, o
earthly creature who are named Hermione.

Listen, listen. The harmony of the airy cicadas is growing gradually duller under the weeping that increases; but a song enters, a
hoarser one that rises from down there, from the far damp shade.
Duller and weaker it dwindles, it fades. Only a note still trembles,
fades, rises again, trembles, fades. We do not hear the voice of the
sea. Now on all the leaves we hear the silver rain beating that

il croscio che varia
secondo la fronda
più folta, men folta.
Ascolta.
La figlia dell'aria
è muta; ma la figlia
del limo lontana,
la rana,
canta nell'ombra più fonda,
chi sa dove, chi sa dove!
E piove su le tue ciglia,
Ermione.

Piove su le tue ciglia nere
sì che par tu pianga
ma di piacere; non bianca
ma quasi fatta virente,
par da scorza tu esca.
E tutta la vita è in noi fresca
aulente,
il cuor nel petto è come pesca
intatta,
tra le palpebre gli occhi
son come polle tra l'erbe,
i denti negli alvèoli
son come mandorle acerbe.

cleanses, the beating that varies according as the leaves are more close, less close. Listen. The daughter of the air is mute, but the distant daughter of the swamp, the frog, sings in the deepest shadow, who knows where, who knows where! And it rains upon your eyelashes, Hermione.

It rains upon your black eyelashes so that you seem to weep but from pleasure; not white, but almost made green, you seem to come out from bark. And all life is fresh, odorous, in us, the heart in our breasts like an untouched peach, the eyes in their eyelids like rivulets in grass, the teeth in their gums like bitter almonds. And we go

E andiam di fratta in fratta,
or congiunti or disciolti
(e il verde vigor rude
ci allaccia i mallèoli
c'intrica i ginocchi)
chi sa dove, chi sa dove!
E piove su i nostri volti
silvani,
piove su le nostre mani
ignude,
su i nostri vestimenti
leggieri,
su i freschi pensieri
che l'anima schiude
novella,
su la favola bella
che ieri
m'illuse, che oggi t'illude,
o Ermione.

I pastori

SETTEMBRE, andiamo. È tempo di migrare.
Ora in terra d'Abruzzi i miei pastori
lascian gli stazzi e vanno verso il mare:

from thicket to thicket, now joined, now separate (and the rough green vigour traps our ankles, entangles our knees) who knows where, who knows where! And it rains upon our woodwild faces, it rains on our naked hands, on our light clothes, on the fresh thoughts which the soul, renewed, discloses, on the lovely fable that yesterday beguiled me, that today beguiles you, o Hermione.

The Shepherds

SEPTEMBER, let us go. It is time to migrate. Now in the land of the Abruzzi my shepherds leave the huts and go towards the sea: they

scendono all'Adriatico selvaggio
che verde è come i pascoli dei monti.

Han bevuto profondamente ai fonti
alpestri, che sapor d'acqua natìa
rimanga ne' cuori esuli a conforto,
che lungo illuda la lor sete in via.
Rinnovato hanno verga d'avellano.

E vanno pel tratturo antico al piano,
quasi per un erbal fiume silente,
su le vestigia degli antichi padri.
O voce di colui che primamente
conosce il tremolar della marina!

Ora lungh'esso il litoral cammina
la greggia. Senza mutamento è l'aria.
Il sole imbionda sì la viva lana
che quasi dalla sabbia non divaria.
Isciacquìo, calpestìo, dolci romori.

Ah perchè non son io co' miei pastori?

go down to the wild Adriatic which is green like the mountain
pastures.

They have drunk deep at alpine springs, so that the taste of native
water may remain in exile hearts as a comfort, to charm their thirst
for long upon the way. They have renewed their staffs of hazel.

And they go along the ancient drove-path to the plain, as if by a
grassy, silent river, upon the traces of the early fathers. O voice
of him who first knows the trembling of the sea!

Now on the shore at its side marches the flock. The air is without
motion. The sun so gilds the living wool that it hardly differs from
the sand. Sea-washing, trampling, sweet sounds.

Ah why am I not with my shepherds?

DINO CAMPANA

La chimera

Non so se tra roccie il tuo pallido
Viso m'apparve, o sorriso
Di lontananze ignote
Fosti, la china eburnea
Fronte fulgente o giovine
Suora de la Gioconda:
O delle primavere
Spente, per i tuoi mitici pallori
O Regina o Regina adolescente:
Ma per il tuo ignoto poema
Di voluttà e di dolore
Musica fanciulla esangue,
Segnato di linea di sangue
Nel cerchio delle labbra sinuose,
Regina de la melodia:
Ma per il vergine capo
Reclino, io poeta notturno
Vegliai le stelle vivide nei pelaghi del cielo,
Io per il tuo dolce mistero
Io per il tuo divenir taciturno,

The Chimera

I do not know if your pale face appeared to me among the rocks,
or if you were the smile of distances unknown, your bent ivory
forehead flashing, o young sister of the Gioconda: o Queen of dead
springtimes for your mythical palenesses, o youthful queen: but
for your unknown poem of voluptuousness and grief, music,
bloodless girl, marked with a line of blood in the round of sinuous
lips, Queen of melody: but for your virgin head bent, I, poet of
the night, watched out the vivid stars in the deeps of the sky, I for
your soft mystery, I for your becoming silent, do not know if the

Non so se la fiamma pallida
Fu dei capelli il vivente
Segno del suo pallore,
Non so se fu un dolce vapore,
Dolce sul mio dolore,
Sorriso di un volto notturno:
Guardo le bianche rocce le mute fonti dei venti
E l'immobilità dei firmamenti
E i gonfii rivi che vanno piangenti
E l'ombre del lavoro umano curve là sui poggi algenti
E ancora per teneri cieli lontane chiare ombre correnti
E ancora ti chiamo ti chiamo Chimera.

L'invetriata

LA sera fumosa d'estate
Dall'alta invetriata mesce chiarori nell'ombra
E mi lascia nel cuore un suggello ardente.
Ma chi ha (sul terrazzo sul fiume si accende una lampada)
  chi ha
A la Madonnina del Ponte chi è chi è che ha acceso la
  lampada? – c'è

pale flame was the tresses' living sign of her paleness, I do not know
if it was a soft mist, soft upon my grief, smile of a face of night. I look
at the white rocks, the dumb fountains of the wind, and the
immobility of firmaments and the swollen streams that pass weeping and the shadows of human labour curved there on icy heights
and still, through tender heavens, far lucid shades running, and still
I call you, I call you Chimera.

The Skylight

THE smoky evening of summer from the high skylight mixes
brightnesses with shade and leaves a burning seal upon my heart.
But who has (on the terrace on the river a lamp is being lit) who
has, for the little Madonna of the Bridge, who is it, who is it that

Nella stanza un odor di putredine: c'è
Nella stanza una piaga rossa languente.
Le stelle sono bottoni di madreperla e la sera si veste di
    velluto:
E tremola la sera fatua: è fatua la sera e tremola ma c'è
Nel cuore della sera c'è,
Sempre una piaga rossa languente.

La sera di fiera

Il cuore stasera mi disse: non sai?
La rosabruna incantevole
Dorata da una chioma bionda:
E dagli occhi lucenti e bruni colei che di grazi imperiale
Incantava la rosea
Freschezza dei mattini:
E tu seguivi nell'aria
La fresca incarnazione di un mattutino sogno:
E soleva vagare quando il sogno
E il profumo velavano le stelle
(Che tu amavi guardar dietro i cancelli
Le stelle le pallide notturne):

has lit the lamp? There is an odour of decay in the room, there is
in the room a red and drooping wound. The stars are buttons of
mother of pearl and the evening is dressed in velvet. The enchanted evening trembles: it is enchanted, the evening, and trembling but there is in the heart of the evening there is, always a red
and drooping wound.

The Evening of the Fair

My heart said to me this evening: do you not know? The charming rose-and-dark girl gilded with fair hair: and with shining brown
eyes, she who with imperial grace charmed the rose-like freshness
of the mornings: and you followed the fresh incarnation of a morning dream through the air: and she would wander when dream and
perfume veiled the stars (for you loved to watch beyond the iron-
gates the stars the pallid night-times): she who used to pass silently

Che soleva passare silenziosa
E bianca come un volo di colombe
Certo è morta: non sai?
Era la notte
Di fiera della perfida Babele
Salente in fasci verso un cielo affastellato un paradiso di
      fiamma
In lubrici fischi grotteschi
E tintinnare d'angeliche campanelle
E gridi e voci di prostitute
E pantomime d'Ofelia
Stillate dall'umile pianto delle lampade elettriche
....
Una canzonetta volgaruccia era morta
E mi aveva lasciato il cuore nel dolore
E me ne andavo errando senz'amore
Lasciando il cuore mio di porta in porta:
Con Lei che non è nata eppure è morta
E mi ha lasciato il cuore senz'amore:
Eppure il cuore porta nel dolore:
Lasciando il cuore mio di porta in porta.

and white as a flight of doves, certainly she's dead: do you not
know? It was the night of the fair of treacherous Babel towering in
clusters towards a gathered heaven, a paradise of flames, in lewd
whistlings grotesquely, and tinkling of angelic bells and shouts and
cries of prostitutes and burlesques of Ophelia distilled from the
humble weeping of electric bulbs. A vulgarish song was dead and
had left my heart in grief, and I wandered on without love, leaving
my heart at this door and the next one: with Her who is not born
and yet is dead who has left my heart without love: yet she takes
my heart to grief: leaving my heart in this door and the next one.

Giardino autunnale

Al giardino spettrale al lauro muto
De le verdi ghirlande
A la terra autunnale
Un ultimo saluto!
A l'aride pendici
Aspre arrossate nell'estremo sole
Confusa di rumori
Rauchi grida la lontana vita:
Grida al morente sole
Che insanguina le aiole.
S'intende una fanfara
Che straziante sale: il fiume spare
Ne le arene dorate: nel silenzio
Stanno le bianche statue a capo i ponti
Volte: e le cose già non sono più.
E del fondo silenzio come un coro
Tenero e grandioso
Sorge ed anela in alto al mio balcone:
E in aroma d'alloro,
In aroma d'alloro acre languente,
Tra le statue immortali nel tramonto
Ella m'appar, presente.

Autumnal Garden

To the ghostly garden, to the dumb laurel with the green garlands, to the autumnal earth, a last farewell! To the hard, barren slopes, reddened in the final sun, distant life cries in a confusion of harsh noises: it cries to the dying sun that has stained the flowerbeds with blood. A blast of trumpets, rising and tearing is heard: the river vanishes in the gilded sands: in the silence white statues stand, turned at the ends of bridges: and former things are no more. And from the distance silence like a chorus, tender and majestic, rises and breathes on high at my balcony: and in the odour of laurel, in the bitter, failing smell of laurel, from between the statues immortal in the sunset she appears to me, present.

Firenze

(Uffizi)

Entro dei ponti tuoi multicolori
L'Arno presago quietamente arena
E in riflessi tranquilli frange appena
Archi severi tra sfiorir di fiori.

....

Azzuro l'arco dell'intercolonno
Trema rigato tra i palazzi eccelsi:
Candide righe nell'azzurro: persi
Voli: su bianca gioventù in colonne.

Vecchi versi

(San Petronio, Bologna)

....
....
....
....

Le rosse torri altissime ed accese
Dentro dell'azzurrino tramonto commosso di vento
Vegliavano dietro degli alti palazzi le imprese
Gentili del serale animamento

Florence

(The Uffizi)

Between your many-coloured bridges the Arno, prophetic, is quietly silting, and in calm reflections hardly breaks the strict arches in the space when flowers are deflowered.

..... *Blue, the arch joining the columns trembles, limned between exalted palaces: white lines on the blue: lost flights: over white youth on columns.*

Old Lines

(San Petronio, Bologna)

.... The red and glowing towers so tall in the blue twilight disturbed by wind watched the kindly purposes of the evening animation behind high palaces.

. . . .
. . . .
Esse parlavano lievi e tacevano: gli occhi levati
Invan seguendo la scìa sconosciuta nell'aria
De le parole rotte che il vicendevole vento
Diceva per un'ansia solitaria.

Bastimento in viaggio

L'ALBERO oscilla a tocchi nel silenzio.
Una tenue luce bianca e verde cade dall'albero.
Il cielo limpido all'orizzonte, carico verde e dorato dopo
    la burrasca.
Il quadro bianco della lanterna in alto
Illumina il segreto notturno: dalla finestra
Le corde dall'alto a triangolo d'oro
E un globo bianco di fumo
Che non esiste come musica
Sopra del cerchio coi tocchi dell'acqua in sordina.

. . . . They spoke low and went silent: upturned eyes vainly
followed the unknown wake in the air of broken words which the
wind, self-willed, spoke for a lonely anxiety.

Ship under Way

THE mast swings, beat for beat, in the silence. A faint white and
green light falls from the mast. The sky clear to the horizon, loaded
green and gilt after the squall. The white square of the ship's light
on high illuminates the night's secret: from the window the ropes
from above in a gold triangle and a globe white with smoke which
does not exist like music above the circle with the muted beating of
the water.

Quattro liriche per S.A.

i. I piloni fanno il fiume più bello

I PILONI fanno il fiume più bello
E gli archi fanno il cielo più bello
Negli archi la tua figura.
Più pura nell'azzurro è la luce d'argento
Più bella la tua figura.
Più bella la luce d'argento nell'ombre degli archi
Più bella della bionda Cerere la tua figura.

ii. Sul più illustre paesaggio

Sul più illustre paesaggio
Ha passeggiato il ricordo
Col vostro passo di pantera
Sul più illustre paesaggio
Il vostro passo di velluto
E il vostro sguardo di vergine violata
Il vostro passo silenzioso come il ricordo
Affacciata al parapetto
Sull'acqua corrente
I vostri occhi forti di luce.

Four Lyrics for S.A.

i. The Piers of the Bridge make the River more Beautiful

THE piers of the bridge make the river more beautiful and its
arches make the sky more beautiful – in the arches the form of
you – purer on the blue is the silver light – more beautiful the form
of you – more beautiful the silver light in the shade of the arches –
more beautiful than fair Ceres the form of you.

ii. On the most Illustrious Landscape

On the most illustrious landscape memory has walked with your
panther step – on the most illustrious landscape your velvet step
and the look you have, of a virgin violated – your silent step like
the memory – you, turned to the parapet above the flowing water,
your eyes strong with light.

iii. Vi amai nella città dove per sole

Vi amai nella città dove per sole
Strade si posa il passo illanguidito
Dove una pace tenera che piove
A sera il cuor non sazio e non pentito
Volge a un'ambigua primavera in viole
Lontane sopra il cielo impallidito.

iv. In un momento

In un momento
Sono sfiorite le rose
I petali caduti
Perchè io non potevo dimenticare le rose
Le cercavamo insieme
Abbiamo trovato delle rose
Erano le sue rose erano le mie rose
Questo viaggio chiamavamo amore
Col nostro sangue e colle nostre lagrime facevamo le rose
Che brillavano un momento al sole del mattino

iii. I Loved You in the City where ... in Deserted ...

I loved you in the city where the languid step lingers in deserted streets, where a tender peace which rains down at evening turns the heart, not filled and not repentant, to a dubious spring in violet distances above the paler sky.

iv. In a Moment

In a moment the roses have shed their bloom, the petals fallen, because I could not forget the roses. We looked for them together: we found roses: they were her roses, were my roses. This journey we called love. With our blood and our tears we made the roses which shone a moment in the morning sun. We ruined their bloom

Le abbiamo sfiorite sotto il sole tra i rovi
Le rose che non erano le nostre rose
Le mie rose le sue rose

P.S. E così dimenticammo le rose.

Firenze vecchia

Ho visto il tuo palazzo palpitare
Di mille fiamme in una sera calda
O Firenze, il magnifico palazzo.
Già la folla à riempito la gran piazza
E vocia verso il suo palazzo vecchio
E beve la sua anima maliarda.
La confraternità di buona morte
Porta una bara sotto le tue mura:
Questo m'allieta questo m'assicura
Della tua forza di contro alla morte:
Non bruciano le tue feree midolla
I tempi nuovi e non l'amaro agreste
Delle tue genti: in ricordanze in feste
L'aspero sangue sotto a te ribolla.

under the sun, among the briars, the roses which were not our roses
– my roses, her roses.

P.S. And so we forgot the roses.

Old Florence

I saw your palace throb with a thousand flames on a warm evening, o Florence, your magnificent palace. The crowd has already filled the great square and shouts towards its old palace and drinks its witching soul. The Fraternity of the Good Death bear a coffin beneath your walls: this gladdens me, this assures me of your strength against death: new times do not burn your iron marrow, nor the rough hardness of your peoples: in rememberings, in celebrations the crude blood seethes in you. Iron, blood, flame, it is

O ferro o sangue o fiamma è tutto fuoco
Che brucia la viltà dentro le vene!
A te dai petti e dalle gole piene,
Di gioia e forza un'inesausta polla!

Una strana zingarella

Tu sentirai le rime scivolare
In cadenza nel caldo della stanza
Sopra al guanciale pallida a sognare
Ti volgerai, di questa lenta danza
Magnetica il sussurro a respirare.
La luna stanca è andata a riposare
Gli ulivi taccion, solo un ubriaco
Che si stanca a cantare e ricantare:
Tu magra e sola con i tuoi capelli
Sei restata. Nel cielo a respirare
Stanno i tuoi sogni. Volgiti ed ascolta
Nella notte gelata il mio cantare
Sulle tue spalle magroline e gialle
I capelli vorrei veder danzare

one fire that burns the vileness in our veins! To you from breasts
and from full throats, an unfailing stream of joy and strength!

A Strange Gipsy

You will feel my rhymes slipping in cadence in the warmth of the
room, you will turn to dream upon the wan pillow, to breathe
the whisper of this slow, magnetic dance. The tired moon has gone
to rest, the olives are silent, only a drunkard wears himself out,
singing and singing again: you, thin and alone, your hair towards
me, have stayed. Your dreams are hovering in the sky, to breathe.
Turn and listen to my singing in the chilled night. I want to see
your hair dance on your skinny yellow shoulders. You are as pure

Sei pura come il suono e senza odore
Un tuo bacio è acerbetto e sorridente
E doloroso, e l'occhio è rilucente
E troppo bello, l'occhio è perditore.
Sicuramente tu non sai cantare
Ma la vocetta deve essere acuta
E perforante come il violino
E sorridendo deve pizzicare
Il cuore. I tuoi capelli sulle spalluccine?
Ami i profumi? E perchè vai vestita
Di sangue? Ami le chiese?
No tu temi i profumi. Il corpiccino
È troppo fine e gli occhi troppo neri
Oh se potessi vederti agitare
La tua animuccia tagliente tremare
E i tuoi occhi lucenti arrotondare
Mentre il santo linfatico e canoro
Che dovevi tentare
Spande in ginocchio nuvole d'incenso
Ringraziando il Signore
E non lo puoi amare
Christus vicisti

as sound and without scent. A kiss of yours is bitterish and smiling and sorrowful, and your eye is sparkling, is too lovely, your eye is perdition. Certainly you won't sing well, but your little voice must be sharp and piercing like a violin, and, as you smile, must pluck at the heart. Your hair on your slim shoulders? Do you love perfume? And why do you go dressed in blood? Do you love churches? No; you are afraid of perfume. Your little body is too slight and your eyes, too dark. O if I could see you shake, your cutting little soul tremble, and your shining eyes grow round, while the sonorous, pale saint whom you had to tempt kneels and scatters clouds of incense, thanking the Lord, and you cannot love him. *Christus*

L'avorio del crocifisso
Vince l'avorio del tuo ventre
Dalla corona non sì dolce e gloriosa
Nera increspata movente
Nell'ombra grigia vertiginosa
E tu piangi in ginocchio per terra colle mani
      sugli occhi
E i tuoi piedi lunghi e brutti
Allargati per terra come zampe
D'una bestia ribelle e mostruosa.
Che sapore avranno le tue lacrimucce?
Un poco di fuoco? Io vorrei farne
Un diadema fantastico e portarlo
Sul mio capo nell'ora della morte
Per udirmi parlare in confidenza
I demonietti dai piedi forcuti.
Povera bimba come ti calunnio
Perchè hai i capelli tragici
E ti vesti di rosso e non odori.

vicisti. The ivory of the crucifix surpasses the ivory of your belly –
from the crown, not so sweet and glorious, black waving moving
in the grey whirling shade – And you weep kneeling on the earth,
your hands over your eyes, and your long ugly feet splayed on
the the earth like the paws of some monstrous, defiant beast. What taste
will your little tears have? A touch of fire? I would like to make a
fantastic diadem of them and wear it on my head at the hour of my
death to hear the little demons with cloven hooves, speak to me in
confidence. Poor child, how I wrong you with words, because you
have tragic hair, and you dress in red, and have no scent.

Donna genovese

T u mi portasti un po' d'alga marina
Nei tuoi capelli, ed un odor di vento,
Che è corso di lontano e giunge grave
D'ardore, era nel tuo corpo bronzino:
– Oh la divina
Semplicità delle tue forme snelle –
Non amore non spasimo, un fantasma,
Un'ombra della necessità che vaga
Serena e ineluttabile per l'anima
E la discioglie in gioia, in incanto serena
Perchè per l'infinito lo scirocco
Se la possa portare.
Come è piccolo il mondo e leggero nelle tue mani!

GIUSEPPE UNGARETTI

Agonia

M orire come le allodole assetate
sul miraggio

Woman of Genoa

Y ou brought me a little seaweed in your hair, and the breath of a wind, that has come from afar and arrives heavy with sultriness, was in your bronzed body: – oh the divine simplicity of your clean limbs – not love, not sudden unrest, a phantom, a shadow of the necessity which wanders calm and inescapable through the soul and melts it in joy, calm in its spell so that the hot wind can bear it away through the infinite. How small the world is, and light, in your hands!

Agony

T o die like thirst-stricken larks close upon the mirage

O come la quaglia
passato il mare
nei primi cespugli
perchè di volare
non ha più voglia

Ma non vivere di lamento
come un cardellino accecato

Veglia

Un'intera nottata
buttato vicino
a un compagno
massacrato
con la sua bocca
digrignata
volta al plenilunio
con la congestione
delle sue mani
penetrata
nel mio silenzio
ho scritto
lettere piene d'amore

Non sono mai stato
tanto
attaccato alla vita

Or like the quail, once the sea is past, in the first bushes, because
it has no more wish to fly.
　But not to live on lament like a blinded finch.

Watch

A whole night, thrown down beside a friend who has been
slaughtered, with his grinning mouth turned to the full moon, with
the convulsion of his hands reaching into my silence, I have written
letters full of love.
　I have never been so attached to life.

I fiumi

MI tengo a quest'albero mutilato
abbandonato in questa dolina
che ha il languore
di un circo
prima o dopo lo spettacolo
e guardo
il passaggio quieto
delle nuvole sulla luna

Stamani mi sono disteso
in un'urna d'acqua
e come una reliquia
ho riposato

L'Isonzo scorrendo
mi levigava
come un suo sasso

Ho tirato su
le mie quattr'ossa
e me ne sono andato
come un acrobata
sull'acqua

Rivers

I LEAN upon this wounded tree abandoned in this depression that
has the listlessness of a circus before or after the show, and I look
at the clouds quietly passing over the moon.

This morning I stretched out in an urn of water and like a relic
I lay there.

The Isonzo running by polished me like one of its stones.

I took upon me my own four limbs and went away like an acro-
bat over the water .

Mi sono accoccolato
vicino ai miei panni
sudici di guerra
e come un beduino
mi sono chinato a ricevere
il sole

Questo è l'Isonzo
e qui meglio
mi sono riconosciuto
una docile fibra
dell'universo

Il mio supplizio
è quando
non mi credo
in armonia

Ma quelle occulte
mani
che m'intridono
mi regalano
la rara
felicità

Ho ripassato
le epoche
della mia vita

Questi sono
i miei fiumi

I squatted down beside my clothes, filthy with war, and like a
Beduin bent my head to receive the sun.

This is the Isonzo and here, best of all, I know myself a pliant
thread in the universe.

My torture is when I do not think myself in harmony.

But those hidden hands which work me grant me rare happiness.

I have gone through the ages of my life.

These are my rivers.

Questo è il Serchio
al quale hanno attinto
duemil'anni forse
di gente mia campagnola
e mio padre e mia madre

Questo è il Nilo
che mi ha visto
nascere e crescere
e ardere d'inconsapevolezza
nelle estese pianure

Questa è la Senna
e in quel suo torbido
mi sono rimescolato
e mi sono conosciuto

Questi sono i miei fiumi
contati nell'Isonzo

Quest è la mia nostalgia
che in ognuno
mi traspare
ora ch'è notte
che la mia vita mi pare
una corolla
di tenebre

This is the Serchio from which they have drawn for two thousand years perhaps, my country people, both my father and my mother.

This is the Nile which has seen me be born and grow and burn with unknowingness in the stretching plains.

This is the Seine and in that murkiness it has I have been stirred and have known myself.

These are my rivers told over in the Isonzo.

This is my nostalgia which in each of them shines through to me now that it is night and my life appears a flower of shadows.

Mattina

M'ILLUMINO
d'immenso

Nostalgia

QUANDO
la notte è a svanire
poco prima di primavera
e di rado
qualcuno passa

Su Parigi s'addensa
un oscuro colore
di pianto

In un canto
di ponte
contemplo
l'illimitato silenzio
di una ragazza
tenue

Le nostre
malattie
si fondono

E come portati via
si rimane

Morning

I AM filled with light of immensity.

Nostalgia

WHEN the night is about to pass away a little before spring and
rarely does anyone pass
  Upon Paris there gathers an unclear colour of weeping.
  At the corner of a bridge I reflect upon the limitless silence of a
slim girl.
  Our sicknesses run together
  And we remain as if carried away.

In memoria

Si chiamava
Moammed Sceab

Discendente
di emiri di nomadi
suicida
perchè non aveva più
Patria

Amò la Francia
e mutò nome

Fu Marcel
ma non era Francese
e non sapeva più
vivere
nella tenda dei suoi
dove si ascolta la cantilena
del Corano
gustando un caffè

E non sapeva
sciogliere
il canto
del suo abbandono

In Memory

He was called Mohammed Sceab.

A descendant of the emirs of the nomads, a suicide because he no longer had a native land.

He loved France and changed his name.

He was Marcel but he was not French and he no longer knew how to live in the tent of his own where they listen to the singsong of the Koran, sipping coffee.

And he did not know how to loose the song of his abandonment.

L'ho accompagnato
insieme alla padrona dell'albergo
dove abitavamo
a Parigi
dal numero 5 della rue des Carmes
appassito vicolo in discesa

Riposa
nel camposanto d'Ivry
sobborgo che pare
sempre
in una giornata
di una
decomposta fiera

E forse io solo
so ancora
che visse.

Quiete

L' UVA è matura, il campo arato,

Si stacca il monte dalle nuvole.

I accompanied him together with the proprietress of the hotel
where we lived at Paris, at number 5 rue des Carmes, faded little
downhill alley.
   He rests in the cemetery of Ivry, a suburb that always has the
look of a broken-up fair,
   And perhaps I alone still know that he lived.

Quiet

THE grapes are ripe, the field, ploughed,
   The mountain detaches itself from the clouds.

Sui polverosi specchi dell'estate
Caduta è l'ombra,

Tra le dita incerte
Il loro lume è chiaro
E lontano.

Colle rondini fugge
L'ultimo strazio.

Sera

APPIÈ dei passi della sera
Va un'acqua chiara
Colore dell'uliva,

E giunge al breve fuoco smemorato

Nel fumo ora odo grilli e rane,

Dove tenere tremano erbe.

On the dusty mirrors of summer the shadow has fallen.
Between uncertain fingers their light is clear and distant.
With the swallows flies the last tearing pain.

Evening

AT the foot of the evening's passes clear water runs by, olive-coloured,
And reaches the brief fire without memory.
In the smoke I hear now crickets and frogs,
Where the grass trembles tenderly.

La pietà

SONO un uomo ferito.

E me ne vorrei andare
E finalmente giungere,
Pietà, dove si ascolta
L'uomo che è solo con sè.

Non ho che superbia e bontà.

E mi sento esiliato in mezzo agli uomini.

Ma per essi sto in pena.

Non sarei degno di tornare in me?

Ho popolato di nomi il silenzio.

Ho fatto a pezzi cuore e mente
Per cadere in servitù di parole?

Regno sopra fantasmi.

O foglie secche,
Anima portata qua e là ...

Pity

I AM a wounded man.
   And I would go away and finally come, Pity, where the man who
is alone with himself is heard.
   I have only pride and goodness.
   And I feel exiled among men.
   But for them I am in torment.
   Would I not be worthy to come to myself again?
   I have peopled silence with names.
   Have I shattered heart and mind to fall into bondage to words?
   I rule over ghosts.
   O dry leaves, soul borne here and there. ...

No, odo il vento e la sua voce
Di bestia immemorabile.

Dio, coloro che t'implorano
Non ti conoscono più che di nome?

M'hai discacciato dalla vita.

Mi discaccerai dalla morte?

Forse l'uomo è anche indegno di sperare.

Anche la fonte del rimorso è secca?

Il peccato che importa,
Se alla purezza non conduce più.

La carne si ricorda appena
Che una volta fu forte.

È folle e usata, l'anima.

Dio, guarda la nostra debolezza.

Vorremmo una certezza.

No, I hear the wind and its voice, an immemorial beast's.
God, do those who implore you no longer know you but by
name?
You have thrust me away from life.
Will you thrust me from death?
Perhaps man is not even fit for hope.
Is the fountain of remorse dry also?
What does sin matter if it no longer leads to purity.
The flesh scarce remembers that once it was strong.
Mad and unregenerate is the soul.
God, look upon our weakness.
We would have a certainty.

Di noi nemmeno più ridi?

E compiangici dunque, crudeltà.

Non ne posso più di stare murato
Nel desiderio senza amore.

Una traccia mostraci di giustizia.

La tua legge qual'è?

Fulmina le mie povere emozioni,
Liberami dall'inquietudine.

Sono stanco di urlare senza voce.

2

Malinconiosa carne
Dove una volta pullulò la gioia,
Occhi socchiusi del risveglio stanco,
Tu vedi, anima troppo matura,
Quel che sarò, caduto nella terra?

È nei vivi la strada dei defunti,

Do you not even laugh at us any longer?
Weep for us then, cruelty.
I can only stay walled-up in desire without love.
Show us a sign of justice.
What is your law?
Blast my poor feelings, free me from restlessness.
I am tired of howling voicelessly.
Melancholy flesh, where joy once teemed, eyes half-opened in
tired awakening, do you see, my too mature soul, what I shall be,
fallen to earth?
The road of the deceased is among the living,

Siamo noi la fiumana d'ombre.

Sono esse il grano che ci scoppia in sogno,

Loro è la lontananza che ci resta,

E loro è l'ombra che dà peso ai nomi.

La speranza d'un mucchio d'ombra
E null'altro è la nostra sorte?

E tu non saresti che un sogno, Dio?

Almeno un sogno, temerari,
Vogliamo ti somigli.

È parto della demenza più chiara.

Non trema in nuvole di rami
Come passeri di mattina
Al filo delle palpebre.

In noi sta e langue, piaga misteriosa.

We are the great river of shades.
They are the grain which breaks open in dream,
Theirs is the distance which keeps with us,
And theirs is the shadow which gives weight to names.
The hope of a mound of shadow and nothing else, is that our fate?
And you would prove nothing but a dream, God?
We want you, rashly, to be at least like a dream.
It is the offspring of clearest insanity.
It does not tremble in the clouds of branches like sparrows at morning on the thread of eyelids.
It stays and worsens in us, a mysterious wound.

3

La luce che ci punge
È un filo sempre piu sottile.

Più non abbagli tu, se non uccidi?

Dammi questa gioia suprema.

4

L'uomo, monotono universo,
Crede allargarsi i beni
E dalle su mani febbrili
Non escono senza fine che limiti.

Attaccato sul vuoto
Al suo filo di ragno,
Non teme e non seduce
Se non il proprio grido.

Ripara il logorio alzando tombe.
E per pensarti, Eterno,
Non ha che le bestemmie.

The light which pricks us is a thread that is each time more
slender.
Can you not dazzle more, without killing?
Give me this supreme joy.
Man, monotonous universe, believes he pours blessings on himself and from his feverish hands nothing but limitations endlessly
come.
Tied to the void by his spider thread, he does not fear and does
not compel anything except his own cry.
He covers up his wasting away by raising tombs, and to think of
you, Eternal One, he has no words but blasphemies.

Tutto ho perduto

TUTTO ho perduto dell'infanzia
E non potrò mai più
Smemorarmi in un grido.

L'infanzia ho sotterrato
Nel fondo delle notti
E ora, spada invisibile,
Mi separa da tutto.

Di me rammento che esultavo amandoti,
Ed eccomi perduto
In infinito delle notti.

Disperazione che incessante aumenta
La vita non mi è più,
Arrestata in fondo alla gola,
Che una roccia di gridi.

I Have Lost Everything

I HAVE lost everything of childhood and I shall no longer be
able to lose memory in a cry.

I have buried childhood in the deep of nights and now it divides
me, invisible sword, from everything.

Of myself I recall that I gloried in loving you, and here I am,
lost in infinity of nights.

Despair endlessly growing, life, stuck in my throat, is now no
more than a rock of cries.

379

Da «Giorno per giorno»

PASSA la rondine e con essa estate,
E anch'io, mi dico, passerò ...
Ma resti dell'amore che mi strazia
Non solo segno un breve appannamento
Se dall'inferno arrivo a qualche quiete ...

*

NON più furori reca a me l'estate,
Nè primavera i suoi presentimenti;
Puoi declinare, autunno,
Con le tue stolte glorie:
Per uno spoglio desiderio, inverno
Distende la stagione più clemente! ...

Non gridate più

CESSATE d'uccidere i morti
Non gridate più, non gridate
Se li volete ancora udire,
Se sperate di non perire.

From 'Day by Day'

THE swallow passes and with it summer, and I too, I tell myself, shall pass. ... But do not let a brief darkening remain as the sole sign of the love that tears me, if I am to come from hell to some calm. ...

SUMMER no longer brings me furies, nor spring its presagings; you can decline, autumn, with your stupid glories: for a bared desire, winter unfolds the mildest season! ...

Do Not Cry Out Any More

STOP killing the dead, do not cry out any more, do not cry out if you want to hear them, if you hope not to perish.

Hanno l'impercettibile sussurro,
Non fanno più rumore
Del crescere dell'erba,
Lieta dove non passa l'uomo.

EUGENIO MONTALE

Falsetto

ESTERINA, i vent'anni ti minacciano,
grigiorosea nube
che a poco a poco in sè ti chiude.
Ciò intendi e non paventi.
Sommersa ti vedremo
nella fumèa che il vento
lacera o addensa, violento.
Poi dal fiotto di cenere uscirai
adusta più che mai,
proteso a un'avventura più lontana
l'intento viso che assembra
l'arciera Diana.
Salgono i venti autunni,
t'avviluppano andate primavere;
ecco per te rintocca
un presagio nell'elisie sfere.

Theirs is the imperceptible whisper, they make no more sound
than the grass growing, happily where no man passes.

Falsetto

DEAR HESTER, your twenty years of age threaten you, a grey and
flushing cloud that little by little takes you into itself. You understand this and are not afraid. We shall see you going under the
smokiness which the wind tears or curdles in its violence. Then you
will emerge from the flood of ashes more burnt up than ever, your
rapt face lifted to a more distant adventure, seeming the huntress
Diana. Twenty autumns rise, departed springtimes wind you
about; there, a prophecy sounds for you among the heavenly

Un suono non ti renda
qual d'incrinata brocca
percossa!; io ti prego sia
per te concerto ineffabile
di sonagliere.

La dubbia dimane non t'impaura.
Leggiadra ti distendi
sullo scoglio lucente di sale
e al sole bruci le membra.
Ricordi la lucertola
ferma sul masso brullo;
te insidia giovinezza,
quella il lacciòlo d'erba del fanciullo.
L'acqua è la forza che ti tempra,
nell'acqua ti ritrovi e ti rinnovi:
noi ti pensiamo come un'alga, un ciottolo,
come un'equorea creatura
che la salsedine non intacca
ma torna al lito più pura.

Hai ben ragione tu! Non turbare
di ubbie il sorridente presente.
La tua gaiezza impegna già il futuro
ed un crollar di spalle

spheres. Let it be no sound of jug cracking as it is struck!; I pray that for you it will be an ineffable melody of little bells.

Doubtful tomorrow doesn't frighten you. Glad you stretch out on the rock shining with salt, and burn your limbs in the sun. Remember the lizard motionless on the naked boulder; youth lies in wait for you, and for him, the boy's grass noose. The water is the force that tries you, in the water you find and renew yourself: and we think of you as a sea-plant, a pebble, some equatorial creature whom the saltiness does not corrode, but who comes purer to shore.

How right you are! Do not disturb the smiling present with misgivings. Your gaiety already involves the future and a shrug of

dirocca i fortilizi
del tuo domani oscuro.
T'alzi e t'avanzi sul ponticello
esiguo, sopra il gorgo che stride:
il tuo profilo s'incide
contro uno sfondo di perla.
Esiti a sommo del tremulo asse,
poi ridi, e come spiccata da un vento
t'abbatti fra le braccia
del tuo divino amico che t'afferra.

Ti guardiamo noi, della razza
di chi rimane a terra.

MERIGGIARE pallido e assorto
presso un rovente muro d'orto,
ascoltare tra i pruni e gli sterpi
schiocchi di merli, frusci di serpi.

Nelle crepe del suolo o su la veccia
spiar le file di rosse formiche
ch'ora si rompono ed ora s'intrecciano
a sommo di minuscole biche.

your shoulders throws down the citadels of your dark tomorrow.
You rise and advance along the slender springboard above the
shouting whirlpool; your profile is chiselled upon a pearly ground.
You hesitate upon the trembling plank, then laugh, and as if
snatched off by the wind, throw yourself into your divine lover's
arms and he holds you.

We watch you, we who belong to the race of those who are
earth-bound.

To laze at noon, pale and abstracted, by a white-hot garden wall,
to listen to clicking of blackbirds and snakes' rustling among the
thorns and the undergrowth.

To make out the files of red ants in the cracks in the ground or
upon the weeds, breaking order and then twining together on top
of their miniature ricks.

Osservare tra frondi il palpitare
lontano di scaglie di mare
mentre si levano tremuli scricchi
di cicale dai calvi picchi.

E andando nel sole che abbaglia
sentire con triste meraviglia
com'è tutta la vita e il suo travaglio
in questo seguitare una muraglia
che ha in cima cocci aguzzi di bottiglia.

Portami il girasole ch'io lo trapianti
nel mio terreno bruciato dal salino,
e mostri tutto il giorno agli azzurri specchianti
del cielo l'ansietà del suo volto giallino.

Tendono alla chiarità le cose oscure,
si esauriscono i corpi in un fluire
di tinte: queste in musiche. Svanire
è dunque la ventura delle venture.

To observe through leaves the far pulsing of the scales of the sea
while the wavering screech of cicadas rises from the bare summits.

And as you walk in the dazzling sun to feel with sad wonder how
life and its struggle is in this following a high wall that has broken
bits of bottle along its top.

Bring me the sunflower so that I can transplant it to my ground
that is burnt with the sea-salt, and show the anxiety of its yellowed
face all day to the mirroring blues of the sky.

Obscure things tend towards clearness, bodies consume themselves in a flowing of shades: these in music. To vanish is then the
chance of chances.

Portami tu la pianta che conduce
dove sorgono bionde trasparenze
e vapora la vita quale essenza;
portami il girasole impazzito di luce.

Da « Mediterraneo»

ANTICO, sono ubriacato dalla voce
ch'esce dalla tue bocche quando si schiudono
come verdi campane e si ributtano
indietro e si disciolgono.
La casa delle mie estati lontane,
t'era accanto, lo sai,
là nel paese dove il sole cuoce
e annuvolano l'aria le zanzare.
Come allora oggi in tua presenza impietro,
mare, ma non più degno
mi credo del solenne ammonimento
del tuo respiro. Tu m'hai detto primo
che il piccino fermento
del mio cuore non era che un momento
del tuo; che mi era in fondo

Bring me the plant which leads to where the sunny depths rise
and life evaporates like spirit; bring me the sunflower maddened
with the light.

From 'Mediterranean'

ANCIENT one, I am drunken with the voice that escapes from
your mouths when they lift clear like green bells and throw themselves back and break up. The home of my far-away summers was
by your side, as you know, there in the country where the sun
broils and mosquitoes cloud the air. Just as then today I am stilled
by your presence, my sea, but no longer think myself worthy of the
grave warning that you breathe. You were first to tell me that the
tiny seething of my heart was simply an impulse of yours; that in

la tua legge rischiosa: esser vasto e diverso
e insieme fisso:
e svuotarmi così d'ogni lordura
come tu fai che sbatti sulle sponde
tra sùgheri alghe asterie
le inutili macerie del tuo abisso.

*

DISSIPA tu se lo vuoi
questa debole vita che si lagna,
come la spugna il frego
effimero di una lavagna.
M'attendo di ritornare nel tuo circolo,
s'adempia lo sbandato mio passato.
La mia venuta era testimonianza
di un ordine che in viaggio mi scordai,
giurano fede queste mie parole
a un evento impossibile, e lo ignorano.
Ma sempre che traudii
la tua dolce risacca su le prode
sbigottimento mi prese
quale d'uno scemato di memoria
quando si risovviene del suo paese.

my depth of being there was your perilous law: to be vast, mani-
fold, and yet, to be bound: and so to clear myself of every filthiness
as you do who dash upon the shores among cork-fragments, seaweed, starfishes, the fruitless rubbish of your void.

OBLITERATE, if you want to, this weak life with its complaining,
as the sponge does the ephemeral stroke upon a blackboard. I am
waiting to re-enter your circle, let my broken-up past be fulfilled.
My coming was witness to an order which I forgot upon my journey, my words swear allegiance to an impossible event and do not
know it. But always when I half-heard your gentle surf upon the
shore, alarm seized me as it does a person of powerless memory when
he recalls his home. Having learnt my lesson, not so much from

Presa la mia lezione
più che dalla tua gloria
rabida, dall'ansare
che quasi non dà suono
di qualche tuo meriggio desolato,
a te mi rendo in umiltà. Non sono
che favilla d'un tirso. Bene lo so, bruciare,
questo, non altro, è il mio significato.

Delta

LA vita che si rompe nei travasi
secreti a te ho legata:
quella che si dibatte in sè e par quasi
non ti sappia, presenza soffocata.

Quando il tempo s'ingorga alle sue dighe
la tua vicenda accordi alla sua immensa,
ed affiori, memoria, più palese
dall'oscura regione ove scendevi,
come ora, al dopopioggia, si riaddensa
il verde ai rami, ai muri il cinabrese.

your raving glory, as from that panting, which hardly makes a
sound, on some deserted afternoon of yours, I give myself up to
you in humility. I am no more than a spark from a faggot. Well do
I know it, to burn, this and nothing else, is the significance I am to
have.

Delta

I BIND that life which breaks off in secret transfusings to you:
the life that contends with itself and seems almost not to know you,
stifled presence.

When time floods high against its dykes, you attune your fortune to its huge one, and rise, memory of mine, clearer from the
dim region where you descended, as now, in the after-rain, the
green once more intensifies upon the branches, and on the walls
their wash of red.

Tutto ignoro di te fuor del messaggio
muto che mi sostenta sulla via:
se forma esisti o ubbìa nella fumea
d'un sogno t'alimenta
la riviera che infebbra, torba, e scroscia
incontro alla marea.

Nulla di te nel vacillar dell'ore
bigie o squarciate da un vampo di solfo
fuori che il fischio del rimorchiatore
che dalle brume approda al golfo.

Mottetto

Lo sai: debbo riperderti e non posso.
Come un tiro aggiustato mi sommuove
ogni opera, ogni grido e anche lo spiro
salino che straripa
dai moli e fa l'oscura primavera
di Sottoripa.

I do not know anything about you except for the mute message which supports me on my way: whether you exist as an ideal, or whether the shore which goes feverish, troubled, and crashes with the rising tide, nourishes you, a delusion, in the haze of a dream.

Nothing of you in the wavering of the hours, grey or rent by a sulphur flame, except the hooting of the tug as, from the mists, it comes to harbour in the gulf.

Motet

You know: I have to lose you again and I can't. Like a well-aimed shot, every action, every cry startles me, and even the salt breath that overflows the harbour-wall and makes the uncertain spring of Sottoripa.

Paese di ferrame e alberature
a selva nella polvere del vespro.
Un ronzìo lungo viene dall'aperto,
strazia com'unghia ai vetri. Cerco il segno
smarrito, il pegno solo ch'ebbi in grazia
da te.
      E l'inferno è certo.

Dora Markus

Fu dove il ponte di legno
mette a Porto Corsini sul mare alto
e rari uomini, quasi immoti, affondano
o salpano le reti. Con un segno
della mano additavi all'altra sponda
invisibile la tua patria vera.
Poi seguimmo il canale fino alla darsena
della città, lucida di fuliggine,
nella bassura dove s'affondava
una primavera inerte, senza memoria.

Place of iron and ship-masts in a forest amid the dust of evening.
A long hum comes from the open, unbearable as nails on glass. I
look for the lost-sight-of sign, the only pledge you granted me.
    And hell-fire is certain.

Dora Markus

It was where the wooden pier thrusts out on the high sea at Porto
Corsini and a few men, almost unmoving, drop and hoist up the
nets. With a wave of your hand you pointed towards your true
native land on the invisible opposite shore. Then we followed the
canal right to the basin of the town, shining with soot, in the flat
landscape where a motionless spring was sinking, without
memories.

E qui dove un'antica vita
si screzia in una dolce
ansietà d'Oriente,
le tua parole iridavano come le scaglie
della triglia moribonda.

La tua irrequietudine mi fa pensare
agli uccelli di passo che urtano ai fari
nelle sere tempestose:
è una tempesta anche la tua dolcezza,
turbina e non appare,
e i suoi riposi sono anche più rari.
Non so come stremata tu resisti
in questo lago
d'indifferenza ch'è il tuo cuore; forse
ti salva un amuleto che tu tieni
vicino alla matita delle labbra,
al piumino, alla lima: un topo bianco,
d'avorio; e così esisti!

2

Ormai nella tua Carinzia
di mirti fioriti e di stagni,
china sul bordo sorvegli
la carpa che timida abbocca

And here where an old life is variegated in a soft oriental anxiety,
your words flashed a rainbow like the scales on the dying sea-fish.

Your restlessness makes me think of birds of passage dashing
themselves against lighthouses on stormy evenings: your sweetness itself is a tempest, whirling and not showing, and its pauses are
even rarer. I do not know how you resist, though spent, in this lake
of indifference which is your heart; perhaps some charm saves you,
one you keep near your lipstick, your powder-puff, your nail-file:
a white mouse, in ivory; and so you subsist!

2

Now in your Carinzia of flowering myrtles and ponds, bent upon
the brink you watch the carp gaping timidly, or follow in the lime-

o segui sui tigli, tra gl'irti
pinnacoli le accensioni
del vespro e nell'acque un avvampo
di tende da scali e pensioni.

La sera che si protende
sull'umida conca non porta
col palpito dei motori
che gemiti d'oche e un interno
di nivee maioliche dice
allo specchio annerito che ti vide
diversa una storia di errori
imperturbati e la incide
dove la spugna non giunge.

La tua leggenda, Dora!
Ma è scritta già in quegli sguardi
di uomini che hanno fedine
altere e deboli in grandi
ritratti d'oro e ritorna
ad ogni accordo che esprime
l'armonica guasta nell'ora
che abbuia sempre più tardi.

trees, the kindling of early night between the ragged pinnacles and
in the water a blazing of awnings from the quays and lodging-
houses.

The evening that stretches out over the humid basin brings,
with the throbbing of motors, only the geese's crying and an in-
terior of snow-white porcelain tells the blackened mirror, that sees
you changed, a story of cool mistakes and engraves it where the
sponge cannot reach.

Your legend, Dora! But it is already written in the looks of those
men who have high-set, weak whiskers in large golden portraits and
it recurs with each chord that the broken harmonica articulates in
the moment of darkening, later and later.

È scritta là. Il sempreverde
alloro per la cucina
resiste, la voce non muta,
Ravenna è lontana, distilla
veleno una fede feroce.
Che vuole da te? Non si cede
voce, leggenda o destino. ...
Ma è tardi, sempre più tardi.

La Casa dei doganieri

Tu non ricordi la casa dei doganieri
sul rialzo a strapiombo sulla scogliera:
desolata t'attende dalla sera
in cui v'entrò lo sciame dei tuoi pensieri
e vi sostò irrequieto.

Libeccio sferza da anni le vecchia mura
e il suono del tuo riso non è più lieto:
la bussola va impazzita all'avventura
e il calcolo dei dadi più non torna.
Tu non ricordi; altro tempo frastorna
la tua memoria; un filo s'addipana.

It is written there. The evergreen laurel survives for the kitchen,
the voice does not change, Ravenna is far away, a ferocious faith
distils poison. What does it want of you? Voice, legend, or destiny
are not to be surrendered. But it is late, always later.

The Shore-watchers' House

You don't remember the shore-watchers' house on the cliff sheer
above the rocky coast: it waits for you unhappily since the night
the swarm of your thoughts came there and stayed without peace.

South winds have lashed the old walls for years and the sound
of your laugh is no longer gay: the compass turns crazily, at ran-
dom, and the guess about the dice is no longer lucky. You don't
recall; another time prevents your memory; a thread is wound.

Ne tengo ancora un capo; ma s'allontana
la casa e in cima al tetto la banderuola
affumicata gira senza pietà.
Ne tengo un capo; ma tu resti sola
nè qui respiri nell'oscurità.

Oh l'orizzonte in fuga, dove s'accende
rara la luce della petroliera!
Il varco è qui? (Ripullula il frangente
ancora sulla balza che scoscende ...)
Tu non ricordi la casa di questa
mia sera. Ed io non so chi va e chi resta.

Eastbourne

«Dio salvi il re» intonano le trombe
da un padiglione erto su palafitte
che aprono il varco al mare quando sale
a distruggere peste
umide di cavalli nella sabbia
del litorale.

I still hold an end of it; but the house recedes and the blackened weathervane on top of its roof spins pitilessly. I hold an end of it; but you stay alone and do not breathe here in the dark.

Oh the retreating sky-line where the tanker's light flares rarely! Is this the crossing point? (The breakers still seethe at the crumbling height ...) You don't remember the house of this my evening. And I do not know who leaves and who stays.

Eastbourne

'God save the king', the brass band intones from a pavilion built high on piles that open a passage to the sea when it rises to destroy the marks of horse-hooves damp in the sand upon the shoreline.

Freddo un vento m'investe
ma un guizzo accende i vetri
e il candore di mica delle rupi
ne risplende.

Bank Holiday ... Riporta l'onda lunga
della mia vita
a striscio, troppo dolce sulla china.
Si fa tardi. I fragori si distendono,
si chiudono in sordina.

Vanno su sedie a ruote i mutilati,
li accompagnano cani dagli orecchi
lungi, bimbi in silenzio o vecchi. (Forse
domani tutto parrà un sogno.)
      E vieni
tu pure voce prigioniera, sciolta
anima ch'è smarrita,
voce di sangue, persa e restituita
alla mia sera.

Come lucente muove sui suoi spicchi
la porta di un albergo
– risponde un'altra e le rivolge un raggio –

A chilling wind assails me but a glimmer lights the windows and
with it the white of mica shines in the cliffs.

Bank Holiday. ... It brings back the long drawn wave of my life
glidingly, too pleasant in its lapse. It grows late. The crashes resound more widely, but end in a mutedness.

Upon their wheel-chairs invalids pass, attended by long eared
dogs, silent children, or the old. (Perhaps tomorrow all this will
be like a dream.) And you too come, imprisoned voice, soul set
free who have strayed, lost voice of blood restored to my own
evening.

As, flashing light from its leaves, a hotel door revolves – another answers, sending back a ray – a roundabout disturbs me that

m'agita un carosello che travolge
tutto dentro il suo giro; ed io in ascolto
(«mia patria!») riconosco il tuo respiro,
anch'io mi levo e il giorno è troppo folto.

Tutto apparirà vano: anche la forza
che nella sua tenace ganga aggrega
i vivi e i morti, gli alberi e gli scogli
e si svolge da te, per te. La festa
non ha pietà. Rimanda
il suo scroscio la banda, si dispiega
nel primo buio una bontà senz'armi.

Vince il male. . . . La ruota non s'arresta.

Anche tu lo sapevi, luce-in-tenebra.

Nella plaga che brucia, dove sei
scomparsa al primo tocco delle campane, solo
rimano l'acre tizzo che già fu
Bank Holiday.

within its track overturns all: and I intently listening ('my country!') know your breathing, I too rise up and the day is far too crowded.

Everything will seem empty, even the force which unites in its untiring hold the living and the dead, trees and rocks, and is moved by you, for you. The holiday is without mercy. The band puts away its clamour, in the first dusk a goodness without armament unfolds.

Evil conquers. . . . The wheel will not stop.

You knew this too, light-in-darkness.

In that burning streak, where you have vanished at the bells' first note, only the bitter torch is left that once was Bank Holiday.

Corrispondenze

Or che in fondo un miraggio
di vapori vacilla e si desperde,
altro annunzia, tra gli alberi, la squilla
del picchio verde.

La mano che raggiunge il sottobosco
e trapunge la trama
del cuore con le punte dello strame,
è quella che matura incubi d'oro
a specchio delle gore
quando il carro sonoro
di Bassareo riporta folli mùgoli
di arieti sulle toppe arse dei colli.

Torni anche tu, pastora senza greggi,
e siedi sul mio sasso?
Ti riconosco; ma non so che leggi
oltre i voli che svariano sul passo.
Lo chiedo invano al piano dove una bruma
èsita tra baleni e spari su sparsi tetti,
alla febbre nascosta dei diretti
nella costa che fuma.

Correspondences

Now that in the distance a mirage of vapours wavers and is scattered, the drumming of the green woodpecker, among the trees, announces something different.

The hand that reaches the undergrowth and pierces through the heart's web with the littered points is the one that nurses portents of gold in the mirror of ponds when the rumbling car of Bacchus brings back wild yells of rams from burnt patches in the hills.

Are you coming back too, shepherdess without flocks, and will you sit on my stone? I recognize you; but do not know what you read beyond the flights that weave over the pass. I vainly ask the plain where a haze lingers among flashes and shots upon the scattered roofs, ask the hidden fever of expresses in the coast that steams.

La primavera hitleriana

> Nè quella ch'a veder lo sol si gira …
> (Dante(?) a Giovanni Querini)

FOLTA la nuvola bianca delle falene impazzite
turbina intorno agli scialbi fanali e sulle spallette,
stende a terra una coltre su cui scricchia
come su zucchero il piede; l'estate imminente sprigiona
ora il gelo notturno che capiva
nelle cave segrete della stagione morta,
negli orti che da Maiano scavalcano a questi renai.

Da poco sul corso è passato a volo un messo infernale
tra un alala di scherani, un golfo mistico acceso
e pavesato di croci a uncino l'ha preso e inghiottito,
si sono chiuse le vetrine, povere
e inoffensive benchè armate anch'esse
di cannoni e giocattoli di guerra,
ha sprangato il beccaio che infiorava
di bacche il muso dei capretti uccisi,
la sagra dei miti carnefici che ancora ignorano il sangue
s'è trasformata in un sozzo trescone d'ali schiantate,

Hitler Spring

> Nor her whom to see the sun turns …
> (Dante(?) to Giovanni Querini)

DENSE the white cloud of moths, maddened, whirls about the dim
lamps and parapets, spreads a sheet on the earth that crackles like
sugar underfoot; the nearing summer liberates now the nightly chill
that was held in the secret quarries of the dead season, in the orchards that from Maiano slither down to these sand-banks.

A short white ago on the main-street a hellish messenger flashed
past amid the chanting of henchmen, a mystic gulf, alight and
bannered with hooked crosses, took and swallowed him, the shop-
windows are shuttered, poor and harmless, though armed, even
they, with cannons and toys of war, the butcher has put up bars, he
who used to decorate the young goats' heads with berries, the rite
of mild killers who still do not know blood, has been transformed

di larve sulle golene e l'acqua seguita a rodere
le sponde e più nessun è incolpevole.

Tutto per nulla, dunque? – e le candele
romane, a San Giovanni, che sbiancavano lente
l'orizzonte, ed i pegni e i lunghi addii
forti come un battesimo nella lugubre attesa
dell'orda (ma un gemma rigò l'aria stillando
sui ghiacci e le riviere dei tuoi lidi,
gli angeli di Tobia, i sette, la semina
dell'avvenire) e gli eliotropi nati
dalle tue mani – tutto arso e succhiato
da un polline che stride come il fuoco
e ha punto di sinibbio ...

                    Oh la piagata
primavera è pur festa se raggela
in morte questa morte! Guarda ancora
in alto, Clizia, è la tua sorte, tu
che il non mutato amor mutata serbi,
fino a che il cieco sole che in te porti

into a sickening reel of crushed wings, of larva upon the mud-flats
and the water keeps gnawing the banks and no one now is blameless.

All for nothing, then? – and the roman candles, at Saint John's
day, that slowly paled the skyline, and the tokens and the long fare-
wells strong as a baptism in the mournful waiting of the horde (but
a gem streaked the air, scattering on the ice, and the shores of your
coastline, Tobias's angels, the seven, the seed of the future) and the
heliotropes born from your hands – all burnt and sucked dry by a
pollen that hisses like fire, and has the sharpness of driving snow.

Oh the wounded springtime is still holiday if it freezes this death
in death! Look up again, Clizia, it is your fate, you who, though
changed, keep your love unchanged, until the blind sun you bear

si abbacini nell'Altro e si distrugga
in Lui per tutti. Forse le sirene, i rintocchi
che salutano i mostri nella sera
della loro tregenda si confondono già
col suono che slegato dal cielo, scende, vince –
col respiro d'un'alba che domani per tutti
si riaffacci, bianca ma senz'ali
di riccapriccio, ai greti arsi del sud ...

Lungomare

IL soffio cresce, il buio è rotto a squarci,
e l'ombra che tu mandi sulla fragile
palizzata s'arriccia. Troppo tardi

se vuoi esser te stessa! Dalla palma
tonfa il sorcio, il baleno è sulla miccia,
sui lunghissimi cigli del tuo sguardo.

in you is dazzled in the Other and is destroyed in Him for everyone. Perhaps the sirens, the tolling bells that greet the monsters on
the evening of their witches' Sabbath are already mingling with the
sound that, unloosed from heaven, descends, conquers, – with
the breathing of a dawn that tomorrow, for everyone, breaks again,
white, but without wings of horror, over the scorched wadis of the
south. ...

Sea-front

THE blowing strengthens, the dark is torn to rags, and the shadow
which you cast upon the light fencing crinkles. Too late
 if you want to be yourself! The rat has thudded down from
the palm-tree, the lightning is playing about the fuse, about the
long, long eyelashes of your gaze.

Su una lettera non scritta

Per un formicolìo d'albe, per pochi
fili su cui s'impigli
il fiocco della vita e s'incollani
in ore e in anni, oggi i delfini a coppie
capriolano coi figli? Oh ch'io non oda
nulla di te, ch'io fugga dal bagliore
dei tuoi cigli. Ben altro è sulla terra.

Sparir non so nè riaffacciarmi; tarda
la fucina vermiglia
della notte, la sera si fa lunga,
la preghiera è supplizio e non ancora
tra le rocce che sorgono t'è giunta
la bottiglia dal mare. L'onda vuota,
si rompe sulla punta a Finisterre.

On a Letter Never Written

For a swarming of dawns, for a few wires upon which the loose
wool of life is caught and looped into hours and years, today are
the dolphins in pair cavorting with their children? Oh that I might
hear nothing of you, might fly from the lightning of your brow. It
is far otherwise on earth.

I cannot vanish, nor turn my face again; the red furnace of the
night is lingering, the evening drawing out, prayer is torture, and
not yet among rocks that jut has the bottle from the sea come to
you. The wave breaks emptily upon the headland at Finisterre.

Giorno e notte

Anche una piuma che vola può disegnare
la tua figura, o il raggio che gioca a rimpiattino
tra i mobili, il rimando dello specchio
di un bambino, dai tetti. Sul giro delle mura
strascichi di vapore prolungano le guglie
dei pioppi e giù sul trespolo s'arruffa il pappagallo
dell'arrotino. Poi la notte afosa
sulla piazzola, e i passi, e sempre questa dura
fatica di affondare per risorgere eguali
da secoli, o da istanti, d'incubi che non possono
ritrovare la luce dei tuoi occhi nell'antro
incandescente; e ancora le stesse grida e i lunghi
pianti sulla veranda
se rimbomba improvviso il colpo che t'arrossa
la gola e schianta l'ali o perigliosa
annùnziatrice dell'alba
e si destano i chiostri e gli ospedali
a un lacerìo di trombe ...

Day and Night

Even a feather gliding by can sketch your shape, or the ray which plays hide-and-seek among the furniture, the reflection of the child's mirror, from the roofs. Upon the circuit of the walls streaks of smoke prolong the spires of poplars and below, upon the trestle, the knife-grinder's parrot ruffles its feathers. Then the sultry night upon the little square, and the footsteps, and ever this hard struggle to sink only to rise unchanged for centuries, moments, of nightmares which cannot find the light of your eyes again in the glowing cave; and still the same cries and the drawn-out weeping on the verandah if the shot suddenly echoes that makes your throat flush and shatters your wings, o dangerous messenger of dawn, and the cloisters and the hospitals awake at a rending of trumpets. ...

Vento sulla mezzaluna

Il grande ponte non portava a te.
T'avrei raggiunta anche navigando
nelle chiaviche, a un tuo comando. Ma
già le forze, col sole sui cristalli
delle verande, andavano stremandosi.

L'uomo che predicava sul Crescente
mi chiese «Sai dov'è Dio?» Lo sapevo
e glielo dissi. Scosse il capo. Sparve
nel turbine che prese uomini e case
e li sollevò in alto, sulla pece.

Edimburgo. 1948

L'ombra della magnolia

L'ombra della magnolia giapponese
si sfoltisce or che i bocci paonazzi
sono caduti. Vibra intermittente
in vetta una cicala. Non è più
il tempo dell'unisono vocale,

Wind in the Crescent

The great bridge did not lead to you. I would have reached you
navigating the sewers at a command from you. But already my
powers were, with the sun on the verandah windows, gradually
spending themselves.

The man preaching on the Crescent asked me 'Do you know
where God is?' I did, and told him. He shook his head. He vanished
in the whirling wind that snatched up men and houses and lifted
them on high, upon pitch blackness.

Edinburgh, 1948

The Magnolia's Shade

The shade of the Japanese magnolia is thinned out now that the
purplish buds have fallen. A cicada quivers at intervals from the
height. It is no longer the time of the unison of voices, Clizia, the

Clizia, il tempo del nume illimitato
che divora e rinsangua i suoi fedeli.
Spendersi era più facile, morire
al primo batter d'ale, al primo incontro
col nemico, un trastullo. Comincia ora
la via più dura: ma non te consunta
dal sole e radicata, e pure morbida
cesena che sorvoli alta le fredde
banchine del tuo fiume, – non te fragile
fuggitiva cui zenit nadir cancro
capricorno rimasero indistinti
perchè la guerra fosse in te e in chi adora
su te le stime del tuo Sposo, flette
il brivido del gelo .... Gli altri arretrano
e piegano. La lima che sottile
incide tacerà, la vuota scorza
di chi cantava sarà presto polvere
di vetro sotto i piedi, l'ombra è livida, –
è l'autunno, è l'inverno, è l'oltrecielo
che ti conduce e in cui mi getto, cefalo
saltato in secco al novilunio.

Addio.

time of the limitless deity who devours his faithful and restores
them with blood again. To be consumed was easier, dying at the
first flutter of a wing, at the first encounter with the enemy, a game.
Now the harder way begins: but not you, consumed by the sun
and rooted and yet a tender thrush who fly high above the cold
wharves of your river, the shiver of frost does not bend you, frail
fugitive, for whom zenith nadir cancer capricorn remained undistin-
guished so that the war might be in you and in who adores upon
you the marks of your Bridegroom. ... The others fall back, and
buckle. The file which finely cuts its way will be silenced, the
empty shell of him who sang will soon be a powder of glass underfoot, the shadow is livid, it is autumn, it is winter, it is the beyond
which leads you and into which I throw myself, sea-fish jumped
clear of the water under the new moon.

Farewell.

L'anguilla

L'ANGUILLA, la sirena
dei mari freddi che lascia il Baltico
per giungere ai nostri mari,
ai nostri estuari, ai fiumi
che risale in profondo, sotto la piena avversa,
di ramo in ramo e poi
di capello in capello, assottigliati,
sempre più addentro, sempre più nel cuore
del macigno, filtrando
tra gorielli di melma finchè un giorno
una luce scoccata dai castagni
ne accende il guizzo in pozze d'acquamorta,
nei fossi che declinano
dai balzi dell'Appennino alla Romagna;
l'anguilla, torcia, frusta,
freccia d'Amore in terra
che soli i nostri botri o i disseccati
ruscelli pirenaici riconducono
a paradisi di fecondazione;
l'anima verde che cerca
vita dove là solo
morde l'arsura e la desolazione,

The Eel

THE eel, the siren of cold seas that leaves the Baltic to reach our seas, our estuaries, the rivers which, deep down, it follows upwards. under the opposing spate, from branch to branch, from tendril to tendril, thinned down, ever more inland, ever more into the heart of rock, slipping through little channels of slime, until one day the light glancing from chestnut-trees illuminates its streak in the stagnant pools, in the hollows that go down from the steeps of the Apennines to the Romagna; the eel, torch, lash, arrow of Love upon earth, which our gullies and fiery, dried-up streams alone lead back to paradises of fertility; the green soul that looks for life in places where only heat and desolation gnaw, the spark which says every-

la scintilla che dice
tutto comincia quando tutto pare
incarbonirsi, bronco seppellito,
l'iride breve gemella
di quella che incastoni in mezzo ai cigli
e fai brillare intatta in mezzo ai figli
dell'uomo, immersi nel tuo fango, puoi tu
non crederla sorella?

Se t'hanno assomigliato
alla volpe sarà per la falcata
prodigiosa, pel volo del tuo passo
che unisce e divide, che sconvolge
e rinfranca il selciato (il tuo terrazzo,
le strade presso il Cottolengo, il prato,
l'albero che ha il mio nome ne vibrano
felici, umili e vinti) – o forse solo
per l'onda luminosa che diffondi
dalle mandorle tenere degli occhi,
per l'astuzia dei tuoi pronti stupori,
per lo strazio
di piume lacerate che può dare
la tua mano d'infante in una stretta;

thing begins when everything seems blackened, a buried stump, the
brief rainbow, twin-sister to the one which you set in the middle
of your eye, and let shine in the midst of the sons of men, sunk in
your mud, – can you not believe her a sister?

If they have likened you to the fox, it will be for the miraculous
leap, for the flight of your step that draws together and divides,
that turns up and freshens the gravel (your balcony, the streets near
the Cottolengo, the meadow, the tree that has my name quiver with
it, happy, humble, and defeated) – or perhaps only for the luminous
wave that you shed from the tender almonds of your eyes, for the
shrewdness of your quick amazements, for the hurt of torn feathers
that your child's hand can give in a clasp; if they have likened you

se t'hanno assomigliato
a un carnivoro biondo, al genio perfido
delle fratte (e perchè non all'immondo
pesce che dà la scossa, alla torpedine?)
è forse perchè i ciechi non ti videro
sulle scapole gracili le ali,
perchè i ciechi non scorsero il presagio
della tua fronte incandescente, il solco
che vi ho graffiato a sangue, croce cresima
incantesimo jattura voto vale
perdizione e salvezza; se non seppero
crederti più che donnola o che donna,
con chi dividerò la mia scoperta,
dove seppellirò l'oro che porto,
dove la brace che in me stride quando,
lasciandomi, ti volgi dalle scale?

Per album

Ho cominciato anzi giorno
a buttar l'amo per te (lo chiamavo «il lamo»).

to a fair carnivore, to the treacherous genius of the undergrowth
(and why not to the unclean fish that gives the shock, the torpedo-
fish?) it is perhaps because the blind did not see the wings on your
fine shoulder-blades, because the blind did not make out the omen
of your glowing forehead, the groove that I have scratched there in
blood, cross, chrism, enchantment, misfortune, prayer meaning
perdition and salvation; if they did not know how to think of you
as more than weasel or woman, whom can I share my discovery
with, where shall I bury the gold I bear, where the live coal that
rages in me when, leaving me, you turn from the stairs?

For an Album

I BEGAN before daylight to cast my hook for you (I called it
by a nickname, 'I-love-her'). But no flash of a tail could I catch

Ma nessun guizzo di coda
scorgevo nei pozzi limosi,
nessun vento veniva col tuo indizio
dai colli monferrini,
Ho continuato il mio giorno
sempre spiando te, larva girino
frangia di rampicante francolino
gazzella zebù ocàpi
nuvola nera grandine
prima della vendemmia, ho spigolato
tra i filari inzuppati senza trovarti.
Ho proseguito fino a tardi
senza sapere che tre cassettine
– SABBIA SODA SAPONE; la piccionaia
da cui partì il tuo volo: da una cucina, –
si sarebbero aperte per me solo.
Così sparisti nell'orizzonte incerto.
Non c'è pensiero che imprigioni il fulmine
ma chi ha veduto la luce non se ne priva.
Mi stesi al piede del tuo ciliegio, ero
già troppo ricco per contenerti viva.

in the muddy wells, no wind came with a sign of you from the hills
of Monferrato. I went on with my day, always watching for you
larva, tadpole, creeper-fringe, ptarmigan, gazelle, zebu, okapi,
black cloud, hailstone, before the wine-harvest I went gleaning
among the soaking rows without finding you. I carried on till late
without knowing that three containers – SAND, SODA, SOAP, the
pigeon-house from which you took flight, from a kitchen, – were
to be opened for me alone. So you vanished on the uncertain sky-
line. There is no thought to capture lightning, but he who has seen
the light will not be robbed of it. I stretched out at the foot of your
cherry-tree, I was already far too rich to hold you living.

SALVATORE QUASIMODO

Vento a Tìndari

TÌNDARI, mite ti so
fra larghi colli pensile sull'acqua
dell'isole dolci del dio,
oggi m'assali
e ti chini in cuore.

Salgo vertici aerei precipizi,
assorto al vento dei pini,
e la brigata che lieve m'accompagna
s'allontana nell'aria,
onda di suoni e amore,
e tu mi prendi
da cui male mi trassi
e paure d'ombre e di silenzi,
rifugi di dolcezze un tempo assidue
e morte d'anima.

A te ignota è la terra
ove ogni giorno affondo
e segrete sillabe nutro:

Wind at Tindari

TINDARI, I know you to be mild between broad hills, over-
hanging the waters of the sweet islands of the god, today you
assail me and bend within my heart.

I climb peaks, airy precipices, intent on the wind from the pines,
and the troop that gaily keep me company go off into the air, wave
of sounds and love, and you take me from whom I wrongly drew
myself away, and fears of shadows and silences, retreats of blessed-
ness once unfailing, and death of soul.

The land is unknown to you where each day I go deep and feed

altra luce ti sfoglia sopra i vetri
nella veste notturna,
e gioia non mia riposa
sul tuo grembo.

Aspro è l'esilio,
e la ricerca che chiudevo in te
d'armonia oggi si muta
in ansia precoce di morire;
e ogni amore è schermo alla tristezza,
tacito passo nel buio
dove mi hai posto
amaro pane a rompere.

Tìndari serena torna;
soave amico mi desta
che mi sporga nel cielo da una rupe
e io fingo timore a chi non sa
che vento profondo m'ha cercato.

Strada di Agrigentum

Là dura un vento che ricordo acceso
nelle criniere dei cavalli obliqui
in corsa lungo le pianure, vento

secret syllabry: another light unfoils you above your windows,
against night's dress, and joy not mine lies in your lap.

Harsh is exile, and my search for harmony which ended in you
is changed today into early anxiety at dying; and every love is a
shield against sadness, muted step in the gloom where you have
placed me to break bitter bread.

Tìndari, come back serene; sweet friend, wake me that I may
lift myself from a rock to heaven and I pretend fear for whoever
does not know what deep wind has searched me.

Street in Agrigentum

There a wind endures that I remember afire in the manes of the
slanting horses racing over the plains, wind that soils and gnaws

che macchia e rode l'arenaria e il cuore
dei telamoni lugubri, riversi
sopra l'erba. Anima antica, grigia
di rancori, torni a quel vento, annusi
il delicato muschio che riveste
i giganti sospinti giù dal cielo.
Come sola allo spazio che ti resta!
E più t'accori s'odi ancora il suono
che s'allontana largo verso il mare
dove Espero già striscia mattutino:
il marranzano tristemente vibra
nella gola al carraio che risale
il colle nitido di luna, lento
tra il murmure d'ulivi saraceni.

Antico inverno

DESIDERIO delle tue mani chiare
nella penombra della fiamma:
sapevano di rovere e di rose;
di morte. Antico inverno.

the sandstone and the heart of the gloomy statued columns, thrown
back upon the earth. Ancient soul, grey with resentment, go back
to that wind, breathe in the fine musk scent that once more clothes
the giants thrown down by heaven. How lonely in the space that is
still yours! And you are the more stricken, if you hear the sound
that goes off far towards the sea which Hesperus already streaks
with morning. The jew's harp sadly quivers in the carter's mouth
as he goes up the hill that is clean with moonlight, slow amid the
murmur of saracenic olives.

Ancient Winter

DESIRE of your clear hands in the half light of the flame: they
smelt of oakwood and roses; of death. Ancient winter.

Cercavano il miglio gli uccelli
ed erano sùbito di neve;
così le parole:
un po' di sole, una raggiera d'angelo,
e poi la nebbia; e gli alberi,
e noi fatti d'aria al mattino.

Imitazione della gioia

Dove gli alberi ancora
abbandonata più fanno la sera,
come indolente
è svanito l'ultimo tuo passo,
che appare appena il fiore
sui tigli e insiste alla sua sorte.

Una ragione cerchi agli affetti,
provi il silenzio nella tua vita.
Altra ventura a me rivela
il tempo specchiato. Addolora
come la morte, bellezza ormai
in altri volti fulminea.
Perduto ho ogni cosa innocente,
anche in questa voce, superstite
a imitare la gioia.

The birds looked for their grain and were suddenly of snow;
similarly words; a little sun, an angel's glory, and then the mist;
and the trees, and us made of air in the morning.

Imitation of Joy

Where the trees make the evening even more abandoned, how
languidly your last step has vanished, as the flower on the linden
trees hardly shows and insists upon its fate.

You search a motive for feelings, experience silence in your life.
Mirrored time reveals a different adventure to me. Beauty now
flashing in other faces makes me sad, like death. I have lost every
innocent thing, even in this voice, surviving to imitate joy.

Ed è sùbito sera

OGNUNO sta solo sul cuor della terra
traffitto da un raggio di sole:
ed è sùbito sera.

Oboe sommerso

AVARA pena, tarda il tuo dono
in questa mia ora
di sospirati abbandoni.

Un òboe gelido risillaba
gioia di foglie perenni,
non mie, e smemora;

in me si fa sera:
l'acqua tramonta
sulle mie mani erbose.

Ali oscillano in fioco cielo,
làbili: il cuore trasmigra
ed io son gerbido,

e i giorni una maceria.

And in No Time it's Evening

EACH one stands alone on the heart of the earth pierced through
by a ray of sunlight: and in no time it's evening.

Sunken Oboe

GRASPING pain, delay your gift in this my hour of longed-for
abandon.
    An icy oboe rephrases joy of evergreen leaves, not mine, and
takes away memory;
    in me it is evening: the water fades upon my grassy hands.
    Wings waver in dim heaven changefully: the heart migrates and
I am untilled,
    and the days a heap of rubble.

Lettera alla madre

«Mater *dulcissima*, ora scendon le nebbie,
il Naviglio urta confusamente sulle dighe,
gli alberi si gonfiano d'acqua, bruciano di neve;
non sono triste nel Nord: non sono
in pace con me, ma non aspetto
perdono da nessuno, molti mi devono lacrime
da uomo a uomo. So che non stai bene, che vivi
come tutte le madri dei poeti, povera
e giusta nella misura d'amore
per i figli lontani. Oggi sono io
che ti scrivo.» Finalmente, dirai, due parole
di quel ragazzo che fuggì di notte, con un mantello corto
e alcuni versi in tasca. Povero, così pronto di cuore,
lo uccideranno un giorno in qualche luogo.
«Certo, ricordo, fu da quel grigio scalo
di treni lenti che portavano mandorle e arance,
alla foce dell'Imera, il fiume pieno di gazze,
di sale, d'eucalyptus. Ma ora ti ringrazio,
questo voglio, dell'ironia che hai messo
sul mio labbro mite come la tua.

Letter to my Mother

'Mater dulcissima, now the mists come down, the canal of the
Naviglio thrusts vaguely against its banks, the trees swell with
water, burn with snow; I am not sad in the North, am not at peace
with myself, but do not expect pardon from any one, many owe
me tears as from man to man. I know you are not well, that you live
like all the mothers of poets, poor and perfect in the measure of
their love for far-off sons. Today it is I who am writing to you.'
At last, you will say, two words from the boy who fled by night
in a short cape, a few lines in his pocket. Poor thing, so open-
hearted, they'll kill him one day in some place. 'Certainly, I remember, it was from that grey yard of slow trains that bore almonds
and oranges to the estuary of the Imera, the river full of magpies,
salt, eucalyptus. But now I thank you, I want to, for the irony which
you laid upon my lip as mild as yours. That smile has saved me from

Quel sorriso m'ha salvato da pianti e da dolori.
E non importa se ora ho qualche lacrima per te,
per tutti quelli che come te aspettano,
e non sanno che cosa. Ah, gentile morte,
non toccare l'orologio in cucina che batte sopra il muro,
tutta la mia infanzia è passata sullo smalto
del suo quadrante, su quei fiori dipinti:
non toccare le mani, il cuore dei vecchi.
Ma forse qualcuno risponde? O morte di pietà,
morte di pudore. Addio, cara, addio, mia
dulcissima mater.»

O miei dolci animali

ORA l'autunno guasta il verde ai colli,
o miei dolci animali. Ancora udremo,
prima di notte, l'ultimo lamento
degli uccelli, il richiamo della grigia
pianura che va incontro a quel rumore
alto di mare. E l'odore di legno
alla pioggia, l'odore delle tane,
com'è vivo qui fra le case,
fra gli uomini, o miei dolci animali.

weeping and from griefs. And it does not matter if I have some
tears for you now, for all those who, like you, await and do not
know what. O kind death, do not touch the clock in the kitchen
ticking upon the wall. All my childhood has passed on the enamel
of its face, on those painted flowers. Do not touch the hands, the
hearts of the old. Perhaps some one will answer? O death of mercy,
death of shame. Goodbye, dear, goodbye, my dulcissima mater.'

O My Sweet Animals

NOW autumn spoils the green of hills, o my sweet animals. We
shall hear again, before nightfall, the final lament of the birds, the
call of the grey plain that goes towards that high noise of the sea.
And the smell of wood in the rain, the smell of the hollows, how
keen it is here between the houses, o my sweet animals. This face

Questo volto che gira gli occhi lenti,
questa mano che segna il cielo dove
romba un tuono, sono vostri, o miei lupi,
mie volpi bruciate dal sangue.
Ogni mano, ogni volto, sono vostri.
Tu mi dici che tutto è stato vano,
la vita, i giorni corrosi da un'acqua
assidua, mentre sale dai giardini
un canto di fanciulli. Ora lontani,
dunque, da noi? Ma cedono nell'aria
come ombra appena. Questa la tua voce.
Ma forse io so che tutto non è stato.

Dalla Rocca di Bergamo Alta

H AI udito il grido del gallo nell'aria
di là dalle murate, oltre le torri
gelide d'una luce che ignoravi,
grido fulmineo di vita, e stormire
di voci dentro le celle, e il richiamo
d'uccello della ronda avanti l'alba.
E non hai detto parole per te:
eri nel cerchio ormai di breve raggio:

that slowly turns its eyes about, this hand that marks the heavens
where a peal of thunder resounds, are yours, o my wolves, my
foxes burnt with blood. Every hand, every face is yours. You tell
me everything has been in vain, life, the days worn away by a
steady flow of water, while from the garden rises a singing of children. Perhaps far from us now? But they yield in the air like
shadows, if as much. This your voice. But perhaps I know everything has not been.

From the Castle-rock of High Bergamo

You heard the cry of the cock in the air beyond the walls, beyond
the towers icy with a light you were not aware of, a cry startling
with life, and the murmur of voices from the cells, and the cry of
the sentinel bird before dawn. And you said nothing for yourself:
you were now in the orbit of short rays: and the antelope and the

e tacquero l'antilope e l'airone
persi in un soffio di fumo maligno,
talismani d'un mondo appena nato.
E passava la luna di febbraio
aperta sulla terra, ma a te forma
nella memoria, accesa al suo silenzio.
Anche tu fra i cipressi della Rocca
ora vai senza rumore; e qui l'ira
si quieta al verde dei giovani morti,
e la pietà lontana è quasi gioia.

heron were silent, lost in a gust of malignant smoke, magic em-
blems of a world all but unborn. And the February moon passed
openly above the earth, but to you, a form in memory, lit with its
own silence. You too are going now, between the cypresses of the
Fortress, without sound; and here anger is made quiet by the green
of the young dead, and distant pity is almost joy.

INDEX OF FIRST LINES

417